The Mirth of a Nation

The Mirth of a Nation

America's Great Dialect Humor

Edited by
Walter Blair and
Raven I. McDavid, Jr.

UNIVERSITY OF MINNESOTA PRESS □ MINNEAPOLIS

190427

Published by the University of Minnesota Press,
2037 University Avenue Southeast, Minneapolis, MN 55414
Printed in the United States of America.

Library of Congress Cataloging in Publication Data
Main entry under title:

The Mirth of a nation.

   Bibliography: p.
   Includes index.
   1. American fiction—19th century. 2. American
wit and humor. I. Blair, Walter, 1900-
II. McDavid, Raven I., Jr., 1911-
PS653.M5   813'.3'09   81-16403
ISBN 0-8166-1022-3   AACR2
ISBN 0-8166-1168-8 (pbk.)

The University of Minnesota is an
equal-opportunity educator and employer.

Cover illustration: "Sam Lawson" from *Oldtown Fireside
Stories* by Harriet Beecher Stowe (Boston: Osgood, 1872,
frontispiece).

Dedicated to

_____

Our former students,
who learned us plenty,
and to our doctors,
who kept us fitten and feisty.

Contents

Introduction

Outstanding — But Unread — American Humor

This book makes available in a readable form some outstanding American humor that has been unread by anyone but scholars for far too long. The writings sampled, produced from about 1830 until the end of the nineteenth century, in their day were very popular. Throughout seven decades, Americans savored them in almanacs, newspapers, and magazines; they read them to one another and quoted them from memory; they clipped them and carried them around or pasted them in scrapbooks for rereading; and they made books collecting them big sellers.

In the 1860s, when several humorists took sides in a bitter civil war, Abraham Lincoln in the White House helped swell their fame. News stories told how he read them during the dark nights to alleviate tensions. Lincoln offered to swap the presidency for the skill to write as well as one of these authors. He announced that another, "next to William Shakespeare, was the greatest judge of human nature the world has ever seen." And he read a piece written by a contemporary humorist to his cabinet before introducing the Emancipation Proclamation.

After the war, well-attended comic lectures on platforms from the Atlantic to the Pacific, newspaper syndications, best-selling books, and reports about the considerable prosperity of funny people attested to and built up their popularity. It is probable that these humorists were the first group of professional authors to make good livings in the United States.

For years, America's most respected critics badmouthed much of the humor that this book collects. Many unbookish readers loved it—a suspicious circumstance. Such humor often deals in earthy language with common folk of a sort foreign commentators long had claimed were uncouth yokels, and so our authors were generally held to be inferior to more conventional writers. But before long some critics who were quite influential—*British* critics—began to pay these writings impressive compliments, and throughout the century growing numbers of their fellow countrymen praised them. "H. W.", in the *Westminster Review* for 1838, for example, said that his compatriots were giving such writings "extensive circulation and notice" because at long last "American literature has ceased to be exclusively imitative" and had become something new and fine. Again in 1844, the *Illustrated London News* called ours "the most racy and thoroughly diverting and exhilarating . . . humour that ever obtained vogue and prevailed among men." *All the Year*, a London magazine, in 1878 printed an article about "Caricature in America," in which the writer worried about its good taste and its sacrifice of "graver considerations" but granted its preeminence.

Everybody knows that the newspaper fun of the world is now mainly of transatlantic origin. . . . Over five thousand journals keep us pretty well supplied with mirth, even as the Gulfstream is said to warm our climate. They have, indeed, somewhat superseded, if not eclipsed, the native article. These facts are patent to everybody.

In 1889, Andrew Lang noticed that it was chiefly the transatlantic humorists that his compatriots were enjoying, and, as a folklorist, he attributed Americans' superiority to their habit of retelling oral stories — "a rich soil in which the plant . . . grows with vigour and puts forth fruit and flowers."

A number of British critics, though they were unenthusiastic about most of our humorists, wrote about some with great enthusiasm. The following at times were ranked with or above Britain's best: Thomas Chandler Haliburton, James Russell Lowell, Charles Farrar Browne, Henry Wheeler Shaw, and Samuel L. Clemens. Not only critics but also creative artists such as Robert Louis Stevenson, Rudyard Kipling, and George Bernard Shaw considered the last of these (Mark Twain) the greatest English-speaking comic writer of their day.

In the United States, as early as 1844, Ralph Waldo Emerson cited such British encomiums to argue that native humorous writers had created characters who were "genuine growths, which are sought with avidity in Europe, where our Europeanlike books are of no value" and that they were sounding "a new and stronger tone in literature." The next year, magazine editor William T. Porter held that recent frontier humorists had opened "a new vein of literature, as original as it is inexhaustible in its source" and that they had described "in a masterly style" the West, "the extraordinary characters occasionally met with — their strange language and habitudes, and the peculiar and sometimes fearful characteristics of the 'squatters' and early settlers." And as the century ended, Bret Harte praised our humor for its originality, its style, and its artistry.

. . . While the American literary imagination was still under the influence of English tradition, an unexpected factor was developing to diminish its power. . . . *Humor —* of a quality as distinct and original as the country and civilization in which it was developed. . . . Crude at first, it received a literary polish in the press, but its dominant quality remained. It was concise and condensed, yet suggestive, . . . delightfully extravagant—or a miracle of understatement. It voiced not only the dialect, but the habits of thought of a people or locality. . . . By degrees, it developed character with incident, often, in a few lines, gave a striking photograph of a community or a section, but always reached its conclusion without an unnecessary word.

Beginning in the 1930s, a century after our humor's birth was announced, scholars and critics weighed its values. They agreed with earlier commentators that, as our first distinctive homebred literary creation, it gave us the first American fiction that writers fashioned "out of the life about them," portraying authentically native men and women and "living communities." An impressive share of it was said to have been written by artists who had "a gift not only for dramatic story-telling but for style as well." Its drift toward realism gave our fiction an important direction. Paradoxically, "The depictions of native characters . . . and tensions between them and representatives of the older heroic traditions in world mythology, contribute much to the sense of largeness, of archetypal representativeness, which we find in American prose romance." And the tall tales prepared the way for fantasy. The genre's innovative manner began "a steady infiltration of the new American words and ways of speech, and the laying of foundations for a genuinely colloquial and natural style of writing." So it "forced the seasoning of American writing with the pungent herbs of the vernacular."

Historians also have found the nonliterary contributions of American humor noteworthy. They have noticed that it has preached homely sermons that have been heeded and that have hit off our people's foibles, flaws, and finaglings, stubbornly resisting some reforms but at times "acting as a catalytic agent for change." By constantly playing up the incongruity "between the ideals of freedom, equality, and self-government" and "the fact that the individual citizens of a democracy are indeed ordinary people who speak, think and act in ordinary terms," it has helped us understand ourselves and our society. Finally, historians have argued, it has served as "a fashioning instrument . . . creating fresh bonds, a new unity, the semblance of a society and the rounded completion of an American type" and forming "a consistent native tradition."

American humor has been important because it has at least some of these virtues. In addition, as the selections that follow show, a great deal of it continues to be very amusing.

Antebellum Comedy—Rustic Yankees

About 1830 then, as critics of that day and as critics and historians of today agree, American humor became a recognizable phenomenon.

During the years until about 1865, comic writers shared certain techniques and notions about what was funny.

The techniques helped writers make merry with a belief that had been developing for many years and that events during the period strengthened—that the inhabitants of different parts of the country were quite unlike one another. Sectional conflicts that would climax in a civil war underlined contrasting basic concepts. Foreigners' travel books as well as natives' folklore stressed alleged regional quiddities. Actors and playwrights found ways to dramatize these peculiarities. So did popular British fiction writers such as Walter Scott and Maria Edgeworth and imitative American fiction writers—a group that used as major ingredients local traits, occupations, and modes of living, thinking, and—quite importantly—talking.

The incongruity, one that would be a favorite for decades, was related to moss-covered Old World jokes about pedantic professors and doctors as they contrasted with sensible ignoramuses. The appeal of the subject flourished in the New World because much of the time our democrats were hostile toward intellectuals and friendly with relatively uneducated men and women. As early as the eighteenth century, Puritan, Quaker, and Methodist reformers had attacked scholars and praised "plain country men." So had Deists, who held that common sense was all that was needed to understand those natural laws that were truly important. And, having found that they could prosper without book learning, American farmers and frontiersmen joined such antiintellectuals in upgrading horse-sensible perceptions based upon sound thinking and practical experience rather than on study. "Tim was so learned," wrote Franklin's Poor Richard in his *Almanack* (1733-1758), "that he could name a horse in nine languages. So ignorant, that he bought a cow to ride on." During the 1840s, a comic frontiersman named Simon Suggs told of his similar prejudice: "Booklarnin spoils a man if he's got motherwit, and if he ain't got that it don't do him no good." Though such attitudes were widely shared, Americans in some moods weren't all that sure that education was useless or silly. When they felt sickly, they called in physicians; they hailed scientists for discoveries; they respected doctors of divinity; and they financed schools and colleges. Therefore, jokes about educated dumbbells and uneducated sages always had a slightly devilish quality about them. The ambivalence, of course, made such characters useful for humor and helped make vocabularies and speech patterns revealing either education or its lack comic.

With unimportant exceptions, the dialect humor of the antebellum period dealt with people and events of two regions, rural New England and the frontier.

Heralded by a few Yankee letter writers and monologists who appeared during the 1820s and then shortly disappeared, Seba Smith's

Jack Downing started to write letters to a newspaper in 1830 and continued—with a few breaks—to hold forth for nearly three decades. This Maine Yankee was the first in a long series of this nation's homespun commentators who would be extraordinarily popular and influential, one after another, for more than a century. Traveling the country and hobnobbing with politicians, including presidents and cabinet members, Jack exchanged letters with editors and the Downingville home folk. These letters were widely reprinted in newspapers and collected in successful books. The communications appealed partly because they commented amusingly on local and national politics and because they portrayed Jack's home village, his relatives, and his friends evocatively. They also appealed because of Jack's rather complex character, the way he looked at things, and the way he expressed himself. Jack, as Daniel Royot pointed out recently, is an incongruous combination—"oracle of the village, comic demigod and picaro." Part sage, part swaggerer, and part wandering opportunist "entangled in the contradictions of his period," he simultaneously mocks Jacksonian democracy and exposes his own fallibility, thereby creating satire that isn't unilateral. His commentaries on politics, though hilarious in their time, depend for appreciation upon more familiarity with historical contexts than most modern readers have. But his picture of Grandpa Downing, which we reprint, with its mingling of affection and sly derision, suggests the enduring quality of his comedy.

In the latter part of the decade of Downing's debut, the 1830s, Thomas Chandler Haliburton of Nova Scotia introduced Yankee peddler Sam Slick, Canada's contribution to dialect humor about New Englanders. Sam's creator said that he initiated pieces about him to urge in "a popular style, under the guise of amusement," the development of his province's natural resources and the building of a railroad and to criticize not only Canucks but also old and New Englanders. But the preachments, which many now find euphoric, didn't turn contemporary readers away, and for a time newspaper diffusion and a dozen briskly selling books about Sam made him the most popular comic vernacular character among English-speaking readers. Reviews show that readers particularly went for the portrait of this cunning itinerant salesman, his wide wanderings, his shrewd aphorisms, his incisive characterizations, and the anecdotes he told to make points. "The Clockmaker," though it only touches briefly on politics, is a fairly typical piece.

Home and fireside comedy such as Downing's relatives and neighbors provided surfaced once in James Russell Lowell's *Biglow Papers* in "The Courtin,'" written to fill a blank page in the first volume, which was published in 1848. The poem was one of the best among scores of narratives about bashful bumpkins who had trouble popping the question. Not only the events and the comic description of them but also the vivid background appealed to readers. By Lowell's own account, he launched the rustic's series of poems because he'd noticed that "self-educated men" were "all the rage" and were, therefore, effective spokesmen and he wanted to use one to protest against the war with Mexico. He invented a Yankee farmer, Hosea Biglow, whom he described as "homely common-sense vivified and heated by conscience," and he had him blast the war and its backers in dialect verses. Some years after the first series appeared in book form, Lowell resurrected the character and his dialect to support the North's cause during the Civil War. Some of the most bitter — and, for modern taste, the most amusing — poems were those in the first series versifying the reports of Birdofredum Sawin, Hosea's boyhood friend. Sawin, a farmer who was carried away by wartime hoopla, told about his enlistment and his wartime experiences. On the battlefield, he lost an eye, a leg, and an arm; as a veteran, he was mistreated and neglected. He became a complete cynic, a drunk, and a crook whose post-war occupation was to exploit his record and rip off his countrymen.

As has been mentioned, influential British critics impressed Americans by giving the comic poems extravagant praise. Thomas Hughes, for instance, put Hosea in a class with Aristophanes, Cervantes, Moliere, and Swift. F. G. Stephens wrote that "those grand elements of fiction" — "individuality and truth of portraiture" — "are to be found in abundance" in the *Biglow Papers*. When Oxford and Cambridge gave Lowell honorary degrees, both indicated that the dialect poems, rather than the author's "serious" poems or learned criticisms, were largely responsible. With such extravagant tributes in mind, Mark Twain held that the *Papers* "placed America inapproachably first in humorous literature."

Yankee home life was a subject for a very popular feminine writer of dialect humor in the period, Frances M. Whitcher. Though Mrs. Whitcher lived in Elmira, New York, and contributed to newspapers and magazines published outside of New England, her *Widow Bedott Papers*, as one contemporaneous critic said, were called "the best Yankee papers ever written." Her Widow Bedott and other ladies were firsts among America's comic feminine characterizations. Mrs. Whitcher did more than picture the life of the time: she also attacked the sentimental fiction that was fashionable. As Daniel Royot notices, her creations are antiheroines who burlesque gushy excesses by themselves overindulging in emotions on occasion. The books were popular, going into numerous editions; and, late in the century, a dramatization of Widow Bedott's story had long runs. In "Hezekiah Bedott," some of the widow's sentimentality shows itself in her reminiscences about her dead spouse, but it merits reprinting chiefly because it is a fine example of what today would be called a shaggy-dog story, still a favorite among American humorists. Max Eastman admiringly described tales of this sort as "loose, rambling, fantastically inconsequential monologues" whose appeal derives in part from their "total want of structure," "a mess, the messier . . . within the limits of patience, the better."

Antebellum Comedy — Frontier Storytellers

Hamilton C. Jones's "Cousin Sally Dilliard," the first piece of frontier fun making reprinted in this volume, offers another fine example of the way a meandering mind works. In addition, it handily illustrates some typical differences between the humor of the settled and staid Northeast and that of the less populated and more rambunctious prewar frontier. (This, the Old Southwest, included part of the Carolinas, Tennessee, Georgia, Alabama, Louisiana, Mississippi, Arkansas, and Missouri.) A violent rumpus has taken place during a party, and some alleged trouble-makers are being tried. Three witnesses haven't been very helpful, one because he had been too drunk to remember what happened. Harris, the fourth witness, in addition to being "a little corned," can't testify unless he is allowed to reminisce over and over about some completely irrelevant matters. He knows nothing, in fact, that is relevant. And, as he ends his deposition, he tells about a performance of his wife that, during that prissy period, was considered quite indelicate. Compared with the humor of Yankee land, the humor of the "new" country as a general rule was more vigorous, rather less refined, and rowdier.

In the next selection, James Kirke Paulding's Nimrod Wildfire is the chief character in a play that had its premier in 1830 as *The Lion of the West*. A revised version of the play — the only one surviving — was retitled *The Kentuckian*. Wildfire acts and talks in the way frontier-type figures had been doing in scores of jokes and sketches for a good many years. Contrasting comically with his two interviewers, the uncouth, boastful Wildfire is a hard drinker, a sure shot, a rough-and-tumble-no-holts-barred fighter, and a teller of soaring tall tales. The broadly comic drama about him, in which a very popular comedian enacted his role, did well in both Great Britain and the United States during three decades.

Though the representation of Wildfire drew upon popular lore about frontier ring-tailed roarers, the gossip of the day, with reason, had it that a real-life prototype was David Crockett, a United States congressman from Tennessee who was the subject of scads of newspaper anecdotes. He himself, helped by ghost-writers, contributed to his reputation by publishing other stories about his life in the canebrakes, in Washington, D.C., and on the campaign trail. Trading on his fame, several series of *Crockett Almanacks* were published in scattered cities between 1835 and 1856. These featured skits written by anonymous but often gifted journalists who hitched oral tales about others to him and invented imaginative windies enlarging the Crockett legend. Three fairly representative samples are "Colonel Coon's Wife Judy," "A Sensible Varmint," and "Crockett's Morning Hunt." Mrs. Coon, a striking contrast, say, with New England's sentimentering Widow Bedott and the demure Huldy of "The Courtin," is a fit mate for a fabulously obstreperous Westerner. The other two sketches, though based upon anecdotes about the real Davy Crockett, imaginatively endow him with the abilities of a comic demigod.

T. B. Thorpe's equally imaginative, cunningly crafted "The Big Bear of Arkansas" (1841) was in its day one of the most famous of all prewar American tall tales. In modern times, it has fascinated scholars and critics galore. No other short humorous narrative of its period has been as thoroughly studied and discussed. It deals with a topic that, naturally enough, was a favorite of the place and the time — hunting.

Between them, antebellum frontier writers compiled a remarkably thorough record of life along the shifting boundary between civilization and wilderness. As Bernard DeVoto said in *Mark Twain's America*:

No aspect of the life in the simpler America is missing from this literature. The indigo tub and the bearskin rug are here, as well as the frontier gentry's efforts to speak French. In the solitude of the upper rivers, trappers practice their ferocity. . . . The panorama of religion passes: camp meetings, christenings, Millerism, Mormonism, spiritualism. So does the comedy of the land — claim jumpers, false locators, Regulators, auctions, surveyors, roof-raisings, husking bees — and of the law courts, the bench and bar, sheriffs, muster days, legislatures, election campaigns. . . . Itinerants pass by, those strange travellers from abroad, peddlers, actors, singers, mesmerists, prophets, temperance agitators, physicians, census takers, circus clowns, bear leaders, accordionists. The folk labor at their vocations in the fields and the woods, the doggeries, the still-houses, the swamps, the bayous; at the spinning wheel, the loom, the churn. They frolic always, and if Betsy Smith, the fair offender, isn't married to John Bunce, why, jedge, "we oughter been, long ago." . . . Cataloguing is futile. Here is the complete life of the frontier.

Quite a number of these characters and scenes have been treated in the amusing stories and sketches not only by the writers just discussed — lawyer Jones, Paulding, the *Crockett Almanack* journalists, and artist Thorpe — but also by the other Old Southwestern authors sampled in this volume. They were a varied and widely dispersed crowd well equipped to cover many aspects with their yarns: Dr. Henry Clay Lewis of Louisiana, journalist Johnson J. Hooper of Alabama, planter Phillip B. January of Mississippi, printer John S. Robb, editor William Tappan Thompson of Georgia, reporter William C. Hall of Louisiana, artist-engraver William Penn Brannan of Mississippi, the Reverend Harden E. Taliaferro of Alabama, and jack-of-all-trades George Washington Harris of Tennessee.

Students of the history of American humor have been particularly fond of this school of exuberant, down-to-earth, wide-ranging yarn spinners. And a number have called the last one named, George Washington

Harris, the best of the lot, ranking second only to Mark Twain as a creator of our country's comedy. Such leading specialists as Franklin J. Meine, Bernard DeVoto, F. O. Matthiessen, Donald Day, Brom Weber, M. Thomas Inge, Milton Rickels, Hamlin Hill, Robert Penn Warren, Edmund Wilson (reluctantly), and Donald Davidson have called him great. William Faulkner placed Harris's chief comic character alongside such immortals as Falstaff, Don Quixote, Sairie Gamp, and Huck Finn. Mark Twain praised Harris and imitated him. Willard Thorp called Harris's Sut Lovingood a "brilliant creation." Thorp's description— an accurate one—indicates the content and tone of much of the young mountaineer's humor, and they may seem surprising when one considers the sophistication of many of his admirers. Thorp calls him "the prince of practical jokers" and cited rough pranks that he plays on a parson, wedding guests, and an Irishman—only a few of the battered victims of this ignorant, hard-drinking, "loudmouthed, sex-ridden, and brutal" Westerner whose chief pastime is raising particular hell. Sut's ferocity and its results make him a forerunner of the characters portrayed by today's writers of black humor. His frankness anticipates today's fun and games with scatology and pornography.

Postwar Comedy— Funny Fellows

Two groups of comic writers who began to emerge during the 1850s have been labeled "postwar humorists" because they were most numerous and most successful after the Civil War ended— Funny Fellows and Local Colorists. Each group flourished, moreover, because it reacted in its own way to the sectional conflict that had led to the war and that the war had been expected to resolve.

In their early writings, some Funny Fellows perpetuated an activity that had been important before the war. Seba Smith and James Russell Lowell in New England and William Tappan Thompson on the frontier had used comic characters to further political causes. Beginning in 1856, George Washington Harris used Sut Lovingood's storytelling skills to advocate his creator's views on political controversies. Notably he did this in a series of articles in which the mountaineer purportedly told how he helped President-elect Lincoln avoid violence during his trip to the inaugural by disguising him and smuggling him into Washington. According to Sut's account, the man he helped was ugly, filthy, stupid, tricky, and cowardly. Therefore, Harris's satire worked this way: he had a clownish yarn spinner traitorously collaborate with the faction that his creator opposed and tell about what happened in such a way as to show up the enemy.

Other satirists used similar formulas. David Ross Locke of Ohio, sympathetic with the North, had rascally Petroleum Vesuvius Nasby—a lying braggart, a loafer, a drunkard, a bigamist, a hypocrite, a racist, and a coward—do his best to sabotage the Union cause. A counterpart in the South, though a far less disreputable fellow, was Charles H. Smith's Bill Arp of Georgia. Smith, a Confederate soldier, had his man write sympathetic letters to "Mr. Linkhorn," which really, as though inadvertently, showed the Northern cause and the president to be unreasonable and immoral. The bitter satires of Locke and Smith were much admired during the impassioned years of the Civil War. Lincoln, for instance, was one of Locke's greatest fans; it was Nasby's creator with whom he offered to trade the presidency for the author's comic gift.

For the most part, the brutal political satire died away after the conflict ended. Locke was unusual in continuing to produce it into the 1880s. Charles Farrar Browne (whose Artemus Ward also was admired by Lincoln—and by Britons quite uninterested in American political fights), when he dabbled in politics occasionally, was much more tolerant, and much more typical. Typical, too, were the genial pontifications of Finley Peter Dunne's Mr. Dooley late in the century. A number of them, like "Mr. Dooley to Mr. Hennessy "on the Victorian Era," weren't concerned with his country's politics at all. Many of Mr. Dooley's most prized remarks concerned human nature rather than controversial issues. Charles H. Smith followed a general postwar trend when he turned his Bill Arp into a rustic philosopher who was able to produce a great many witty aphorisms.

A leading exploiter during the era of that ancient favorite incongruity between illiteracy and shrewdness, or even wisdom, was Henry Wheeler Shaw's Josh Billings, whose outstanding gift was writing amusing aphorisms. As in the piece that we reprint, "Live Yankees," he wrote many essays made up, one after another, of loosely related smart commentaries. A long run of *Josh Billings' Farmer's Allminaxes* made him a rich man because he stuffed issues with sayings such as these.

It is better to kno less, than to kno so much that aint so.

The more yung ones in a family, the eazier they are tew raize.

One chicken alwus makes more klucking for a hen than a dozen duz.

Don't forget *one* thing, yu hav got tew be wize before yu kan be witty; and don't forget *two* things, a single paragraff haz made sum men immortal, while a volume haz bin wuss than a pile-driver tew others—but what would Amerikans dew if it want for their sensations?

As the quotations indicate, Billings got much mileage out of the very eccentric way he said things. He was typical in this respect of the Funny Fellows, sometimes spelled "Phunny Phellows" because of their initial habit of spelling badly. Even after most of their creators cut down on the cacography, the group in general tended to macerate grammar; to mix metaphors; to commit malapropisms, spoonerisms, and "unintentional" puns; and to use eccentric sentences, which readers found funny. For another thing, the humorists tended to reduce characters to a few traits instead of individualizing them: they were uneducated fools or genial idiots, period. Other particularizations tended to disappear—localized locutions, scenes, occupations, attitudes, and actions. Consciously or unconsciously, probably the latter, the "Literary Comedians" (as their habit of lecturing caused them to be called) produced humor that in most instances scanted sectional differences and that followed the advice of an editor who wrote in 1866, "Let them seek to embody the wit and humor of all parts of the country, not of one city . . . for the benefit of all. Let them form a nucleus which will draw to itself all the waggery and wit of America."

Local Colorists

The Local Colorists fostered national unity (or believed that they did) in what might be described as almost the opposite way—by playing up regional backgrounds, characters, and mores. Not every writer in this group was a humorist. They often wrote tragic or at least sombre stories. But they produced a great deal of humor, and a large share of them went to extremes in using dialects. So, with some important differences, they perpetuated trends evident among the works of the prewar comic writers.

One important contrast resulted from their treating, as a rule, scattered happenings in areas that were smaller and more thoroughly differentiated than those their predecessors had treated. Typically, the dialect storytellers in our samples were very specific about their locales. Harriet Beecher Stowe wrote about a puritanical small town in Massachusetts; George Washington Cable, southern Louisiana; Joel Chandler Harris, a Georgia plantation; F. Hopkinson Smith, aristocratic tidewater Virginia; Mary E. Wilkins Freeman, rural Massachusetts; Charles W. Chesnutt, the North Carolina of the blacks; James Whitcomb Riley, Hoosier farm country; Alfred Henry Lewis, the Arizona of ranchers and cowboys; and Edward Noyes Westcott, upstate New York.

The Local Colorists differed in another way from prewar humorists. These writers, as a rule, even in their fun making, manifested an emotional involvement with their characters that was largely absent from the earlier comic writings. Although the group claimed that it carefully mirrored regional realities—in Mrs. Stowe's words "real characters, real scenes, and real incidents"—they generally avoided anything sordid, violent, or tragic. Instead of setting stories during the postwar era, they usually chose to portray the rose-tinted past. Mrs. Stowe set her stories in the New England of her childhood, "a simple, pastoral, germ-state of society . . . forever gone." Harris and Smith pictured happy plantations "befo the waw." The atmosphere was idyllic; the mood was nostalgic. Both literary and social critics believed that such sympathetic portrayals fostered intersectional affection and understanding. Theodore Roosevelt praised Harris for performing an important service: "He has written what exalts the South in the mind of every man who reads it, and yet has no bitterness toward any other part of the Union. There is not another American anywhere who can read Mr. Harris's stories . . . who does not rise up with a more earnest desire to do his part in solving America's problems aright."

A third difference between Local Colorists and both prewar humorists and postwar Literary Comedians was related to the way their stories were published. Instead of having their works published in newspapers, almanacs, and books sold door to door, most members of this group had their stories published by highly respected literary magazines, such as the *Atlantic Monthly, Harper's Monthly Magazine, Scribner's,* and *Lippincott's,* and in book form by reputable publishers, rather than by the issuers of subscription books. Though fairly popular, these regionalists didn't have the wide appeal of other groups of humorists.

Mark Twain, despite the fact that he was a journalist and a very popular writer himself, greatly admired several Local Colorists. He called George Washington Cable "the only master in the writing of French dialect that the country has produced." Partly because he thought Cable a great writer, partly for purposes of contrast, Twain traveled with him throughout the country on a joint lecture tour. Twain hailed Joel Chandler Harris as "the only master in writing Negro dialect" and called him "a fine genius . . . whose immortal tales charmed the world." Twain claimed that when his friend F. Hopkinson Smith retold a story he had heard in Virginia, he outdid Boccaccio's telling of the same story in his *Decameron* long before, turning a "curt and meager" version into "a good and tellable thing" that "transmuted . . . dross into golden words, and by the art of delivery made you shout." James Whitcomb Riley's "The Old Soldier's Story," Twain realized, was another recycling of a chestnut that had been passing from country to country all over the world for centuries. But he believed that Riley's way of telling it made it not only superb as art but also "about the funniest thing I ever listened to."

Mark Twain

Mark Twain's recognition that the comic writers of whom he had a high opinion retold old stories is interesting because he himself retold a goodly number and sometimes talked about doing so. The man who generally has been called the greatest American humorist, furthermore, knew that other leading writers had literary affiliations and consciously or unconsciously made use of literary sources. Marginal comments that he wrote in a book that treated bookish influences show that he took for granted that Dumas, Shakespeare, and others borrowed from their predecessors and that he approved. And, in his old age, he remarked that "all our phrasings are spiritualized shadows cast multitudinously from our readings."

He had close ties with each of the four groups of dialect humorists discussed above. Brought up in the antebellum Southwestern town of Hannibal, Missouri, as a boy and as a young man he read the rustic Yankee and the frontier humor of the era. As a printer's devil and a wandering journeyman printer, he pretty surely set some of it in type, since newspapers everywhere used humorous snippets for fillers. When he became a newspaper reporter and, somewhat later, a full-time humorist, he commented specifically on some of it and included selections in an anthology called *Mark Twain's Library of Humor*. He copied some of its characters and techniques, and he retold some stories earlier humorists had told. A few of many instances are these: Several traits and actions of both Tom Sawyer and his Aunt Polly echoed earlier American comedy loud and clear. The twentieth chapter of *Adventures of Huckleberry Finn* repeats Hooper's "Simon Suggs Attends a Camp Meeting" with several improvements; the twenty-second repeats a joke about a circus acrobat that several prewar humorists, among them Thompson, had told; the twenty-fourth chapter repeats, with variations, another of Suggs's adventures. A passage in *A Tramp Abroad* is much like "A Coon Hunt in a Fency Country," and a chapter in *Joan of Arc* retells a yarn that had been told by a number of humorists, among them George Washington Harris.

Mark Twain's affection for several Local Colorists has been noticed. It isn't surprising, since he himself in his most admired books was a Local Colorist, revisiting his boyhood home in *The Adventures of Tom Sawyer*, the river of his youth in "Old Times on the Mississippi" and *Adventures of Huckleberry Finn*, the Far West of his days out there in *Roughing It*. A critic wrote in the *Atlantic Monthly* in 1897, "He has recorded the life of certain southwestern portions of our country, at one fleeting stage of their development, better than it is possible it will ever be done again. . . . [His pictures are] both absolutely accurate and surprisingly comprehensive." The kinds of details he sets down, the humor, and often the nostalgic tone are typical of the school.

But during the postwar days when Mark Twain rose to international prominence, it was as a Funny Fellow, and now and then during the rest of his life he replayed that role. Like other literary comedians, he soon became a top comic lecturer; he continued to be one for thirty years; and his chief stock-in-trade on the platform, like that of Artemus

Ward and others, was the funereal demeanor of a successful mortician. In writing, as well as in lecturing, he borrowed from Ward tricks that he praised his friend for perfecting. Like Ward and other Funny Fellows, he dropped practically all afflicted spellings. But he never abandoned eccentrically built sentences, plague-stricken grammar, striking tropes, or vernacular expressions when they were in character for someone he was impersonating. Also, like Josh Billings, whose writings he knew well and praised, Twain was a great one to turn out aphorisms, some of which became popular enough to take on the guise of folk sayings.

What Mark Twain wrote, then, was very much the sort of humor other Americans wrote. But, as historians often have remarked, he did it better. "He was very funny," wrote Barry Paine in 1910, the year of the humorist's death, "and he knew every trick of the trade."

The pair of selections that we reprint are in the mainstream of American humor, but nevertheless they show Mark Twain at his best. In the manner of many an antebellum frontier humorist, he based "Jim Baker's Blue-Jay Yarn" on a tale he'd heard told during a fireside storytelling session. Like some successful prewar artists (for example, T. B. Thorpe), he introduced the raconteur's monologue with a framework using relatively formal language in sharp contrast with the easygoing dialect of the quoted narrative that follows it, the content of which helps bring the eccentric vernacular narrator to life. Jim tells a typical tall tale, which imaginatively and comically humanizes California woodland critters and that ends with a snapper. "Were one asked," DeLancey Ferguson wrote in *Mark Twain: Man and Legend*, "to choose from all Mark Twain's works the most powerful example of the Western tall story, . . . the choice would probably come down at last to Jim Baker's blue-jay yarn."

"Frescoes from the Past," like other local-color narratives, represents a picturesque way of life in a certain area during the past, "illustrating keelboat talk and manners, and that now departed and hardly-remembered raft-life," as Twain puts it. As in some superior antebellum pieces, there is an amusing contrast between the author's literate introduction and the sparkling vernacular styles, here of the ragamuffin Huck Finn and the rambunctious raftsmen. The passage uses a pattern utilized in hundreds of old-time stories: Two lions of the West take turns boasting about their toughness in language so outrageous that it is laughable. (An earlier example is the exchange of boasts by Nimrod Wildfire and the boatman in the excerpt from Paulding's 1830 play.) In most American antebellum narratives, such vauntings are followed by a ferocious fight in which both brave battlers are badly damaged and one finally wins. Similar incredible comic vauntings had been the stock-in-trade of Old World comic writers from classic times on; but abroad, the windup had differed. There, when the moment of truth comes, both boasters show that they are bluffing cowards by backing down. Since in typical pre-Civil War American accounts both contestants are brutally injured, one worse than the other, intrinsically the Old World ending is funnier than the New World ending is. For this reason and no doubt for others, most postwar American versions use the Old World pattern, as Mark Twain does. But the best parts of his account, like those in either classic or American stories, are the boasts themselves. And Twain's boasts, because of their fantastic imaginings and their inventive language, outdo the best concocted by other humorists, both domestic and foreign.

Sympathetic Translations

The story of American humor and its reception, and the critics' evaluations, show that it is of interest as a historical phenomenon and, what's more, that it has real merit as comic literature. But, except for the writings of Mark Twain, still read and admired seven decades after his death, very little of it is being read today. Two related causes for the neglect are (1) changes in the attitude of readers toward dialect as an important part of humorous works and (2) developments in the way humorists represent vernacular speech.

During much of the nineteenth century, readers in the United States found good, indifferent, and even bad renderings of dialect deliciously funny. There were several reasons for the popularity of works that featured dialect. During a period when many of the orators and highly admired literati used styles that were particularly elegant and highfalutin, less structured, less ornate, and more earthy writings seemed both refreshingly lifelike and incongruous. It was an age, too, when schoolmarms and dictionary makers were stuffy and stern about spelling, elegant diction, and grammar; therefore, assaults on all three seemed both naughty and funny. Sectional and class differences were more marked, important, and interesting then than they now are. Readers evidently were familiar with unlearned speech and more tolerant and comfortable with it than many of us are today. And people felt no need, it seems, to hurry their fireside reading.

At least some learned commentators on regional ways of talking spoke up for them, and, regardless of the fact that Americans found pedantry ridiculous, they were impressed. Particularly important were four editions of *A Dictionary of Americanisms*, the first issued in 1848 and the last—twice as long—in 1877, by John Russell Bartlett, with comments and definitions that, as H. L. Mencken said, showed that Bartlett "obviously relished" neologisms. In 1859, James Russell Lowell, by then a Harvard professor and therefore a person respected as an authority, reviewed the second edition and waxed eloquent in praise of "common-folk-talk."

No language, after it has faded into *diction*, none that cannot suck up feeding juices from the mother-earth of rich common-folk-talk, can bring forth a sound and lusty book. True vigor of expression does not pass from page to page, but from man to man, where the brain is kindled and the lips are limbered by downright living interests and passions in the very throe. Language is the soil of thought; and our own especially is a rich leaf-mould, the slow growth of ages . . . .

Again, in introducing the second series of the *Biglow Papers*, Lowell added hosannas, claiming that "our popular idiom is racy with life and vigor and originality, bucksome . . . to our new occasions."

Understandably, a number of regional writers not only practiced but preached the lavish use of dialect in humor. One instance perhaps will do as an example. Joel Chandler Harris wrote, "The fact remains that the vernacular, as distinct from literary form and finish, is the natural vehicle of the most popular variety of American humor; hence the frequent employment of . . . dialect." Humor based upon the speech of common folk, he added, is "the cream of the best."

Despite such praise, in time the enthusiasm—for various reasons—waned. Respected literary works came to be written in a less stuffy and a more talklike style, so vernacular phrasings were less incongruous. Some kinds of prejudices became less popular, and as a result so did jokes about class and racial mispronunciations. In 1873, critic E. C. Stedman spoke for many readers when he groaned about "the *horrible* degeneracy of public taste" that fostered the writings of both Funny Fellows and Local Colorists. A bit later, expatriate Henry James, over in Britain, was struck by "the invasive part played by the element of dialect in . . . American fictions," far more predominant than anything "in English, in French, in German work of the same order." And he bewailed "the riot of the vulgar tongue" in writings that used "dialect with its literary rein loose on its agitated back and with its shambling power of traction." This was in 1909. Forty years later, looking back, Lionel Trilling spoke for many of his contemporaries when he said, "Today the carefully spelled out dialects of nineteenth-century humorists are likely to seem dull." Hosts of readers have decided that, considering the rewards, they just don't have time to slog their way through swamps of dialect and to hell with them.

The attitudes and procedures of creators of comedy also changed as time went by. Some very early writers, none represented in this book, either didn't know or didn't care about setting down authentic popular speech. By the 1830s, however, several who knew regional speech quite well were satisfied to do no more than sample enough of its rhythms and quiddities to convey its flavor, Seba Smith in Maine and T. B. Thorpe in the Old Southwest, for instance. Constance Rourke, a pioneering scholar of American humor, praised the former writer because he "created an effect of Yankee speech without making its oddities obtrusive, in a medium that is all but transparent, and, if one cares to notice it very beautiful, revealing without effort the slow abundant satire." Rourke gave some contemporaries of Smith similar praise. She believed, though, that "these early conquests were nearly obliterated" when some humorists (she cited Lowell) tried to achieve "crackling realism." Thereafter, for years, "many another dark abyss in the use of native language yawned" and "the more sensitive uses" tended to be forgotten.

Doing their well-meaning but uninformed best to echo vulgar speech exactly, a number of humorists created works that became much too wearing for most moderns to read. Here is a brief passage of Sut Lovingood's talk recorded by the humorist many have called second only to Mark Twain, George Washington Harris.

" . . . the year afore las'—in struttin an' gobblin time, Wat felt his keepin right warm, so he sot intu bellerin an' pawin up dus in the neighborhood roun the ole widder McKildrin's. The more dus he flung up, the wus he got, ontil at las' he jis cudn't stan the ticklin sensahuns anuther minnit; so he put fur the county clark's offis, wif his hans sock'd down deep intu his britchis pockets, like he wer fear'd ove pick-pockets, his bach roach'd roun, an' a-chompin his teef ontil he splotch'd his whiskers wif foam. Oh! he wer yearnis' hot, an' es restless es a cockroach in a hot skillit."

Here is a passage in a story of 1882 by F. Hopkinson Smith, "Ginger and the Goose," which, it will be remembered, Mark Twain held to be a work of art told in "golden words."

Now Dolly, you know, is de gal I lub, an' wen she cum in de kitchen, she hole up her nose, an' she say, wid a long sniff: "He-e-e-e! wha' dat smell so good?" An' I say: "G'long, gal; . . . what you got to do wid dat smell?" An' she say: "Ginja, dat is de nicerest smell I eber hab had. What is dat?" An' I say: "G'long, gal; what you got to do wid de white folks' goose?" An' Dolly cum close to me, an' look ober my shoulder, an' she say: "Dat is a splendid goose. Oh, Ginga, but dat goose smell nice!"

Here, not only the spelling of *come* with the meaningless *cum* but also other bad spellings, and the failure to paragraph, add to the needless confusion brought about by excessive representations of black speech.

As a final horrifying example, here is a paragraph quoting a Funny Fellow, Petroleum V. Nasby, whom Lincoln admired.

I see in the papers last nite that the Governmenet hez institooted a draft, and that in a few weeks sum hundreds uv thousands uv peecable citizens will be dragged to the tented field. I know not wat uthers may do, but ez for me, I cant go. Upon a rigid eggsaminashun uv my fizzleckle man, I find it wood be wus nor madnis for me to undertake a campane. . . .

Academic editors of nineteenth-century dialect humor such as that by Harris, Smith, and Locke have tended to be unyielding in their demand that it be reprinted exactly as it first came into print. We believe that scholarly editors of much older English works of undisputed excellence have chosen a better way. Look at a passage on the opening page of the first folio edition of William Shakespeare's *Tragedie of Ivlivs Caesar.*

Cob. Truly ſir, all that I line by, is with the Aule: I meddle with no Tradeſmans matters, nor womens matters; but withal I am indeed Sir, a Surgeon to old ſhooes: when they are in great danger, I recouer them. As proper men as euer trod vpon Neats Leather, haue gone vpon my handy-worke.

Although the first folio has been painstakingly reproduced in facsimile for study by specialists, scholars have put this into a form that general readers can grasp and appreciate.

Sec. Commoner. Truly, sir, all that I live by is with the awl: I meddle with no tradesman's matter, nor women's matters, but with awl. I am, indeed, sir, a surgeon to old shoes; when they are in great danger, I recover them. As proper men as ever trod upon neat's leather have gone upon my handiwork.

The meaning of the speech and practically all of its wording, including a pun ("with awl"), have been preserved; but, thanks to modernizations of typography, punctuation, and spelling and the insertion of a *the* where it is needed, this becomes readable today. Similar changes in a revered work called on its 1611 title page *The Newe Teſtament of our Lord and Sauiour Iesvs Christ* have made the New Testament accessible to modern readers. And editors of eighteenth- and nineteenth-century classics have felt that they weren't profaning the works of great authors when they modernized capitalizations, spellings, and punctuation in the interest of readability.

We think that it is significant that some nineteenth-century dialect humorists in America moved in the same direction. "As for Hosea," Lowell wrote as early as 1847, "I am sorry that I began by making him such a detestable speller. There is no fun in bad spelling itself. . . . I am getting him out of it gradually." Several Funny Fellows forsook cacography and the wilder eccentricities. Charles H. Smith went so far as to rewrite some of Bill Arp's first pieces in a style that was far more literate. George Washington Cable, though he didn't get around to doing it, gave thought to simplifying some of his dialect passages. Mark Twain wrote dialect that can be read without any changes, as in *Adventures of Huckleberry Finn,* for instance, and in "Jim Baker's Blue-Jay Yarn." Twain saw that "written things have to be . . . colloquialized [with] a touch of indifferent grammar . . . flung in *here and there,* apparently at random." Thus he discovered what H. Allen Smith in our time called "the secret of dialect writing": it was "always to stop some distance short of perfection." "Rigid consistency," Smith said, "is a sin of many who try to write in dialect. It's the spacing of the dialect words that is important."

The aim in editing the selections that follow has been to do for them what past- and present-day writers who are read and liked have done for their own vernacular imitations. Sharing as he does H. L. Mencken's admiration and love for the American language, editor Raven McDavid has tried to retain the qualities that Mencken believed our dialect humorists imparted to their renderings of this nation's speech—"its rich disdain of all scholastic rules and precedents, its tendency toward bold and often bizarre tropes, its rough humors, its not infrequent flights of what might be called poetic fancy, its love of neologisms for their own sake." Raven McDavid hopes to have made as few changes as possible but enough to make the pieces accessible to modern readers. The grammar, however eccentric by academic standards, will be left like she done been writ. Choices of words haven't been disturbed. But paragraphing, capitalization, and punctuation have been modernized. Most important, except when cacography creates hilarity, eccentric but meaningless, unfunny, or confusing spellings have been normalized. Thanks to the retention of the structures, the rhythms, and the vocabularies, we devoutly hope that essential excellences have been retained, along with the gusto and the humor that made the writings popular. If McDavid has succeeded, hereafter the following versions will serve as standard "translations" of outstanding comic works that have been unduly neglected.

Walter Blair
Chicago

Note: Although the coeditors planned this book together, frequently discussed procedures, and even helped one another avoid some errors, they divided responsibility as follows: Walter Blair selected the humorous works included, supplied the texts, wrote the introduction and the headnotes, and prepared the bibliography. Raven McDavid tamed the dialect where needed, wrote the Linguistic Note, provided dialect studies to be included in the bibliography, and compiled the list of Forgotten Words and Personalities. We are grateful to the English Department of Odense University, Denmark, for clerical assistance that hastened the completion of the manuscript.

Rustic Yankees

Seba Smith

(1792-1868)

Seba Smith, born in Buckfield, Maine, went to grade school
and college in the state of his birth and later worked there as a journalist until he was forty-seven years old. So, though he lived elsewhere
during his remaining twenty-nine years, he was well prepared to picture
Down Easters and to imitate their speech. He first put these skills to use
in 1830 when, hoping "by some out of the common trick of newspaper
writing to give increased interest and popularity to his little newspaper"
(the Portland Daily Courier), he invented Jack Downing of Downingville, Maine, and had him write letters "to his friends at home in their
own plain language." So lifelike were Smith's representations of Jack
and his correspondents that some readers were sure that Jack was a real
person and Downingville a real village; the letters were received so well
in Maine and beyond that his creator sent Jack on travels that allowed
him to comment on national events and controversies. From 1830 until
the eve of the Civil War, with few interruptions, Smith's rustic Yankee
and his relatives had their say to a large audience in newspapers and
books. The Life and Writings of Major Jack Downing (1833) and My
Thirty Years Out of the Senate (1859), which collected most of them,
had sales that proved the Yankee cracker-box philosopher had many
followers. Further evidence of his appeal was supplied by a group of
writers who imitated his style, in some cases even purloined his name,
to preach their beliefs, as well as by playwrights who put him into successful comedies.

Jack thus became the first of a long line of nationally admired humorous commentators speaking in the vernacular—a parade that would
include such figures as Davy Crockett, Hosea Biglow, Josh Billings, Mr.
Dooley, Mark Twain, Will Rogers, and others.

"*Jack's Grandfather,*" *part of Downing's introduction to his* Life and Writings, *not only characterizes Jack but also charmingly introduces and quotes the old war veteran. The choice of details and the style, as well as the shrewd maneuvers of Mr. Johnson, make the account of a bloody battle comic.*

Jack's Grandfather

Jack Downing

My Thirty Years Out of the Senate
(New York, 1859, p. 261).

As I said afore, my grandfather, old Mr. Zebedee Downing, was the first settler in Downingville. Bless his old heart, he's living yet; and although he is eighty-six years old, he attended a public caucus for the good of his country about two years ago, and made a speech, as you will find somewhere before you get through this book, where it tells about my being nominated for Governor of the State of Maine.

As it is the fashion, in writing the lives of great folks, to go back and tell something about their posterity, I s'pose I ought to give some account of my good old grandfather, for he was a true patriot, and as strong a republican as ever Uncle Joshua was. He was born somewhere in the old Bay State away back of Boston, and when the Revolutionary War come on, he went a-soldierin. Many and many a time, when I was a little boy, I've sot on the dye-pot in the corner till most midnight, to hear him tell over his going through the *fatigue of*

Burgoyne. If one of the neighbors came in to chat awhile in the evening, my grandfather was always sure to go through with the fatigue of Burgoyne, and if a stranger was traveling through Downingville and stopped at my grandfather's in a warm afternoon to get a drink of water, it was ten chances to one if he could get away till my grandfather had been through the whole story of the fatigue of Burgoyne.

He used to tell it the best to old Mr. Johnson, who used to come in regularly about once a week to spend an evening and drink a mug of my grandfather's cider. And he would set so patiently and hear my grandfather through from beginning to end, that I never could tell which took the most comfort, Mr. Johnson in drinking the cider, or my grandfather in going through the fatigue of Burgoyne. After Mr. Johnson had taken about two or three drinks, he would smack his lips and, says he, "I guess, Mr. Downing, you would have been glad to get such a mug of cider as this in the battle of Burgoyne."

"Why, yes," said my grandfather, "or when we was on the march from Cambridge to Peekskill, either, or from Peekskill to Albany, or from Albany to Saratogue, where we went through the fatigue of Burgoyne.

"Old Schuyler was our general," said my grandfather, bracing himself back in his chair, "and he turned out to be a traitor, and was sent for, to go to General Washington to be court-martialed! Then General Gates was sent to us to take the command, and he was a most capital officer, every inch of him. He had his cocked hat on, and his regimentals, and his furbelows on his shoulders, and he looked nobly," said my grandfather.

"I can see him now as plain as if 'twas yesterday. He wore a plaguy great stub queue, as big as my wrist, sticking out at the back of his neck as straight as a handspike. Well, when Gates came, we were all reviewed, and everything was put in complete order, and he led us on, ye see, to take Burgoyne. By daylight in the morning we were called out by the sound of the drum, and drawn up in regiments, and the word was, 'On your posts, march!' And there we stood, marching on our posts without moving forward an inch, heads up, looking to the right. We didn't dare to move an eye, or hardly to wink.

"By and by along comes the old General to inspect us, riding along so stately, and that old stub queue sticking out behind his head so straight, it seems as though I can see him right here before me. And then he addressed us, like a father talking to his children.

"'Fellow soldiers,' says he, 'this day we are going to try the strength of Burgoyne's forces. Now let every man keep a stiff upper lip, go forward boldly and attack them with courage, and you've nothing to fear.' Oh, he addressed us completely; and then we marched off to meet the enemy.

"By and by we begun to hear the balls whizzing over our heads, and the enemy's guns begun to roar like thunder. I felt terribly for a minute or two, but we kept marching up, marching up," said my grandfather, rising and marching across the floor, "for we had orders not to fire a gun till we got up so near we could almost reach 'em with our bayonets. And there was a hundred drums in a bunch, rattling enough to craze a nation, and the fifes and bugles," continued my grandfather, still marching across the floor, "went 'tootle, tootle, tootle, tootle!'—Oh, I can hear that very tune ringing in my ears now, as plain as if 'twas yesterday, and I shall never forget it to my dying day.

"When we got up so near the enemy that we could fairly see the whites of their eyes, the word was 'Halt!' " said my grandfather, suddenly halting in the middle of the floor, and sticking his head back straight as a soldier, " 'Make ready!'

" 'Twas did in a moment," continued my grandfather, throwing his staff up against his shoulder, " 'Take aim!'

" 'Twas did in a moment," fetching his staff down straight before his eyes. " 'Fire!' Then, O mercy, what a roar," said my grandfather, striking his staff down on the floor, "and such a smother and smoke you couldn't hardly see your hand afore you.

"Well, in an instant the word was 'Prime and load!' And as fast as we fired we fell back in the rear to let others come up and take their turn, so by the time we were loaded we were in front and ready to fire again, for we kept marching all the time," said my grandfather, beginning to march again across the floor.

"But the enemy stood their ground and kept pouring in upon us tremendously, and we kept marching up and firing, marching up and firing, but didn't gain forward an inch. I felt streaked enough, for the balls were whistling over our heads, and sometimes a man would drop down on one side of me and sometimes on t'other; but it wouldn't do to flinch a hair; we must march up and fire and wheel to the right and left, and keep it going.

"By and by the word was 'advance columns!' Then, heavens and earth, how light I felt," said my grandfather, quickening his march across the floor. "I knew in a moment the enemy was retreating, and it seemed to me I could have jumped over the moon. Well, we marched forward, but still kept firing, and presently we came to the enemy's ground. And then, O mercy! such a sight I never see before and never want to again: stepping over the dead bodies, and the poor wounded wretches wallowing in their blood, mangled all to pieces, and such screeches and groans— some crying out, 'Don't kill me! don't kill me!' and others begging us to kill 'em to put 'em out of misery. Oh, it was enough to melt the very heart of a stone," said my grandfather, wiping the tears from his eyes.

"But they needn't have been afraid of being hurt, for our General was one of the best men that ever lived. He had the carts brought up immediately and all the poor wounded souls carried off as fast as possible where they would be taken good care of. He wouldn't let one of 'em be hurt more than he would one of his own men. But it was a dreadful hot battle; we fit and skirmished all the afternoon and took a good many prisoners, and some cannon and ammunition. When it come night, the enemy retreated to their fortifications, and we camped all night on the ground with our guns in our hands, ready at a moment's warning to pitch battle again.

"As soon as it was daylight, we were all mustered and paraded again, and round come the old General to see how we looked. He held up his head like a soldier, and the old stub queue stuck out as straight as ever. I can see it now as plain as I can see my staff," said my grandfather. "And O my stars, how he addressed us; it made our hearts jump to hear him. 'Fellow soldiers,' says he, 'this day we shall make Burgoyne tremble. If you are only as brave as you were yesterday, we shall have him and his army before night.'

"But Burgoyne had slipped away in the night and got into a place stronger fortified. But he couldn't get away; he was hemmed in all round, so we got him before it was over. We were five or six days skirmishing about it; but I can't tell you all, nor a quarter part on't."

"But how was it you took Burgoyne at last?" said Mr. Johnson, taking another drink of cider.

"O, he had to give up at last," said my grandfather. "After we had skirmished a day or two longer, General Gates sent word to Burgoyne, that if he had a mind to march his army back into Canada and leave everything this side unmolested, he'd let him go peaceably. But Burgoyne would not accept it; he sent word back that he was going to winter with his troops in Boston. Well, after we had skirmished round two or three days longer, and Burgoyne got into such close quarters that he couldn't get away anyhow, he sent word to General Gates that he'd accept the offer and march back to Canada. But Gates sent word back to him again, 'You said you meant to winter in Boston, and I mean to make you as good as your word.'

"At last Burgoyne see it was no use for him to hold out any longer, so he give all of his men up prisoners of war. Then we were all paraded in lines a little ways apart to see them surrender. And they marched right out and marched along towards us; and it was a most noble sight to see them all dressed out in their regimentals, and their bayonets glistening in the sun enough to dazzle anybody's eyes. And they marched along and stacked their arms, and they all marched through between our lines, looking homesick enough. I guess we felt as well as they did, if our clothes wa'n't so good.

"Well, that was the end of the war in the northern states. There was a little skirmishing away off to the South afterwards, but nothing to be compared to that. The battle of Burgoyne was what achieved our independence; it was the capstone of the war; there never was such a glorious battle as that since the days of Caesar, nor Methusaleh, no, nor clear back to Adam."

"I don't think there ever was," said Mr. Johnson, handing me the quart mug and telling me to run and get another mug of cider; for before my grandfather could get through the fatigue of Burgoyne, Mr. Johnson would most always get to the bottom of the mug.

When I brought in the second mug, Mr. Johnson took another sip and smacked his lips, and says he, "Mr. Downing, I should like to drink a toast with you; so here's health and prosperity to the apple trees of Downingville. Mr. Downing, what will you drink to us?" said he, handing the mug to my grandfather.

"Why, I don't care about any cider," said my grandfather (for he is a very temperate man, and so are all the Downings remarkably temperate), "but I will just drink a little to the memory of the greatest and the bravest general that this world ever see yet. So here's my respects to old General Gates's stub queue." By this time my grandfather having poured out of him the whole fatigue of Burgoyne, and Mr. Johnson having poured into him about three pints of cider, they would both of them feel pretty considerably relieved, and Mr. Johnson would bid us good night and go home.

I take it that it was hearing these stories of my grandfather's bravery told over so often in my younger days that made me such a military character as to induce the President to appoint me to the command at Madawaska, and also to go to South Carolina to put down the Nullifiers. But I'm getting a little before my story, for I haven't got through with my grandfather yet, and my father comes before I do, too.

As I said afore, my grandfather was the first settler in Downingville. When he got through soldiering in the Revolutionary War, he took a notion he'd go and pick him out a good lot of land away down East to settle on, where there was land enough to be had just for whistling for it, and where his boys would have a chance to do something in the world. So he took grandmother and the two boys, for father and Uncle Joshua were all the boys he had then, and packed them into a horse-wagon, and took an axe and a hoe and a shovel, and some victuals, and a bed tick to put some straw in, and a gun and some blankets and one thing and another, and started off down East.

He drove away into Maine till he got clear to the end of the road, and then he picked his way along through the woods and round the pond five miles further, till he got to the very spot where Downingville now is, and there he stopped and baited his horse, and while grandmother and the boys sot down and took a bit of a luncheon, grandfather went up top of one of the hills to take a view of the country. And when he come down again, says he, "I guess we may as well untackle, for I don't believe we shall find a better place if we travel all summer."

So he untackled the old horse, and took the wagon and turned it over against a great oak tree, and put some bushes up round it and made a pretty comfortable sort of a house for 'em to sleep in a few nights, and then he took his axe and slashed away amongst the trees. But that old oak tree never was cut down; it's the very same one that stands out a little ways in front of grandfather's house now.

And poor old grandmother, long as she lived—for she's been dead about five years—always made it a practice once a year, when the day come round that they first camped under the old oak, to have the table carried out and set under the tree. And all hands, children and grandchildren, had to go and eat supper there, and the good old lady always used to tell over the whole story—how she slept eight nights under the wagon, and how they were the sweetest nights' rest she ever had.

Thomas Chandler Haliburton

(1796-1865)

*T*homas Chandler Haliburton, though a Canadian, was an important pioneer in the popularization of south-of-the-border American humor. True, several United States-born authors of humor about Yankees preceded him; but V. L. O. Chittick, Haliburton's biographer, was probably right when he claimed that for years his Sam Slick was "the best known character in the field of ludicrous 'down east' sayings and doings." Between 1836 and 1860, books about that wandering peddler ran through at least 200 editions in Canada, the United States, and England. In addition, Haliburton edited a couple of anthologies, each in three volumes, that popularized Yankee dialect humor in England—Traits of American Humour, by Native Authors *(1852) and* Americans at Home *(1854).*

In the preface to the former work, he listed ninety-some words "common to various parts of the Union" that were pronounced differently in New England, the South, and the West and sorted out the pronunciations. In addition to his travels, Haliburton's background helped him do this. His father was a transplanted Yankee, and, as Haliburton knew and had Slick say, his home province (Nova Scotia) had imported a large share of its inhabitants from New England. So his literary representations of Down East ways of talking were based upon a lifelong acquaintance.

As a wandering salesman of clocks and other items, Sam Slick earned his living the way a great many comic Yankees did. Again and again, tales about acute peddlers and their clever tricks had turned up in almanacs, newspapers, and books. Haliburton enlarged Sam's shrewdness to let him say keen things about many matters, often embodying what his good brain, sharp eyes, and wide experience had taught him in memorable aphorisms. One of Haliburton's books played up Sam's skill in its title, Sam Slick's Wise Saws and Modern Instances *(1853), but earlier volumes had amply proved he had it—* The Clockmaker, *three series (1837, 1838, 1840), and* The Attache, *two series (1843, 1844). Sam's monologues filled three other books, the last of which was published in 1855. In each, the peddler's speech was rich in Yankee provincialisms, though, as Haliburton had a character in his 1855 book say, over the years he tended to speak "purer English." This led Prof. Walter S. Avis (who in 1969 edited a number of selections "for modern readers" by adopting "modern style in spelling, punctuating, and paragraphing") to "feel confident that the editing would meet with Judge Haliburton's full approval."*

The Clockmaker

Sam Slick
*Judge Haliburton's
Yankee Stories*
(Philadelphia: T. B. Peterson and Brothers,
1838, title page).

I had heard of Yankee clock peddlers, tin peddlers, and Bible peddlers, especially of him who sold Polyglot Bibles (*all in English*) to the amount of sixteen thousand pounds. The house of every substantial farmer had three substantial ornaments: a wooden clock, a tin reflector, and a Polyglot Bible. How is it that an American can sell his wares, at whatever price he pleases, where a Bluenose would fail to make a sale at all? I will inquire of the Clockmaker the secret of his success.

"What a pity it is, Mr. Slick (for such was his name), what a pity it is," said I, "that you, who are so successful in teaching these people the value of clocks, could not also teach them the value of *time*."

"I guess," said he, "they have got that ring to grow on their horns yet, which every four-year-old has in our country. We reckon hours and minutes to be dollars and cents. They do nothing in

13

these parts, but eat, drink, smoke, sleep, ride about, lounge at taverns, and talk about 'House of Assembly.' If a man don't hoe his corn and he don't get a crop, he says it is all owing to the bank. And if he runs into debt and is sued, why he says the lawyers are a curse to the country. They are a most idle set of folks, I tell you."

"But how is it," said I, "that you manage to sell such an immense number of clocks (which certainly cannot be called necessary articles, among a people with whom there seems to be so great a scarcity of money?"

Mr. Slick paused, as if considering the propriety of answering the question, and looking me in the face, said in a confidential tone, "Why I don't care if I do tell you, for the market is glutted and I shall quit this circuit. It is done by a knowledge of *soft sawder* and human natur. But here is Deacon Flint's," said he. "I have but one clock left, and I guess I will sell it to him."

At the gate of a most respectable looking farm house stood Deacon Flint, a respectable old man, who had understood the value of time better than most of his neighbors, if one might judge from the appearance of everything about him. After the usual salutation, an invitation to "light" was accepted by Mr. Slick, who said he wished to take leave of Mrs. Flint before he left Colchester.

We had hardly entered the house, before the Clockmaker pointed to the view from the window, and, addressing himself to me, said, "If I was to tell them in Connecticut there was such a farm as this away down east in Nova Scotia, they wouldn't believe me—why there ain't such a location in all New England. The deacon has a hundred acres of land."

"Seventy," said the Deacon, "only seventy."

"Well, seventy; but then there is your fine deep bottom. Why I could run a ramrod in it."

"Interval, we call it," said the Deacon, who though evidently pleased at this eulogism, seemed to wish the experiment of the ramrod to be tried in the right place.

"Well, interval if you please (though Professor Eleazer Cumstick, in his work on Ohio, calls them bottoms), is just as good as dyke. Then there is that water privilege, with three thousand or four thousand dollars, twice as good as what Governor Cass paid fifteen thousand dollars for. I wonder, Deacon, you don't put up a turning lathe, a shingle machine, a circular saw, grind bark, and—"

"Too old," said the Deacon. "Too old for all these speculations."

"Old," repeated the Clockmaker, "not you! why you are worth half a dozen of the young men we see, nowadays. You are young enough to have—" Here he said something in a lower tone of voice, which I did not distinctly hear. But whatever it was, the Deacon was pleased; he smiled and said that he did not think of such things now.

"But your beasts, dear me; your beasts must be put in and have a feed." Saying which, he went out to order them to be taken to the stable.

As the old gentleman closed the door after him, Mr. Slick drew near to me, and said in an undertone, "That is what I call *'soft sawder'*: An Englishman would pass that man as a sheep passes a hog in a pasture, without looking at him; or," said he, looking rather archly, "if he was mounted on a pretty smart horse, I guess he'd trot away, if he could. Now I find—"

Here his lecture on *"soft sawder"* was cut short by the entrance of Mrs. Flint.

"Just come to say good bye, Mrs. Flint."

"What, have you sold all your clocks?"

"Yes, and very low, too, for money is scarce, and I wished to close the concern. No, I am wrong in saying all, for I have just one left. Neighbor Steel's wife asked to have the refusal of it, but I guess I won't sell it. I had but two of them, this one and the fellow of it, that I sold Governor Lincoln. General Green, the Secretary of State for Maine, said he'd give me fifty dollars for this here one. It has composition wheels and patent axles; it is a beautiful article—a real first chop—no mistake—genuine superfine, but I guess I'll take it back; and beside, Squire Hank might think kinda harder, that I did not give him the offer.

"Dear me," said Mrs. Flint, "I should like to see it. Where is it?"

"It is in a chest of mine, over the way, at Tom Tape's store. I guess he can ship it on to Eastport."

"That's a good man," said Mr. Flint. "Just let's look at it."

Mr. Slick, willing to oblige, yielded to these entreaties, and soon produced the clock—a gaudy, highly varnished, trumpery looking affair. He placed it on the chimney-piece, where its beauties were pointed out and duly appreciated by Mrs. Flint, whose admiration was about ending in a proposal, when Mr. Flint returned from giving directions about the care of the horses. The Deacon praised the clock; he too thought it a handsome one. But the Deacon was a prudent man; he had a watch—he was sorry, but he had no occasion for a clock.

"I guess you're in the wrong furrow this time, Deacon; it ain't for sale," said Mr. Slick. "And if it was, I reckon neighbor Steel's wife would have it, for she gives me no peace about it."

Mrs. Flint said that Mr. Steel had enough to do, poor man, to pay his interest, without buying clocks for his wife.

"It's no concern of mine," said Mr. Slick, "as long as he pays me, what he has to do, but I guess I don't want to sell it, and besides, it comes too high: that clock can't be made at Rhode Island under forty dollars. Why it ain't possible," said the Clockmaker, in apparent surprise, looking at his watch. "Why as I'm alive it is four o'clock, and if I haven't been two hours here—how on earth shall I reach River Philip tonight? I'll tell you what, Mrs. Flint: I'll leave the clock in your care till I return on my way to the States. I'll set it a-going and put it to the right time."

As soon as this operation was performed, he delivered the key to the Deacon with a sort of serio-comic injunction to wind up the clock every Saturday night, which Mrs. Flint said she would take care should be done, and promised to remind her husband of it, in case he should chance to forget it.

"That," said the Clockmaker as soon as we were mounted, "that I call *'human natur.'* Now that clock is sold for forty dollars; it cost me just six dollars and fifty cents. Mrs. Flint will never let Mrs. Steel have the refusal—nor will the Deacon learn until I call for the clock, that havin once indulged in the use of a superfluity, how difficult it is to give it up. We can do without any article of luxury we have never had; but when once obtained, it is not *'in human natur'* to surrender it voluntarily. Of fifteen thousand clocks sold by myself and partners in this Province, twelve thousand were left in this manner, and only ten clocks were ever returned—when we called for them, they invariably bought them. We trust to *'soft sawder'* to get them into the house, and to *'human natur'* that they never come out of it."

James Russell Lowell

(1819-1891)

*J*ames Russell Lowell, one of the Massachusetts Lowells, was revered in his day for his work as a Harvard professor, a learned scholar,
an outstanding editor, an influential writer on politics, a profound literary critic, and a serious poet. But it is ironic that most of his highly respected writings have weathered badly, and he is remembered today
almost entirely because he created two illiterate Yankees—a disreputable
rascal and a pious hayseed—and let them talk themselves and their
neighbors to life in dialect poems.

Lowell professed Romance languages for many years. He was a found-
ing editor of the Atlantic Monthly and a very successful coeditor of the
North American Review. He served as ambassador to Spain and Great
Britain. And his admired books of criticism and poetry made him a pre-
eminent man of letters during a long career. But it was his Biglow Papers
of 1846-1848 and of 1862-1867, the first series concerning the Mexican
war and the second the Civil War, that caught the fancy of both general
readers and discerning critics of his day and beyond.

Lowell, strongly opposed to the War with Mexico in 1846, was eager
to state his feelings "in a way that would tell." He was aware that his
serious writings in literary English were "almost unread." He also knew
that from Poor Richard's day to his own some of the most effective
satirists had been real or fictitious, uneducated, and horse-sensible commentators, so he decided to let a countrified, unread mouthpiece speak
out for him. His Hosea Biglow accordingly was "an upcountry man . . .
homely commonsense vivified and heated by conscience" who fell back
"into the natural stronghold of his homely dialect when heated to the
point of self-forgetfulness."

Lowell was well qualified to create such a spokesman. The Cambridge
in which he had lived since his birth was a village in the midst of farm-
lands. Having worked and nooned over the years with Yankee farmers,
he knew well their qualities and their way of thinking and talking. He

17

was a trained linguist with a great love for "the language of the divine illiterate"—those speaking "a popular idiom . . . racy with life and vigor and originality."

Although the papers were undoubtedly influential as rhetoric in their day, they have continued to appeal because, as William Dean Howells put it, they are "a creative fiction of unique excellence." In the words of another reviewer, they portray "characters so lifelike . . . so good as individuals and as types that we know not where in literature to look for others that excel them." The authentic language was a chief aid both to the vivid characterization and to the comedy of the poems.

"The Courtin," the best-known paper, actually isn't concerned with war at all; it tells an amusing story about the way shy Ezekiel finally got engaged to the quiet but coquettish Huldy. What it shows about its teller, Hosea Biglow, is his ability to enrich a simple story by vividly picturing a characteristic background and by bringing his characters to life through descriptions, dialogue, and portrayed actions.

"Second Letter from B. Sawin, Esq." is Hosea's versified translation of a letter he received from Birdofredum. This rascally farm boy has let himself be persuaded to enlist in the army, has served and suffered, and now plans to cash in on his disfigurements by going into politics. His disillusioned picture of army life, his wry totting up of his disablements, and his canny calculations about cashing in as a veteran tellingly satirize any war and its grim consequences. And some of Hosea's ingenious rhymes give readers fun like that Ogden Nash's rhymes would provide almost a hundred years later.

Not long after he started to publish the letters, Lowell decided that he had made a mistake when he caused Hosea to spell as badly as he did. Therefore, in subsequent letters, he gradually improved the spelling.

Biglow Papers
The Courtin

God makes such nights, all white and still,
　Far's you can look or listen,
Moonshine and snow on field and hill,
　All silence and all glisten.

Zekle crep up quite unbeknown
　And peeked in through the window,
And there sot Huldy all alone,
　'Ith no one nigh to hinder.

A fireplace filled the room's one side
　With half a cord of wood in;
There warn't no stoves (till comfort died)
　To bake ye to a puddin.

The wa'nut logs shot sparkles out
　Towards the prettiest, bless her;
And little flames danced all about
　The chiny on the dresser.

Agin the chimbley crook-hecks hung,
　And in among them rusted
The old queen's arm that gran'ther Young
　Fetched back from Concord busted.

The very room, cause she was in,
　Seemed warm from floor to ceilin,
And she looked full as rosy again
　As the apples she was peelin.

'T was kind of kingdom-come to look
　On such a blessed creetur,
A dogrose blushin to a brook
　Ain't modester nor sweeter.

He was six foot of man, A 1,
    Clean grit and human natur;
None couldn't quicker pitch a ton
    Nor draw a furrow straighter.

He'd sparked it with full twenty gals,
    Had squired 'em, danced 'em, druv 'em,
First this one, and then that, by spells—
    All is, he couldn't love 'em.

But long of her his veins'd run
    All crinkly like curled maple,
The side she breshed felt full of sun
    As a south slope in Ap'il.

She thought no v'ice had such a swing
    As hisn in the choir;
My! when he made Old Hundred ring,
    She felt the Lord was nigher.

And she'd blush scarlet, right in prayer,
    When her new meetin-bonnet
Felt somehow through its crown a pair
    Of blue eyes sot upon it.

That night, I tell ye, she looked *some!*
    She seemed to've got a new soul,
For she felt sartin-sure he'd come,
    Down to her very shoe-sole.

She heered a foot, and knowed it too,
    A-raspin on the scraper,—
All ways to once her feelins flew
    Like sparks in burnt-up paper.

He kind of l'itered on the mat,
    Some doubtful of the sequel,
His heart kept going pitty-pat,
    But hern went pity Zekle.

And yet she gin her chair a jerk,
    As though she wished him furder,
And on her apples kept to work,
    Parin away like murder.

"You want to see my Pa, I s'pose?"
    Wal . . . no . . . I come designin"—
"To see my Ma? She's sprinklin clothes
    Agin tomorrow's i'nin.'"

To say why gals acts so or so,
  Or don't, 'ould be presumin;
Maybe to mean *yes* and say *no*
  Comes nateral to women.

He stood a spell on one foot first,
  Then stood a spell on t'other,
And on which one he felt the worst
  He could n't ha' told ye nuther.

Says he, "I'd better call agin";
  Says she, "Think likely, Mister";
That last word pricked him like a pin,
  And . . . Wal, he up and kissed her.

When Ma bimeby upon 'em slips,
  Huldy so pale as ashes,
All kind of smily round the lips
  And teary round the lashes.

For she was just the quiet kind
  Whose naturs never vary,
Like streams that keep a summer mind
  Snowhid in January.

The blood close round her heart felt glued
  Too tight for all expressin,
Till mother see how matters stood,
  And gin 'em both her blessin.

Then her red come back like the tide
  Down to the Bay of Fundy,
And all I know is they was cried
  In meetin come next Sunday.

A Second Letter from B. Sawin, Esq.

Birdofredum Sawin
Mark Twain's Library of Humor
(New York: Charles L. Webster Company,
1888, p. 431).

I s'pose you wonder where I be; I can't tell for the soul of me
Exactly where I be myself—meanin by that the whole of me
When I left home, I had two legs, and they worn't bad ones nither
(The scaliest trick they ever played was bringin on me hither).
Now one on 'em's I dunno where; they thought I was a-dyin,
And sawed it off because they said 'twas kinda mortifyin.
I'm willin to believe it was, and yit I don't see, nuther,
Why one should take to feelin cheap a minute sooner 'n t'other.
Since both was equally to blame; but things is as they be:
I took on so they took it off, and that's enough for me.
There's one good thing, though, to be said about my wooden new one—
The liquor can't git into it as used to in the true one.
So it saves drink; and then, besides, a fellow couldn't beg
A greater blessing than to have one alluz sober peg.
It's true a chap's in want of two for followin a drum,
But all the march I'm up to now is just to Kingdom Come.

22

I've lost one eye, but that's a loss it's easy to supply
Out o' the glory that I've got, for that is all my eye.
And one is big enough, I guess, by diligently usin it,
To see all I shall ever git by way o' pay for losin it.
Off'cers, I notice, who git paid for all our thumps and kickins,
Do well by keepin single eyes a'ter the fattest pickins.
So as the eye's put fairly out, I'll larn to go without it,
And not allow *myself* to be no great put out about it.
Now le' me see, that isn't all; I used, 'fore leavin Jaalam,
To count things on my finger ends, but sutthin seems to ail 'em:
Where's my left hand? Oh, darn it, yes, I recollect what's come on't;
I hain't no left arm but my right, and that's got just a thumb on't;
It ain't so handy as it was to cal'late a sum on't.
I've had some ribs broke—six (I b'lieve)—I hain't kept no account on 'em;
When pensions git to be the talk, I'll settle the amount on 'em.
And now I'm speakin about ribs, it kinda brings to mind
One that I couldn't never break—the one I left behind.
If you should see her, just clear out the spout o' your invention
And pour the longest sweetnin in about an annual pension,
And kinda hint (in case, you know, the critter should refuse to be
Consoled) I ain't so 'xpensive now to keep as what I used to be.
There's one arm less, ditto one eye, and then the leg that's wooden
Can be took off and sot away whenever there's a puddin.

I s'pose you think I'm comin back as opulent as thunder,
With shiploads o' gold images and various sorts o' plunder.
Well, 'fore I volunteered, I thought this country was a sorta
Canaan, a reg'lar Promised Land, flowin with rum and water,
Where property growed up like time, without no cultivation,
And gold was dug as 'taters be among our Yankee nation,
Where nateral advantages were perfectly amazin,
Where every rock there was about with precious stones was blazin,
Where mill-sites filled the country up as think as you could cram 'em,
And desperate rivers run about, a-beggin folks to dam 'em.
Then there were meetin houses too, chock full o' gold and silver
That you could take and no one couldn't hand ye in no bill for.
That's what I thought afore I went; that's what them fellows told us
That stayed to home and speechified and to the buzzards sold us.
I thought that gold mines could be got cheaper than china asters
And see myself a-comin back like sixty Jacob Astors.
But such idees soon melted down and didn't leave a grease spot;
I vow my whole share o' the sp'iles wouldn't come nigh a V spot,
Although, most anywheres we've been, you needn't break no locks,
Nor run no kind o' risks, to fill your pocket ful o' rocks.

I guess I mentioned in my last some o' the nateral featurs
O' this all-fired bogey-hole in the way o' awful creaturs,
But I forgot to name (new things to speak on so abounded)
How one day you'll most die o' thirst and fore the next git drownded.
The climate seems to me just like a teapot made o' pewter
Our Prudence had, that wouldn't pour (all she could do) to suit her;
First place the leaves 'ould choke the spout, so's not a drop 'ould dreen
   out,
Then Prue 'ould tip and tip and tip, till the whole kit burst clean out.
The kiver hinge-pin bein lost, tea leaves and tea and kiver
'Ould all come down *kerswosh*! as though the dam broke in a river.
Just so 'tis here, whole months there ain't a day o' rainy weather,
And just as th' officers 'ould be a-layin heads together
As t' how they'd mix their drink at such a milingtary deepot,
'Twould pour as though the lid was off the everlastin teapot.
The cons'quence is, that I shall take, when I'm allowed to leave here,
One piece o' property along, and that's the shakin fever.
It's regular employment, though, and that ain't thought to harm one,
Nor 't ain't so tiresome as it was with t'other leg and arm on;
And it's a consolation, too, although it doesn't pay
To have it said you're some great shakes in any kind o' way.
'T worn't very long, I tell you what, I thought o' fortin-makin—
One day a reg'lar shiver-de-freeze and next as good as bakin,
One day a-broilin in the sand, then smoth'rin in the ma'shes—
Git up all sound, be put to bed a mess o' hacks and smashes.

But then, thinks I, at any rate there's glory to be had;
That's an investment, a'ter all, that mayn't turn out so bad.
But somehow, when we'd fit and licked, I alluz found the thanks
Got kinda lodged afore they come as low down as the ranks.
The generals got the biggest share, the colonels next and so on—
We never got a blasted mite o' glory as I know on,
And s'pose we had, I wonder how you're goin to contrive its
Division so's to give a piece to twenty thousand privates.
If you should multiply by ten the portion o' the brav'st one
You wouldn't git more 'n half enough to speak of on a gravestone.
We git the licks—we're just the grist that's put into war's hoppers.
Leftenants is the lowest grade that helps pick up the coppers.
It may suit folks that go agin a body with a soul in't
And ain't contented with a hide without a bayonet hole in't.
But glory is a kind o' thing *I* shan't pursue no furder
'Cause that's the off'cers' perquisite—yourn's on'y just the murder.

Well, a'ter I gin glory up, thinks I at least there's one
Thing in the bills we ain't had yit, and that's the GLORIOUS FUN;

If once we git to Mexico, we fairly may presume we
All day and night shall revel in the halls o' Montezumy.
I'll tell ye what my revels was, and see how you would like 'em:
We never got inside the halls; the nighest ever *I* come
Was standin sentry in the sun (and fact, it seemed a cent'ry)
A-catchin smells o' b'iled and roast that come out through the entry,
And hearin, as I sweltered through my passes and repasses,
A rat-tat-too o' knives and forks, a clinkety-clink o' glasses.
I can't tell off the bill o' fare the Generals had inside;
All I know is, that out o' doors, a pair o' soles was fried,
And not a hundred miles away from where this child was posted,
A Massachusetts citizen was baked and b'iled and roasted.
The only thing like revellin that ever come to me
Was bein routed out o' sleep by that darned reveille.

They say the quarrel's settled now; for my part I've some doubt on't.
'T'll take more fish-skin than folks think to take the rile clean out on't.
At any rate, I'm so used up I can't do no more fightin;
The only chance is left to me is politics or writin.
Now as the people's got to have a milingtary man,
And I ain't nothin else just now, I've hit upon a plan;
The can'idatin line, you know, 'ould suit me to a T;
And if I lose, 'twon't hurt my ears to lodge another flea;
So I'll set up for can'idate for any kind o' office
(I mean for any that includes good easy chairs and soffies;
For as to runnin for a place where work's the time o' day,
You know that's what I never did—except the other way).
If it's the Presidential chair for which I'd better run,
What two legs anywheres about could keep up with my one?
There ain't no kind o' quality in can'idates, it's said,
So useful as a wooden leg—except a wooden head;
There's nothin ain't so popular—(why, it's a perfect sin
To think what Mexico has paid for Santa Anna's pin),
Then I hain't got no principles, and since I was knee high,
I never did have any great, as you can testify.
I'm a decided peace-man, too, and go agin the war;
For now the whole on't's gone and past, what is there to go *for*?
If, while you're lectioneerin round, some curious chap should beg
To know my views o' state affairs, just answer WOODEN LEG!
If they ain't satisfied with that, and kinda pry and doubt,
And ax for somethin' definite, just say ONE EYE PUT OUT!
That kind o' talk I guess you'll find 'll answer to a charm,
And when you're druv too nigh the wall, hold up my missin arm;
If they should nose round for a pledge, put on a virtuous look
And tell them that's precisely what I never gin—nor took!

Then you can call me "Timbertoes"—that's what the people likes!
Sutthin combinin moral truth with phrases such as strikes;
Some say the people's fond o' this, or that, or what you please—
I tell you what the people wants is just correct idees;
"Old Timbertoes," you see, 's a creed it's safe to be quite bold on,
There's nothin in't the other side can any ways git hold on;
It's a good tangible idee, a sutthin to embody
The valuable class o' men who look through brandy toddy.
It gives a party platform, too, just level with the mind
Of all right-thinkin honest folks that mean to go it blind.
Then there air other good hurrahs to draw on as you need 'em,
Such as the ONE-EYED SLAUGHTERER, the BLOODY BIRDOFRE-
    DUM;
Them's what takes hold o' folks that thinks, as well as o' the masses,
And makes you certain o' the aid o' good men o' all classes.

There's one thing I'm in doubt about: in order to be President,
It's absolutely ne'ssary to be a Southern resident;
The Constitution settles that, and also that a fellow
Must own a nigger o' some sort—jet black or brown or yellow.
Now I hain't no objections agin partic'lar climes
Nor agin ownin anything (except the truth sometimes),
But as I hain't no capital, up there among ye, maybe,
You might raise funds enough for me to buy a low-priced baby,
And then, to suit the Northern folks, who feel obleeged to say
They hate and cuss the very thing they vote for every day,
Say you're assured I go full butt for Liberty's diffusion
And made the purchase on'y just to spite the Institution.
But golly! there's the courier's hoss upon the pavement pawin!
I'll be more 'xplicit in my next.

Yourn,
Birdofredum Sawin

Frances Miriam Whitcher

(1814-1852)

Some of the female chatterboxes created by Frances Miriam Whitcher—gossipy Widow Bedott, tart Aunt Maguire, and others—were greatly liked by nineteenth-century Americans. Mrs. Whitcher modeled them after New York villagers she knew in her birthplace, Whiteboro, and in Elmira, where she lived after her marriage. Their monologues first appeared in a little Rome, New York, newspaper and later became nationally famous when the Saturday Gazette and Godey's Lady's Book gave them wider circulation. At least twenty-five editions of Widow Bedott Papers (1855) sold more than 100,000 copies; and, beginning in 1879, a dramatization had long runs in playhouses throughout the country. Fifteen years after Mrs. Whitcher's death, a New York publishing firm gathered her previously uncollected early pieces in Widow Spriggins, Mary Elmer and Other Sketches. The author's talkative spinsters, wives, and widows commented shrewdly or stupidly and sentimentally or satirically in monologues that revealed their own quirky characters. Widow Bedott's meandering reminiscences about her husband Hezekiah fit perfectly Mark Twain's definition of the American humorous story as one that "bubbles gently along" and that "may be spun out at great length, and may wander around as it pleases, and arrive nowhere in particular." Later creators of similarly fashioned shaggy-dog stories included Mark Twain himself, James Whitcomb Riley, W. C. Fields, Ed Wynn, and Norm Crosby. "Hezekiah Bedott," Mrs. Whitcher's most famous piece, was reprinted scores of times in newspapers, periodicals, and anthologies after it introduced the Widow Bedott Papers.

Hezekiah Bedott

Widow Bedott

The Widow Bedott Papers (New York: Derby & Jackson, 1856, p. 25).

He was a wonderful hand to moralize, husband was, specially after he begun to enjoy poor health. He made an observation once when he was in one of his poor turns that I never shall forget the longest day I live. He says to me one winter evenin as we was a-settin by the fire. I was a-knittin (I always was a wonderful great knitter) and he was a-smokin (he was a master hand to smoke, though the doctor used to tell him he'd be better off to let tobacco alone; when he was well, used to take his pipe and smoke a spell after he'd get the chores done up, and when he wa'n't well, used to smoke the biggest part of the time.)

Well, he took his pipe out of his mouth and turned toward me, and I knowed something was comin, for he had a particular way of lookin round when he was gwine to say anything uncommon. Well, he says to me, says he, "Silly" (my name was Priscilly naterally, but he generally called me "Silly," cause it was handier, you know). Well, he says to me, says he, "Silly," and he looked pretty solemn, I tell you, he had a solemn countenance naterally—and after he got to be deacon 'twas more so, but since he'd lost his health he looked solemner than ever, and certingly you wouldn't wonder at it if you knowed how much he underwent. He was troubled with a wonderful pain in his chest and amazin weakness in the spine of his back, besides the pleurisy in the side, and having the aguer a considerable part of the time, and being broke of his rest of nights, cause he was so put to 't for breath when he laid down. Why it's an unaccountable fact that when that man died he hadn't see a well day in fifteen year, though when he was married and for five or six year after I shouldn't desire to see a ruggeder man than what he was.

But the time I'm speaking of he'd been out of health nigh upon ten year, and O dear sakes! how he had altered since the first time I ever see him! That was to a quiltin to Squire Smith's a spell afore Sally was married. I'd no idee then that Sal Smith was a-gwine to be married to Sam Pendergrass. She'd been keepin company with Mose Hewlitt for better'n a year, and everybody said *that* was a settled thing, and lo and behold! all of a sudding she up and took Sam Pendergrass.

Well, that was the first time I ever see my husband, and if anybody'd a-told me then that I should ever marry him, I should a-said—but lawful sakes! I most forgot, I was gwine to tell you what he said to me that evenin, and when a body begins to tell a thing I believe in finishin on't some time or other. Some folks have a way of talkin round and round and round forevermore, and never comin to the p'int. Now there's Miss Jinkins, she that was Poll Bingham afore she was married. She is the tejusest individual to tell a story that ever I see in all my born days.

But I was a-gwine to tell you what husband said. He says to me, says he, "Silly." Says I, "What?" I didn't say, "What, Hezekiah?" for I didn't like his name. The first time I ever heard it I nearly killed myself a-laughin. "Hezekiah Bedott," says I, "well I would give up if I had such a name." But then you know I had no more idee o' marryin the fellow than you have this minute o' marryin the governor. I s'pose you think it's curious we should a-named our oldest son Hezekiah. Well, we done it to please father and mother Bedott; it's father Bedott's name, and he and mother Bedott both used to think that names had ought to go down from generation to generation. But we always called him Kiah, you know. Speaking of Kiah, he is a blessin, ain't he? and I ain't the only one that thinks so, I guess. Now don't you never tell nobody that I said so, but between you and me I rather guess that if Keziah Winkle thinks she's a-gwine to catch Kiah Bedott she is a *leetle* out of her reckonin.

But I was going to tell what husband said. He says to me, says he, "Silly." I says, says I, "What?" If I didn't say "what?" when he said "Silly," he'd a-kept on saying "Silly" from time to eternity. He always did, because, you know, he wanted me to pay particular attention, and I genuinely did; no woman was ever more attentive to her husband than I was. Well, he says to me, says he, "Silly." Says I, "What?" though I'd no idee what he was gwine to say, didn't know but what t'was something about his sufferings, though he wa'n't apt to complain, but he frequently used to remark that he wouldn't wish his worst enemy to suffer one minute as he did all the time, but that can't be called grumblin — think it can?

Why, I've seen him in sitivations where you'd a-thought no mortal could a-helped grumblin, but he didn't. He and me went once in the sled out to Boonville to see a sister of hisn. You know the snow is amazin deep in that section of the kentry. Well, the hoss got stuck in one of them-ere flambergasted snow-banks, and there we sot, unable to stir, and to cap it all, while we was a-sittin there, husband was took with a dreadful crick in his back. Now *that* was what I call a *predicament*, don't you? Most men would a-swore, but husband didn't. He only says, says he, "Consarn it." How did we get out, did you ask? Well we might a-been sittin there to this day, fur as *I* know, if there hadn't a-happened to come along a mess of men in a double team and they h'isted us out.

But I was gwine to tell you that observation of hisn. Says he to me, says he, "Silly." I could see by the light of the fire (there didn't happen to be no candle burnin if I don't disremember, though my memory is sometimes ruther forgetful, but I know we wa'n't apt to burn candles exceptin when we had company); I could see by the light of the fire that his mind was apt to be uncommon solemnized. Says he to me, says he, "Silly." I says to him, "What?" He says to me, says he, "*We're all poor critters!*"

Frontier Storytellers

Hamilton C. Jones

(1798-1868)

Stories like Whitcher's "Hezekiah Bedott" that wander exten-
sively and get nowhere enjoyed many reincarnations. They also made
many earlier appearances, among them Laurence Sterne's Tristram Shan-
dy (1767), a novel that itself had many forebears, and a number of monologues by stage Yankees dating back to 1824. Norris Yates noticed that
in the backwoods sketches that were quite popular before the war "the
narrator perversely rambles from point to point until he loses the entire
thread of the story, if he ever had one to start with." "Cousin Sally
Dilliard," a variant of this kind of narrative, surfaced in a North Carolina
newspaper about 1830 and was reprinted again and again in many newspapers and at least three times (1836, 1838, and 1844) in The Spirit of
the Times, a leading purveyor of frontier humor. William T. Porter, the
editor of the Spirit, included it in his famous collection, The Big Bear
of Arkansas and Other Sketches, Illustrative of Characters and Incidents
in the South and South-West (1845), as did other anthologists.

In addition to having fun with digressions, the author of "Cousin Sally
Dilliard" plays up the informality of frontier courts, a favorite target in
the new country. Yates suggests that "the witness was only feigning stupidity and had been suborned; this impression is strengthened by the
fact that he gave the lawyer 'a knowing wink' before he began his first
attempt at answering the questions."

The author was Hamilton C. Jones, identified by Henry Watterson, in
Oddities in Southern Life and Character, as "a lawyer of eminence in
his day and generation." Franklin Meine found that he was born in Virginia in 1798, that he graduated from the University of North Carolina,
and that he not only practiced law but also served as state solicitor and,
for four terms, as a state legislator, but Meine was unable to learn when
he died. This one sketch was the only piece of his writing that became
well known.

Cousin Sally Dilliard

The Witness

Cyclopaedia of Wit and Humor
(1858, I.206).

*Scene: A court of justice
in North Carolina.*

A beardless disciple of Themis arises, and thus addressed the court.

"May it please Your Worship, and you, Gentlemen of the Jury, since it has been my fortune (good or bad I will not say) to exercise myself in legal disquisition, it has never befallen me to be obliged to prosecute so direful, marked and malicious an assault—a more wilful, violent, dangerous battery—and finally a more diabolical breach of the peace, has seldom happened in a civilized country; and I dare say it has seldom been your duty to pass upon one so shocking to benevolent feelings, as this which took place at Captain Rice's, in this country. But you will hear from the witnesses."

The witnesses being sworn, two or three were examined and deposed. One said that he heard the noise and did not see the fight; another that he seen the row but didn't know who struck first; and a third, that he was very drunk and couldn't say much about the scrimmage.

Lawyer Chops: "I am sorry, gentlemen, to have occupied your time with the stupidity of the witnesses examined. It arises, gentlemen, altogether from misapprehension on my part. Had I known, as I now do, that I had a witness in attendance who was well acquainted with all the circumstances of the case, and who was able to make himself clearly understood by the court and jury, I should not so long have trespassed upon our time and patience. Come forward, Mr. Harris, and be sworn!"

So forward comes the witness, a fat, shuffly old man, a little corned, and took his oath with an air.

Chops: "Harris, we wish you to tell all about the riot that happened the other day at Captain Rice's; and as a good deal of time has already been wasted in circumlocution, we wish you to be compendious, and at the same time as explicit as possible."

Harris: "Adzactly," giving the lawyer a knowing wink and at the same time clearing his throat. "Captain Rice, he gin a treat; and cousin Sally Dilliard, she came over to my house and axed me if my wife she couldn't go. I told cousin Sally Dilliard that my wife was poorly, being as how she had a touch of the rheumatics in the hip, and the big swamp was in the road, and the big swamp was up, for there had been a heap of rain lately. But howsomever, as it was she, cousin Sally Dilliard, my wife she mout go. Well, cousin Sally Dilliard then axed me if Mose he moutn't go. I told cousin Sally Dilliard that he was the foreman of the crop, and the crop was smartly in the grass; but howsomever as it was she, cousin Sally Dilliard, Mose he mout go—"

Chops: "In the name of common sense, Mr. Harris, what do you mean by this rigmarole?"

Witness: "Captain Rice, he gin a treat, and cousin Sally Dilliard she came over to our house and axed if my wife she moutn't go. I told cousin Sally Dilliard—"

Chops: "Stop, sir, if you please; we don't want to hear anything about your cousin Sally Dilliard and your wife. Tell us about the fight at Rice's."

Witness: "Well, I will, sir, if you will let me."

Chops: "Well, sir, go on."

Witness: "Well, sir, Captain Rice he gin a treat, and cousin Sally Dilliard she came over to my house, and axed me if my wife she moutn't go—"

Chops: "There it is again. Witness, please to stop."

Witness: "Well, sir, what do you want?"

Chops: "We want to know about the fight, and you must not proceed in this impertinent story. Do you know anything about the matter before the court?"

Witness: "To be sure I do."

Chops: "Well, go on and tell it, and nothing else."

Witness: "Well, Captain Rice, he gin a treat—"

Chops: "This is intolerable. May it please the Court; I move that this witness be committed for a contempt; he seems to be trifling with this case."

Court: "Witness, you are now before a court of justice, and unless you behave yourself in a more becoming manner, you will be sent to jail. So begin and tell us what you know about the fight at Captain Rice's."

Witness (alarmed): "Well, gentlemen, Captain Rice, he gin a treat, and cousin Sally Dilliard—"

Chops: "I hope the witness may be ordered into custody."

Court (after deliberating): "Mr. Attorney, the Court is of the opinion that we may save time by telling witness to go on in his own way. Proceed, Mr. Harris, with your story, but stick to the point."

Witness: "Yes, gentlemen. Well, Captain Rice he gin a treat, and cousin Sally Dilliard she came over to our house and axed me if my wife she mout go. I told cousin Sally Dilliard that my wife she was poorly, being as how she had the rheumatics in the hip, and the big swamp was up, but howsomever, as it was she cousin Sally Dilliard, my wife she mout go. Well, cousin Sally Dilliard then axed me if Mose he moutn't go. I told cousin Sally Dilliard as how Mose—he was foreman of the crop, and the crop was smartly in the grass, but howsomever, as it was she, cousin Sally Dilliard, Mose he mout go. So they goes on together—Mose, my wife, and cousin Sally Dilliard—and they come to the big swamp, and it was up, as I was telling you. But being as how there was a log across the big swamp, cousin Sally Dilliard and Mose, like genteel folks, they walked across the log; but my wife, like a darned fool, hoisted her skirts and waded through. And that's all I know about the fight."

James Kirke Paulding
(with W. B. Bernard)

(1778-1860)

A native New Yorker, a close friend of Washington Irving, and the author of sophisticated, gossipy essays, prolific James Kirke Paulding also made some important contributions to the literature about the Old Southwest when it was America's frontier. In 1830, Paulding wrote a note to John Wesley Jarvis, a widely traveled artist and a superb storyteller, asking him to give him "a few sketches, short stories and incidents, of Kentucky or Tennessee manners, and especially of their peculiar phrases and comparisons," perhaps adding or inventing "ludicrous scenes of Col. Crockett in Washington." Paulding wanted these to use in a play he would enter in a contest being conducted by actor-producer James H. Hackett. Using whatever help Jarvis furnished, plus his own experiences and his reading, the New Yorker won the contest with The Lion of the West, or A Trip to Washington *(1830).*

Starring as the comic frontiersman Nimrod Wildfire, Hackett opened the play in New York. There and elsewhere, its reception was bolstered by well-founded rumors that Wildfire was a fictional prototype of Congressman Crockett of Tennessee, whose alleged social gaucheries and extravagant talk were being played up by journalists throughout the country. The play did well not only in America but also in England after it was twice revised. The long-lived final version was doctored by a British dramatist, William Bayle Bernard. In its final form as The Kentuckian, or A Trip to New York *(1833), it proved to be Hackett's most popular vehicle for twenty years. Since Bernard's is the only version that has survived, it is impossible to say how earlier versions were changed. But in the conversation with Percival reprinted here, Wildfire retells a story that Paulding had told in his own words in 1817, and in his talk with Mrs. Wollope he retells a yarn long circulated on the frontier. Mrs. Wollope, however, is a caricature of Mrs. Trollope, whose controversial travel book about America had been published in 1832.*

Jarvis, who was interested in vernacular speech, may have contributed

37

several of Wildfire's "peculiar phrases," such as "lion of the west," "te-totaciously," "exflunctified," "catawampus," and a Western term for lawyers, "catfish," given them, Wildfire explains, because "they're all head, and their head's all mouth." In addition, Jarvis may have helped with the congressman's comic boasts and his repeated shout, "Wake, snakes, June-bugs are coming!" Newspapers cited some of these in reviews. But Paulding deserves credit for the creation of a memorable character and his appropriate words and actions.

Nimrod Wildfire's Tall Talk

Wildfire: Madam, your most obedient.

Mrs. Wollope: Sir.

Wildfire: I believe your name is Mrs. Wollope.

Mrs. Wollope: It is.

Wildfire: Then you know my uncle, Peter Freeman. He tells me you have come among us to take a squint at things in general on this here side of the big pond.

Mrs. Wollope: The big pond? Oh, the Atlantic. That, sir, is my object.

Wildfire: Then I meant to say, madam, on that subject, I can out-talk any fellow in this country—and give him half an hour's start.

Mrs. Wollope: A man of intelligence. Pray be seated.

Wildfire (*brings forward two chairs, sits on one, and as Mrs. Wollope is about to sink into the other, he throws his legs on it*)! Now, Mrs. Wollope.

Mrs. Wollope: The soldier tired. Perhaps, sir, you would prefer an armchair.

Wildfire: No, Madam, if it was just after dinner, I should like to put my legs out of the window.

Mrs. Wollope: His legs out of the window—a very cool proceeding, certainly. May I offer you a cup of tea?

Wildfire: Much objected to you, madam. I never raise the steam with hot water—always go on the high-pressure principle—all whiskey.

Mrs. Wollope: A man of spirit. Are you stationed in New York, sir?

Wildfire: Stationed—yes! But don't mean to stop long. Old Kaintuck's the spot. There the world's made upon a large scale.

Mrs. Wollope: A region of superior cultivation—in what branch of science do its gentlemen excel?

Wildfire: Why, madam, of all the fellows either side of the Allegheny hills, I myself can jump higher—squat lower—dive deeper—stay under longer and come out drier.

Mrs. Wollope: Here's amelioration. And your ladies, sir?

Wildfire: The gals! Oh, they go it on the big figure, too—no mistake in them. There's my late sweetheart, Patty Snaggs. At nine year old she shot a bear, and now she can whip her weight in wildcats. There's the skin of one of 'em. (*Takes off his cap*)

Mrs. Wollope: Feminine accomplishments! Doubtless your soil and people correspond.

Wildfire: The soil—oh, the soil's so rich you may travel under it.

Mrs. Wollope: Travel under ground, sir? I must put this down.

Wildfire: Yes, madam, particularly after the spring rains. Look you here now, t' other day, I was a-horseback, paddling away pretty comfortably through Nobottom Swamp, when suddenly—I wish I may be curry-combed by 50,000 tomcats, if I didn't see a white hat getting along in mightly considerable style all alone by itself on top of the mud—so up I rid, and being a bit dubious, I lifted it with the butt-end of my whip, when a fellow sung out from under it, "Hullo, stranger! Who told you to knock my hat off?" "Why," says I, "what sort of a sample of a white man are you? What's come of the rest of you?" "Oh," says he, "I'm not far off—only in the next county. I'm doing beautifully—got one of the best horses under me that ever burrowed—claws like a mole—no stop in him—but here's a wagon and horses right under me in a mighty bad fix, I reckon, for I heard the driver say a spell ago one of the team was getting a leetle tired."

Mrs. Wollope: What a geological novelty.

Wildfire: "So," says I, "you must be a considerable fellow on your own, but you had better keep your mouth shut or you'll get your teeth sunburnt. So," says I, "good-bye, stranger. I wish you a pleasant ride."

*****

Wildfire: A gentleman? Oh, I'll put it to him *like a gentleman*, but if this had happened about ten years ago—when I was chock full of fun and fight—I wouldn't have minded doing it in Old Mississippi style.

Percival: Some mode peculiar to the wildness of the region?

Wildfire: Well, I'll tell you how it was. I was riding along the Mississippi one day when I came across a fellow floating down the stream, sitting cocked up in the stern of his boat, fast asleep. Well, I hadn't had a fight for as much as ten days—felt as though I must cover myself up in a salt bin to keep—so wolfy about the head and shoulders. So, says I, "Hullo, stranger, if you don't take care your boat will run away wi' you." So he looked up at me slantindicular, and I looked down on him slaunchwise. He took out a chaw of tobacco from his mouth and, says he, "I don't value you tantamount to that," and then he flapped his wings and crowed like a cock. I riz up, shook my mane, crooked my neck, and neighed like a horse. Well, he run his boat foremost ashore. I stopped my wagon and set my triggers. "Mister," says he, "I'm the best man—if I ain't, I wish I may be tetotaciously exflunctified! I can whip my weight in wildcats and ride straight through a crabapple orchard on a flash of lightning—clear meat-axe disposition! And what's more I once backed a bull off a bridge." "Poh," says I, "what do I care for that? I can tote a steamboat up the Mississippi and over the Allegheny Mountains. My father can whip the best man in old Kaintuck, and I can whip my father. When I'm good-natured I weigh about a hundred and seventy, but when I'm mad, I weigh about a *ton.*" With that I fetched him the regular Injun war-whoop. Out he jumped from his boat and down I tumbled from my wagon—and, I say, we came together like two steamboats going sixty mile an hour. He was a pretty severe colt, but no part of a priming to such a fellow as me. I put it to him mightly droll—tickled the varmint till he squealed like a young colt, bellowed "enough" and swore I was a rip-staver. Says I, "*Ain't* I a horse?" Says he, "Stranger, you're a *beauty* any-how, and if you'd stand for Congress, I'd vote for you next 'lection." Says I, "Would you? My name's Nimrod Wildfire. Why I'm the yellow flower of the forest. I'm all *brimstone but the head,* and that's aqua fortis."

Percival: A renowned achievement. Well, Colonel, I feel it my duty be-fore I leave New York to disclose the rumor I have heard to your uncle. Proceed in this affair as you think best, but remember, if you do meet his Lordship, it must be with the weapons of a gentlemen. (*Exit*)

Wildfire: A gentleman's weapons? Oh, of course, he means rifles. Maybe that Lord has heard of mine. She's a noisy varmint made of Powder House lightning-rod steel, and twisted like our Kentucky widow. She's got but one peeper, but if she blinks that at him, his head will hum like a hornet's nest—he'll see the stars dance in the daytime. He'll come off as badly as a fellow I once hit a sledgehammer lick over the head—a real sockdologer. He disappeared altogether; all they could ever find of him was a little grease spot in one corner. (*Exit*)

"Nimrod Wildfire's Tall Talk" is reprinted from *The Lion of the West: A Farce in Two Acts* by James Kirke Paulding; edited and with an Introduction by James N. Tidwell, with the permission of the publishers, Stanford University Press. Copyright 1954 by the Board of Trustees of the Leland Stanford Junior University.

Crockett Almanack Stories

(1837-1853)

*D*avid Crockett (1786-1836) was a meagerly educated man, with perhaps a hundred days of formal schooling. In frontier Tennessee, where he was born and reared, a lack of education probably was more of a help than a handicap in politics, since there was a general distrust of book learning. Helped also by his reputation as a mighty hunter, a good militiaman, a genial drinker, and a fine storyteller, Davy (as he was generally known) was appointed or elected to several local offices and in time was sent to Congress (1827-1831, 1833-1835). While he was serving in Washington, his motto, "Be sure you're right and then go ahead," caught in a few words the formula for the period, and numerous newspaper items played up his colorful personality and his coonskin humor. Anecdote-filled books signed with his name, though partly or wholly written by ghost writers, swelled his fame. So did his picturesque death during the battle of the Alamo.

The best dialect humor about Davy, very loosely based upon actuality, appeared in a series of Crockett Almanacks. The earliest came out in Nashville before Davy's death and was issued annually for several years (1834-1840). Some of the tales in the early series and in Crockett Almanacks published in New York, Boston, Philadelphia, and other cities until 1856 were adapted from The Lion of the West and Crockett's books. But it is doubtful that Crockett himself or even his family had anything to do with these very popular publications or the aphorisms and tales printed between the instructions, predictions, and tables in the almanacs. Most of the material written in dialect was the work of journalists and hack writers who imitated the speech and the methods of tellers of Old Southwestern tall tales. At their best, the anonymous yarns amusingly mingle imaginative inventions of characters, events, and speeches with mundane details and expressions. "Colonel Coon's Wife Judy" (1837) is from the Nashville almanac for 1838. "A Sensible Varmint" (1841), based upon an anecdote told earlier about other frontiersmen, and "Crockett's Morning Hunt" (1853) are from New York almanacs. In the last, as Constance Rourke remarked, the mythical Davy "becomes a demigod, or at least a Prometheus."

Colonel Coon's Wife Judy

It's most likely my readers has all heerd of Colonel Coon's wife Judy. She wore a bearskin petticoat, an alligator's hide for an overcoat, an eagle's nest for a hat, with a wildcat's tail for a feather. When she was fourteen years old, she wrung off a snappin turtle's neck, and made a comb of its shell, which she wears to this day. When she was sixteen years old, she run down a four-year-old colt and chased a bear three mile through the snow, because she wanted his hair to make a toothbrush. She out-screamed a catamount, on a wager, and sucked forty rattlesnake eggs, just to give her a sweet breath, the night she was married.

It was not at all likely that Judy would throw herself away on any young fellow that was a mind to set up a claim to her, and so many of 'em found they were barkin up the wrong tree and gettin their fingers pricked with a chestnut burr.

At last, one Tennessee roarer, that never backed out for anything short of a mammoth, heard of Judy's accomplishments, and 'termined to try his flint ag'in her steel. So he got into a jumper on a cold winter night, and drove through the woods towards her father's house. He begun to scream before he got within sight of the log hut where Judy lived, and his woice was heard five mile off. Judy's heart begun to beat when she heard him, for she knew whoever he was, he was a whole steamboat.

When he got to the house, he give one leap from his jumper, dashed down the door, and bounced into the middle of the room. "Tom Coon, by jingo," cried everone in the house—for he was no stranger by fame, though they had never seen him before. Judy right away set down in a corner to try his spunk, and said not a word, good or bad. He pulled half a dozen eyes out of his pocket, and flingin 'em down on the floor, swore with a round oath that he'd place any man's eyes by the side of them that dared to say a word ag'in Judy! Judy then jumped up like a frog and said, "Tom Coon, I'm yours for life—I know what you've come for, and I'll be your wedded wife without any more fustification about it."

So Tom got Judy and all her plunder. Tom took her into Tennessee with him right away, and begun to make a little clearin in the midst of the wood, when Judy soon gave him a specimen of her talent. For being out one evenin to a tea-squall, about ten mile off, in coming home through the wood she found a nest of young wildcats in the stump of a tree. She said nothin about it when she went home, but let her toenails grow till they were an inch long, when she started all alone, one mornin and went to the nest, and jumpin in upon the young wildcats, stamped them to death with her feet. It was quite a tough job, and they bit her legs most ridiculously, but she stood up to the scratch, though they scratched her backsides so tarnaciously they've never itched since.

A Sensible Varmint

Almost everybody that knows the forest understands perfectly well that Davy Crockett never loses powder and ball, having been brought up to believe it a sin to throw away ammunition, and that is the benefit of a virtuous eddication. I was out in the forest one a'ternoon, and had just got to a place called the Great Gap, when I seed a raccoon setting all alone upon a tree. I clapped the breech of Brown Betsy to my shoulder, and war just going to put a piece of lead between his shoulders, when he lifted one paw, and says he, "Is your name Davy Crockett."

Says I, "You are right for once, my name is Davy Crockett."

"Then," says he, "you needn't take no further trouble, for I may as well come down without another word. And the creatur walked right down from the tree, for he considered himself shot.

I stoops down and pats him on the head, and says I, "I hope I may be shot myself before I hurt a hair of your head, for I never had such a compliment in my life."

"Seeing as how you say that," says he, "I'll just walk off for the present, not doubting your word a bit, d'ye see, but lest you should kinda happen to change your mind."

Crockett's Morning Hunt

Davy Crockett
Davy Crockett's Almanack, 1837,
facsimile in *The Crockett Almanacks, Nashville Series, 1835-1838*
(Chicago: Caxton Club, 1955, title page).

One January mornin it was so all-screwen-up cold that the forest trees war so stiff that they couldn't shake, and the very daybreak froze fast as it war tryin to dawn. The tinder box in my cabin would no more catch fire than a sunk raft at the bottom o' the sea. Seein that daylight war so far behind time, I thought creation war in a fair way for freezin fast.

"So," thinks I, "I must strike a leetle fire from my fingers, light my pipe, travel out a few leagues, and see about it."

Then I brought my knuckles together like two thunder clouds, but the sparks froze up before I could collect 'em—so out I walked, and endeavored to keep myself unfriz by goin at a hop, step and jump gait and whistlin the tune of "fire in the mountains!" as I went along in three double-quick time. Well, a'ter I had walked about twenty-five miles up the peak o' Daybreak Hill, I soon discovered what war the matter. The earth had actually friz fast in her axes, and couldn't turn round; the sun had got jammed between two cakes o' ice under the wheels, and there he had been shinin and workin to get loose, till he friz fast in his cold sweat.

"C-r-e-a-t-i-o-n!" thought I. "This are the toughest sort o' suspension, and it mustn't be endured—somethin must be done, or human creation is done for."

It war then so antediluvian and premature cold that my upper and lower teeth and tongue was all collapsed together as tight as a friz oyster. I took a fresh twenty-pound bear off o' my back that I'd picked up on the road, and beat the animal ag'in the ice till the hot ile began to walk out on him at all sides. I then took and held him over the earth's axes, and squeezed him till I thawed 'em loose, poured about a ton on 't over the sun's face, give the earth's cogwheel one kick backward, till I got the sun loose—whistled, "Push along, keep movin!" and in about fifteen seconds the earth gin a grunt and begun movin—the sun walked up beautiful, salutin me with such a wind o' gratitude that it made me sneeze. I lit my pipe by the blaze o' his top-knot, shouldered my bear, and walked home, introducin the people to fresh daylight with a piece of sunrise in my pocket, with which I cooked my bear steaks, and enjoyed one o' the best breakfasts I had tasted for some time. If I didn't, just wake me some mornin and go with me to the office o' sunrise!

Thomas Bangs Thorpe

(1815-1878)

In recognition of T. B. Thorpe's most admired story and its preeminence, that pioneer scholar of America's humor Bernard DeVoto dubbed antebellum Southern comic writers "the Big Bear School," and his designation has been widely adopted. Thorpe, though born in Massachusetts and educated in New York and Connecticut, between 1836 and 1864 did his best work as a painter and a prolific journalist while living in Louisiana. His masterpiece was written in 1841. In 1864 he moved to New York, where he died in 1878.

In an authoritative study, "The Text, Tradition, and Themes of 'The Big Bear of Arkansas,'" American Literature 47 (1975) 321-42, *J. A. Lee Lemay correctly calls Thorpe's tall tale "the classic story, as well as the most frequently anthologized one, of the humor of the Old Southwest." Moreover, between 1930 and 1979, it has been the humorous story of its period most often analyzed and praised by scholars and critics. Nevertheless, though recent commentators have found in the piece many complexities and mythic significations that led them to admire it, modern readers, like most of those who have enjoyed it over the years, can have fun just reading it as a superb humorous narrative.*

Thorpe begins with a vivid picture of a crowd in the social hall of a Mississippi River steamboat during a trip upstream from New Orleans. The highly miscellaneous crowd is joined by a delightful storyteller, Jim Doggett, who talks tall about Arkansas and his settlement there and then unwinds a wonderful yarn about his hunt for a creation bear.

When a graduate student told William Faulkner that he believed he saw a resemblance between Thorpe's tall tale and Faulkner's famous story, "The Bear," the novelist "looked surprised" and then said, "That's a fine story. A writer is afraid of a story like that. He's afraid he'll try to rewrite it. A writer has to learn when to run from a story."

The Big Bear of Arkansas

A steamboat on the Mississippi frequently, in making her regular trips, carries between places varying from one to two thousand miles apart. And as these boats advertise to land passengers and freight at "all intermediate landings," the heterogeneous character of the passengers of one of these up-country boats can scarcely be imagined by one who has never seen it with his own eyes. Starting from New Orleans in one of these boats, you will find yourself associated with men from every state in the Union, and from every portion of the globe; and a man of observation need not lack for amusement or instruction in such a crowd, if he will take the trouble to read the great book of character so favorably opened before him.

Here may be seen jostling together the wealthy Southern planter and the peddler of tinware from New England—the Northern merchant, and the Southern jockey—a venerable bishop, and a desperate gambler—the land speculator, and the honest farmer—professional men of all creeds and characters—Wolverines, Suckers, Hoosiers, Buckeyes, and Corn-crackers, besides a plentiful sprinkling of the half-horse and half-alligator species of men, who are peculiar to old Mississippi, and who appear to gain a livelihood simply by going up and down the river. In the pursuit of pleasure or business, I have frequently found myself in such a crowd.

On one occasion, when in New Orleans, I had occasion to take a trip of a few miles up the Mississippi, and I hurried on board the well-known "high-pressure-and-beat-everything" steamboat *Invincible*, just as the last note of the last bell was sounding. And when the confusion and bustle that is natural to a boat's getting under way had subsided, I discovered that I was associated in as heterogeneous a crowd as was ever got together. As my trip was to be of a few hours' duration only, I made no endeavors to become acquainted with my fellow passengers, most of whom would be together many days. Instead of this, I took out of my pocket the latest paper, and more critically than usual, examined its contents; my fellow passengers at the same time disposed themselves in little groups.

While I was thus busily employed in reading, and my companions were more busily employed in discussing such subjects as suited their humors best, we were startled most unexpectedly by a loud Indian whoop, uttered in the "social hall," that part of the cabin fitted off for a bar. Then was to be heard a loud crowing, which would not have continued to have interested us—such sounds being quite common in that place of spirits—had not the hero of these windy accomplishments stuck his head into the cabin and hallooed out, "Hurrah for the Big Bear of Arkansas!" And then might be heard a confused hum of voices, unintelligible, save in such broken sentences as "horse," "screamer," "lightning is slow," etc.

As might have been expected, this continued interruption attracted the attention of everyone in the cabin. All conversation dropped, and in the midst of this surprise the "Big Bear" walked into the cabin, took a chair, put his feet on the stove, and looking back over his shoulder, passed the general familiar salute of "Strangers, how are you?" He then expressed himself as much at home as if he had been at the Forks of Cypress, and perhaps a little more so.

Some of the company at this familiarity looked a little angry, and some astonished; but in a moment every face was wreathed in a smile. There was something about the intruder that won the heart on sight. He appeared to be a man enjoying perfect health and contentment; his eyes were as sparkling as diamonds, and good natured to simplicity. Then his perfect confidence in himself was irresistibly droll.

"Perhaps," said he, "gentlemen," running on without a person speaking, "perhaps you have been to New Orleans often. I never made *the first visit before*, and I don't intend to make another in a crow's life. I am thrown away in that-ere place, and useless, that are a fact. Some of the gentlemen there called me *green*—well, perhaps I am, said I, *but I aren't so at home*. And if I ain't off my trail much, the heads of them polite chaps themselves weren't much the hardest. For according to my notion, they were real *know-nothings*, as green as a pumpkin vine— couldn't, in farming, I'll bet, raise a crop of turnips; and as for shooting, they'd miss a barn if the door was swinging, and that, too, with the best rifle in the country.

"And then they talked to me 'bout hunting, and laughed at my calling the principal game in Arkansas poker, and high-low jack. 'Perhaps,' said I, 'you prefer chickens and roulette.' At this they laughed harder than ever, and asked me if I lived in the woods and didn't know what *game* was?

"At this I rather think I laughed. 'Yes,' I roared, and says, 'Strangers, if you'd asked me *how we got our meat* in Arkansas, I'd a-told you at once, and given you a list of varmints that would make a caravan, beginning with the bear and ending off with the cat. That's *meat*, though, not game.'

"Game indeed, that's what city folks call it, and with them it means chippen-birds and shite-pokes. Maybe such trash live in my diggins, but I aren't noticed them yet; a bird anyway is too trifling. I never did shoot at but one, and I'd never forgiven myself for that, had it weighed less than forty pounds. I wouldn't draw a rifle on anything less than that, and when I meet with another wild turkey of the same weight I will drop him."

"A wild turkey weighing forty pounds!" exclaimed twenty voices in the cabin at once.

"Yes, strangers, and wasn't it a whopper? You see, the thing was so fat that it couldn't fly far. And when he fell out of the tree, after I shot him, on striking the ground he bust open behind, and the way the pound gobs of tallow rolled out of the opening was perfectly beautiful."

"Where did all this happen?" asked a cynical-looking Hoosier.

"Happen! happened in Arkansas! Where else could it have happened but in the creation state, the finishing up country—a state where the *sile* runs down to the center of the earth, and government gives you title to every inch of it? Then its airs—just breathe them, and they will make you snort like a horse. It's a state without a fault, it is."

"Excepting mosquitoes," cried the Hoosier.

"Well, stranger, except them; for it are a fact that they are rather *enormous*, and do push themselves in somewhat troublesome. But, stranger, they never stick twice in the same place; and give them a fair chance for a few months, and you will get as much above noticing them as an alligator. They can't hurt my feelings, for they lay under the skin; and I never knew but one case of injury resulting from them, and that was a Yankee. And they take worse to foreigners, anyhow, than they do to natives.

"But the way they used that fellow up! First they punched him until he swelled up and busted. Then he su-per-a-ted, as the doctor called it, until he was as raw as beef. Then he took the aguer, owing to the warm weather, and finally he took a steamboat and left the country. He was the only man that ever took mosquitoes to heart that I know of. But mosquitoes is natur, and I never find fault with her. If they are large, Arkansas is large, her varmints are large, her trees are large, her rivers are large, and a small mosquito would be no more use in Arkansas than preaching in a cane-brake."

This knock-down argument in favor of big mosquitoes used the Hoosier up, and the logician started on a new track, to explain how numerous bear were in his "diggins," where he represented them to be "about as plenty as blackberries, and a little plentifuler."

Upon the utterance of this assertion, a timid little man near me inquired if the bear in Arkansas ever attacked the settlers in numbers.

"No," said our hero, warming with the subject, "no, stranger, for you see it ain't the natur of bear to go in droves; but the way they squander about in pairs and single ones is edifying. And then the way I hunt them the old black rascals know the crack of my gun as well as they know a pig's squealing. They grow thin in our parts, it frightens them so, and they do take the noise dreadfully, poor things. That gun of mine is *perfect epidemic among bear*. If not watched closely, it will go off as quick on a warm scent as my dog Bowie-knife will. And then that dog—whew! Why the fellow thinks that the world is full of bear, he finds them so easy.

"It's lucky he don't talk as well as think, for with his natural modesty, if he should suddenly learn how much he is acknowledged to be ahead of all other dogs in the universe, he would be astonished to death in two minutes. Strangers, the dog knows a bear's way as well as a horse-jockey knows a woman's. He always barks at the right time, bites at the exact place, and whips without getting a scratch. I never could tell whether he was made expressly to hunt bear, or whether bear was made expressly for him to hunt. Anyway, I believe they were ordained to go together as naturally as Squire Jones says a man and a woman is, when he moralizes in marrying a couple. In fact, Jones once said, said he, 'Marriage according to the law is a civil contract of divine origin; it's common to all countries as well as Arkansas, and people take to it as naturally as Jim Doggett's Bowie-knife takes to bear.'"

"What season of the year do your hunts take place?" inquired a gentlemanly foreigner, who, from some peculiarities of his baggage I suspected to be an Englishman, on some hunting expedition, probably at the foot of the Rocky Mountains.

"The season for bear hunting, stranger," said the man of Arkansas, "is generally all the year round, and the hunts take place about as regular. I read in history that varmints have their fat season, and their lean season. That is not the case in Arkansas, feeding as they do upon the *spontenacious* production of the *sile*, they have one continued fat season the year round, though in winter things in this way is rather more greasy than in summer, I admit. For that reason, bear with us run in warm weather, but in winter, they only waddle.

"Fat! fat! it's an enemy to speed; it tames everything that has plenty of it. I have seen wild turkeys, from its influence, as gentle as chickens. Run a bear in this fat condition, and the way it improves the critter is amazing; it sort of mixes the ile up with the meat, until you can't tell t'other from which. I've done this often. I recollect one pretty morning in particular, of putting an old fellow on the stretch, and considering the weight he carried, he ran well. But the dogs soon tired him down, and when I come up with him, wasn't he in a beautiful sweat—I might say fever; and then to see his tongue sticking out of his mouth a foot, and his sides sinking and opening like a bellows, and his cheeks so fat he couldn't look cross. In this fix I blazed at him, and pitch me naked into a briar patch if the steam didn't come out of the bullet hole ten feet in a straight line. The fellow, I reckon, was made on the high-pressure system, and the lead sort of bust his b'iler."

"That column of steam was rather curious, or else the bear must have been *warm*," observed the foreigner, with a laugh.

"Stranger, as you observe, that bear was WARM, and the blowing off of the steam showed it, and also how much the varmint had been run. I have no doubt that if he had kept on two miles further his insides would have been stewed. And I expect to meet with a varmint yet of extra bottom, who will run himself into a skinful of bear's grease. It is possible, much unlikelier things have happened."

"Whereabouts are these bears so abundant?" inquired the foreigner, with increasing interest.

"Why, stranger, they inhabit the neighborhood of my settlement, one of the prettiest places on old Mississippi—a perfect location, and no mistake; a place that had some defects until the river made the cut-off at Shirt-Tail Bend and that remedied the evil, as it brought my cabin on the edge of the river—a great advantage in wet weather, I assure you, as you can now roll a barrel of whiskey into my yard in high water from a boat, as easy as falling off a log. It's a great improvement, as toting it by hand in a jug, as I used to do, *evaporated* it too fast, and it became expensive. Just stop with me, stranger, a month or two, or a year if you like, and you will appreciate my place. I can give you plenty to eat; for beside hog and hominy, you can have bear ham, and bear sausages, and a mattress of bear skins to sleep on, and a wildcat skin, pulled off whole, stuffed with corn shucks, for a pillow. That bed would put you to sleep if you had the rheumatics in every joint in your body. I call that-ere bed a *quietus*.

"Then look at my land—the government ain't got another such a piece to dispose of. Such timber and such bottom land, only you can't preserve anything natural you plant in it unless you pick it young, things there will grow out of shape so quick. I once planted in those diggins a few potatoes and beets; they took a fine start, and after that an ox team couldn't have kept them from growing. I went off to old Kentuck on business, and did not hear from them things in three months, when I accidentally stumbled on a fellow who had stopped at my place with an idea of buying me out.

" 'How did you like things?' said I.

" 'Pretty well,' said he. 'The cabin is convenient, and the timber land is good; but that bottom land ain't worth the first red cent.'

" 'Why?' said I.

" ' 'Cause,' said he.

" ' 'Cause what?' said I.

" ' 'Cause it's full of cedar stumps and Indian mounds,' said he, '*and it can't be cleared.*'

" 'Lord!' said I, 'Them-ere "cedar stumps" is beets, and them-ere "Indian mounds" are tater hills.' As I expected, the crop was overgrown and useless; the sile is too rich, *and planting in Arkansas is dangerous.* I had a good-sized sow killed in that same bottom land. The old thief stole an ear of corn, and took it down where she slept at night to eat. Well, she left a grain or two on the ground, and lay down on them; before morning the corn shot up, and the percussion killed her dead. I don't plant anymore; natur intended Arkansas for a hunting ground, and I go according to natur."

The questioner who thus elicited the description of our hero's settlement seemed to be perfectly satisfied and said no more. But the "Big Bear of Arkansas" rambled on from one thing to another, with a volubility perfectly astonishing, occasionally disputing with those around him, particularly with a "live Sucker" from Illinois, who had the daring to say that our Arkansas friend's stories "smelt rather tall."

In this manner the evening was spent, but conscious that my own association with so singular a person would probably end before morning, I asked him if he would not give me a description of some particular bear hunt, adding that I took great interest in such things, though I was no sportsman. The desire seemed to please him, and he squared himself round towards me, saying that he could give me an idea of a bear hunt that was never beat in this world, or in any other. His manner was so singular, that half of his story consisted in his excellent way of telling it, the great peculiarity of which was the happy manner he had of emphasizing the prominent parts of his conversation. As near as I can recollect, I have italicized them, and give you the story in his own words.

"Stranger," said he, "in bear hunts *I am numerous*, and which particular one, as you say, I shall tell, puzzles me. There was the old she devil I shot at the Harricane last fall—then there was the old hog thief I popped over at the Bloody Crossing, and then, Yes, I have it! I will give you an idea of a hunt, in which the greatest bear was killed that ever lived, *none excepted*; about an old fellow that I hunted, more or less, for two or three years, and if that ain't a particular bear hunt, I ain't got one to tell. But in the first place, stranger, let me say, I am pleased with you, because you ain't ashamed to go in for information by asking, and listening. And that's what I say to Countess's pups every day when I'm home, and I have great hopes of them-ere pups, because they are continually *nosing* about; and although they stick it sometimes in the wrong place, they gain experience anyhow, and may learn something useful to boot.

"Well, as I was saying about this big bear, you see when I and some more first settled in our region, we were driven to hunting naturally. We soon liked it, and after that we found it an easy matter to make the thing our business. One old chap who had pioneered afore us, gave us to understand that we had settled in the right place. He dwelt upon its merits until it was affecting, and showed us, to prove his assertion, more marks on the sassafras trees than I ever saw on a tavern door 'lection time.

" 'Who keeps that-ere reckoning?' said I.

" 'The bear,' said he.

" 'What for?' said I.

" 'Can't tell,' said he; 'but so it is. The bear bite the bark and wood too, at the highest point from the ground they can reach, and you can tell, by the mark,' said he, 'the length of the bear to an inch.'

" 'Enough,' said I; 'I've learned something here a'ready, and I'll put it in practice.'

"Well, stranger, just one month from that time I killed a bear and told its exact length before I measured it, by those very marks. And when I did that, I swelled up considerable—I've been a prouder man ever since. So I went on, larning something every day, until I was reckoned a buster, and allowed to be decidedly the best bear hunter in my district. And that is a reputation as much harder to earn than to be reckoned first man in Congress, as an iron ramrod is harder than a toadstool.

"Did the varmints grow over-cunning by being fooled with by greenhorn hunters, and by this means get troublesome, they send for me as a matter of course; and thus I do my own hunting and most of my neighbors'. I walk into the varmints though, and it has become about as much the same to me as drinking. It is told in two sentences—a bear is started, and he is killed. The thing is somewhat monotonous now—I know just how much they will run, where they will tire, how much they will growl, and what a thundering time I will have in getting them home. I could give you this history of the chase with all particulars at the commencement. I know the signs so well—*stranger*, I'm certain. Once I met with a match, though, and I will tell you about it; for a common hunt would not be worth relating.

"One fine fall day, long time ago, I was trailing about for bear, and what should I see but fresh marks on the sassafras trees, about eight inches above any in the forests that I know of. Says I, 'Them marks is a hoax, or it indicates the damnedest bear that was ever grown.' In fact, stranger, I couldn't believe it was real, and I went on. Again I saw the same marks, at the same height, and *I knew the thing lived*. That conviction came back to my soul like an earthquake. Says I, 'Here is something a-purpose for me. That bear is mine, or I give up the hunting business.' The very next morning what should I see but a number of buzzards hovering over my cornfield. 'The rascal has been there,' said I, 'for that sign is certain.' And sure enough, on examining, I found the bones of what had been as beautiful a hog the day before as was ever raised by a Buckeye. Then I tracked the critter out of the woods, and all the marks he left behind, showed me that he was *the bear*.

"Well, stranger, the first fair chase I had with that big critter, I saw him no less than three distinct times at a distance. The dogs run him over eighteen miles and broke down, my horse gave out, and I was as nearly used up as a man can be, made on *my* principle, *which is patent*. Before this adventure, such things were unknown to me as possible; but, strange as it was, that bear got me used to it before I was done with him. For he got so at last that he would leave me on a long chase *quite easy*. How he did it, I never could understand. That a bear runs at all is puzzling; but how this once could tire down and bust up a pack of hounds and a horse, that were used to overhauling everything they started after, in no time, was past my understanding. Well, stranger, that bear finally got so sassy that he used to help himself to a hog off my premises whenever he wanted one. The buzzards followed after what he left, and so between *bear and buzzard*, I rather think I was *out of pork*.

"Well, missing that bear so often took hold of my vitals, and I wasted away. The thing had been carried too far, and it reduced me in flesh faster than an aguer. I would see that bear in everything I did; *he haunted me*, and that, too, like a devil, which I began to think he was. While in this fix, I made preparations to give him a last brush, and be done with it. Having completed everything to my satisfaction, I started at sunrise, and to my great joy, I discovered from the way the dogs run, that they were near him. Finding his trail was nothing, for that had become as plain to the pack as a turnpike road. On we went, and coming to an open country, what should I see but the bear very leisurely ascending a hill, and the dogs close at his heels, either a match for him in speed, or else he did not care to get out of their way—I don't know which. But wasn't he a beauty, though? I loved him like a brother.

"On he went, until he came to a tree, the limbs of which formed a crotch about six feet from the ground. Into this crotch he got and seated himself, the dogs yelling all around it, and there he sat eyeing them as quiet as a pond in low water. A greenhorn friend of mine, in company, reached shooting distance before me, and blazed away, hitting the critter in the center of his forehead. The bear shook his head as the ball struck it, and then walked down from that tree as gently as a lady would from a carriage. 'Twas a beautiful sight to see him do that—he was in such a rage that he seemed to be as little afraid of the dogs as if they had been sucking pigs. And the dogs warn't slow in making a ring around him at a respectful distance; even Bowie-knife, himself, stood off. Then the way his eyes flashed—why the fire of them would have singed a cat's hair; in fact, that bear was in a *wrath all over*.

"Only one pup came near him, and he was brushed out so totally with the bear's left paw that he entirely disappeared; and that made the old dogs more cautious still. In the meantime, I came up, and taking deliberate aim as a man should do, at his side, just back of his foreleg, *if my gun did not snap*, call me a coward, and I won't take it personal. Yes, stranger, *it snapped*, and I could not find a cap about my person. While in this predicament, I turned round to my fool friend—says I, 'Bill,' says I, 'your're an ass—you're a fool—you might as well have tried to kill that bear by barking the tree under his belly, as to have done it by hitting him in the head. Your shot has made a tiger of him, and blast me, if a dog gets wounded when they come to blows, I will stick my knife into your liver, I will—' My wrath was up. I had lost my caps, my gun had snapped, the fellow with me had fired at the bear's head, and I expected every moment to see him close in with the dogs, and kill a dozen of them at least.

"In this thing I was mistaken, for the bear leaped over the ring formed by the dogs, and giving a fierce growl was off—the pack, of course, in full cry after him. The run this time was short, for coming to the edge of a lake the varmint jumped in, and swam to a little island in the lake, which it reached just a moment before the dogs.

" 'I'll have him now,' said I, for I had found my caps in the *lining of my coat*. So, rolling a log into the lake, I paddled myself across to the island, just as the dogs had cornered the bear in a thicket. I rushed up and fired. At the same time the critter leaped over the dogs and came within three feet of me, running like mad. He jumped into the lake, and tried to mount the log I had just deserted, but every time he got half his body on it, it would roll over and send him under. The dogs, too, got around him and pulled him about, and finally Bowie-knife clenched with him, and they sank into the lake together. Stranger, about this time I was excited, and I stripped off my coat, drew my knife, and intended to have taken a part with Bowie-knife myself, when the bear rose to the surface. But the varmint stayed under—Bowie-knife came up alone, more dead than alive, and with the pack came ashore.

" 'Thank God,' said I, 'the old villain has got his deserts at last.' Determined to have the body, I cut a grapevine for a rope, and dove down to where I could see the bear in the water, fastened my queer rope to his leg, and fished him, with great difficulty, ashore, Stranger, may I be chawed to death by young alligators, if the thing I looked at wasn't a *she bear, and not the old critter after all*. The way matters got mixed on that island was unaccountably curious, and thinking of it made me more than ever convinced that I was hunting the devil himself. I went home that night and took to my bed—the thing was killing me. The entire team of Arkansas in bear hunting, acknowledged himself used up, and the fact sunk into my feelings like a snagged boat will in the Mississippi. I grew as cross as a bear with two cubs and a sore tail.

"The thing got out among my neighbors, and I was asked how come that individ-u-al that never lost a bear when one started? And if that same individ-u-al didn't wear telescopes when he turned a she bear, of ordinary size, into an old he one, a little larger than a horse?

" 'Perhaps,' said I, 'friends' — getting wrathy — 'perhaps you want to call somebody a liar.'

" 'Oh, no,' said they, 'we only heard such things as being *rather common* of late, but we don't believe one word of it, oh, no' — and they would ride off and laugh like so many hyenas over a dead nigger.

"It was too much, and I determined to catch that bear, go to Texas, or die — and I made my preparations accordin. I had the pack shut up and rested. I took my rifle to pieces and iled it. I put caps in every pocket about my person, *for fear of the lining.* I then told my neighbors, that on Monday morning — naming the day — I would start THAT BEAR, and bring him home with me, or they might divide my settlement among them, the owner having disappeared.

"Well, stranger, on the morning previous to the great day of my hunting expedition, I went along into the woods, near my house, taking my gun and Bowie-knife along, just *from habit.* And there sitting down also from habit, what should I see, getting over my fence, but *the bear!* Yes, the old varmint was within a hundred yards of me, and the way he *walked over that fence* — stranger, he loomed up like a *black mist*, he seemed so large, and he walked right towards me.

"I raised myself, took deliberate aim, and fired. Instantly the varmint wheeled, gave a yell, and *walked through that fence* like a falling tree would through a cobweb. I started after, but was tripped up by my inexpressibles, which either from habit or the excitement of the moment, were about my heels, and before I had really gathered myself up I heard the old varmint groaning in a thicket near by, like a thousand sinners, and by the time I reached him, he was a corpse.

"Stranger, it took five niggers and myself to put that carcass on a mule's back, and the old long-ears waddled under the load, as if he was foundered in every leg of his body; and with a common whopper of a bear he would have trotted off, and enjoyed himself. 'Twould astonish you to know how big he was: I made a *bedspread of his skin*, and the way it used to cover my bear mattress, and leave several feet on each side to tuck up, would have delighted you. It was in fact a creation bear, and if it had lived in Samson's time, and had met him, in a fair fight, it would have licked him in the twinkling of a dice box. But stranger, I never like the way I hunted, and *missed him*. There is something curious about it I could never understand — and I never was satisfied at his giving in so easy at the last. Perhaps, he had heard of my preparations to hunt him the next day, so he just come in, like Capt. Scott's coon, to save his wind to grunt with in dying. But that ain't likely. My private opinion is, that that bear was an *unhuntable bear, and died when his time come.*"

When the story was ended, our hero sat some minutes with his auditors in a grave silence. I saw that there was a mystery to him connected with the bear whose death he had just related. It was also evident that there was some superstitious awe connected with the affair—a feeling common with all children of the woods, when they meet with anything out of their everyday experience. He was the first one, however, to break the silence and jumping up, he asked all present to "liquor" before going to bed—a thing which he did, with a number of companions, evidently to his heart's content.

Long before day, I was put ashore at my place of destination, and I can only follow with the reader, in imagination, our Arkansas friend, in his adventures at the Forks of Cypress, on the Mississippi.

Henry Clay Lewis
(Madison Tensas)

(1825-1850)

*F*or an American humorist and a native of Charleston, South
Carolina, Henry Clay Lewis had an unusual mix of ancestors—French,
Indian, and Jewish. His own summary of his experiences indicates that
they too were varied: "I was scarcely sixteen, yet I was a student of
medicine, and had been almost a printer, a cotton-picker, a ploughboy,
gin-driver, gentleman of leisure, cabin boy, cook, scullion, and runaway
. . . ." His steamboat days were spent on the Ohio, Mississippi, and
Yazoo rivers; and, after receiving his medical degree in 1846, he practiced his profession in Yazoo City, Madison Parish, and the surrounding
countryside. His humorous pieces, published under a pseudonym that
combined the names of two adjoining parishes, appeared in newspapers
and magazines before they were collected in his one book, Odd Leaves
from the Life of a Louisiana "Swamp Doctor" (1850). As the title suggests, his sketches for the most part deal with his medical training and
with practice among the planters, "swampers," backwoodsmen, and
blacks in northeastern Louisiana. For instance, "Cupping on the Sternum," his most popular piece, tells what happened when, after his teacher
gave him laconic instructions, he mistranslated the word "sternum."
After blithely explaining to his patient that, though the pain she felt
was in her breast, "the stern and the bosom are not many feet apart,"
he applied the scarifactor and the blister in the wrong area, with results
that were both painful and highly irrelevant. Quite a few of his sketches,
however, were too agonizing or too macabre for lay readers to enjoy.

"A Tight Race Considerin" is one of many frontier stories about
boys, girls, men, and women who somehow find themselves stark naked
and horribly embarrassed in the presence of large crowds. Such unplanned
exhibitionism must have had a racy devilishness about it that helped
make it good material for rough comedy.

A Tight Race Considerin

During my medical studies, passed in a small village in Mississippi, I became acquainted with a family named Hibbs (a *nom de plume*, of course), residing a few miles in the country. The family consisted of Mr. and Mrs. Hibbs and son. They were plain, unlettered people, honest in intent and deed, but overflowing with that which amply made up for all their deficiencies of education, namely, warm-hearted hospitality, the distinguishing trait of Southern character. They were originally from Virginia, from whence they had emigrated in quest of a clime more genial, and a soil more productive than that in which their fathers toiled. Their search had been rewarded, their expectations realized, and now, in their old age, though not wealthy in the Astorian sense, still they had something sufficient to keep the wolf from the door, and drop something more substantial than condolence and tears in the hat that poverty hands round for the kind offerings of humanity.

The old man was like the generality of old planters, men whose ambition is embraced by the family or social circle, and whose thoughts turn more on the relative value of "Sea Island" and "Mastodon," and the improvement of their plantations than the glorious victories of Whiggery in Kentucky or the triumphs of democracy in Arkansas.

The old lady was a shrewd, active dame, kind-hearted and long-tongued, benevolent and impartial, making her coffee as strong for the poor pedestrian, with his all upon his back, as the broadcloth sojourner with his "up-country pacer." She was a member of the church, as well as the daughter of a man who had once owned a race horse; and these circumstances gave her an indisputable right, she thought, to let on all she knew, when religion or horse flesh was the theme. At one moment she would be heard discussing whether the new "circus rider" (as she always called him) was as affecting in Timothy as the old one was pathetic in Paul, and anon (not anonymous, for the old lady did everything above board, except rubbing her corns at supper), protecting dad's horse from

61

the invidious comparisons of some visitor, who having heard, perhaps, that such horses as Fashion and Boston existed, thought himself qualified to doubt the old lady's assertion that her father's horse "Shumach" had run a mile on one particular occasion.

"Don't tell *me*," was her never failing reply to their doubts. "Don't tell me 'bout Fashion or Bosting, or any other beating 'Shumach' a fair race, for the thing was unfeasible. Didn't he run a mile a minute by Squire Dim's watch, which always stopped 'zactly at twelve, and didn't he start a minute afore, and git out just as the long hand war givin its last quiver on catchin the short leg of the watch? And didn't he beat everything in Virginny 'cept once? Dad and the folks said he'd beat then, if young Mr. Spotswood hadn't give 'old Swage,' Shumach's rider, some of that 'Croton water' (that them Yankees is making such a fuss over as bein so good, when gracious knows, nothin but what the doctors call interconception could git me to take a dose) and just 'fore the race Swage or Shumach, I don't 'stinctly member which, but one of them had to '*let down*,' and so Dad's hoss got beat."

The son I will describe in a few words. Imbibing his parents' contempt for letters, he was very illiterate and, as he had not enjoyed the equivalent of travel, was extremely ignorant on all matters not relating to hunting or plantation duties. He was a stout, active fellow, with a merry twinkling of the eye, indicative of humor, and partiality for practical joking. We had become very intimate, he instructing me in forest lore, and I, in return, giving amusing stories or, what was as much to his liking, occasional introductions to my hunting flask.

Now that I have introduced the Dramatis Personae, I will proceed with my story. By way of relaxation, and to relieve the tedium incident more or less to a student's life, I would take my gun, walk out to old Hibbs's, spend a day or two, and return refreshed to my books.

One fine afternoon I started upon such an excursion, and, as I had upon a previous occasion missed killing a fine buck, owing to my having nothing but squirrel shot, I determined this time to go for the antlered monarch, by loading one barrel with fifteen blue whistlers, reserving the other for small game.

At the end of the plantation was a fine spring, and adjacent, a small cave, the entrance artfully or naturally concealed, save to one acquainted with its locality. The cave was nothing but one of those subterraneous varies so common in the west and south and called sink holes. It was known only to the young H. and myself, and we, for peculiar reasons, kept secret, having put it in requisition as the depository of a jug of old Bourbon, which we favored. And as the old folks abominated drinking, we had found convenient to keep there, whither we would repair to get our drinks and return to the house to hear them descant on the evils of drinking, and vow no drap, 'cept in doctor's truck, should ever come on their plantation.

Feeling very thirsty, I took my way by the spring that evening. As I descended the hill overtopping it, I beheld the hind parts of a bear slowly being drawn into the cave. My heart bounded at the idea of killing a bear, and my plans were formed in a second. I had no dogs—the house was distant—and the bear becoming "small by degrees and beautifully less." Every hunter knows, if you shoot a squirrel in the head when it's sticking out of a hole, ten to one he'll jump out. And I reasoned that if this were true regarding squirrels, might not the same principle extract bear, applying it low down in the back?

Quick as thought I leveled my gun and fired, intending to give him the buckshot when his body appeared. But what was my surprise and horror, when, instead of a bear rolling out, the parts were jerked nervously in, and the well-known voice of young H. reached my ears.

"Murder! Hinjuns! hell and cockleburrs! Oh! lordy! 'nough!—'nough! Take him off! Just let me off this once, Dad, and I'll never run mam's colt again! Oh! Lordy! Lordy! *all my brains blowed clean out!* Snakes! snakes!" yelled he, in a shriller tone if possible. "Hell on the outside and snakes in the sink hole! I'll die a Christian anyhow, and if I die before I wake," and out scrambled poor H., pursued by a large black snake.

If my life had depended on it, I could not have restrained my laughter. Down fell the gun, and down dropped I, shrieking convulsively. The hill was steep, and over and over I went, until my head striking against a stump at the bottom, stopped me, half senseless.

On recovering somewhat from the stunning blow, I found Hibbs upon me, taking satisfaction from me for having blowed out his brains. A contest ensued, and H. finally relinquished his hold, but I soon saw from the knitting of his brows that the bear-storm, instead of being over, was just brewing.

"Mr. Tensas," he said, with awful dignity, "I'm sorry I put into you 'fore you come to. But you're yourself now, and as you've tuck a shot at me, it's no more than fair I should have a chance 'fore the hunt's up."

It was with the greatest difficulty that I could get H. to bear with me until I explained the mistake. But as soon as he learned it he broke out into a huge laugh. "Oh, Dod busted! that's 'nough; you has my pardon. I ought to knowed you didn't 'tend it; 'sides, you just scraped the skin. I war worse scared than hurt, and if you'll go to the house and beg me off from the old folks, I'll never let on you couldn't tell copperas britches from bear skin."

Promising that I would use my influence, I proposed taking a drink, and that he should tell me how he had incurred his parents' anger. He assented, and after we had inspected the cave and seen that it held no serpent other than the one we craved, we entered its cool recess, and H. commenced:

"You see, Doc, I'd heered so much from mam 'bout her dad's Shumach and his nigger Swage, and the mile a minute, and the Croton water what was gin him, and how she b'lieved that if it warn't for bettin, and the cussin and fightin, runnin race hosses warn't the sin folks said it war, and if they war anything to make her 'gret gettin religion and j'inin the church, it war 'cause she couldn't 'tend races, and have a race colt of her own to comfort her 'clinin years, such as her daddy had afore her, till she got me. So I couldn't rest for wantin to see a hoss race, and go shares, p'raps, in the colt she war wishin for.

"And then I'd think what sort of a hoss I'd want him to be—a quarter nag, a mile critter, or a hoss what could run (for all mam says it can't be did) a whole four mile at a stretch. Sometimes I'd think I'd rather own a quarter nag, for the suspense wouldn't long be hung, and then we could run up the road to Nick Bamer's cow pen, and Sally is almost alluz out there in the cool of the evenin, and in course we wouldn't be so cruel as to run the poor critter in the heat of the day. But then agin, I'd think I'd rather have a miler,—for the 'citement would be greater and we could run down the road to old Wither's orchard, and his gal Miry is frightfully fond of sunnin herself there, when she 'spects me long, and she'd hear of the race, certain. But then there war the four miler for my thinkin, and I'd knowed in such case the 'citement would be greatest of all, and you know, too, from dad's stable to the grocery is just four miles, and in case of any 'spute, all hands would be willin to run over, even if it had to be tried a dozen times.

"So I never could 'cide on which sort of a colt to wish for. It war first one and then t'others, till I was nearly 'stracted, and when mam, makin me religious, told me one night to say grace, I just shut my eyes, looked pious, and yelled out, 'Damn it, go!' and in 'bout five minutes a'ter, came near kickin dad's stomach off, under the table, thinkin I war spurrin my critter in a tight place. So I found the best way war to get the hoss first, and then 'termine whether it should be Sally Bamer and the cow pen; Miry Wither and the peach orchard; or Spellman's grocery, with the bald face.

"You've seed my black colt, that one that dad's father gin me in his will when he died, and I 'spect the reason he wrote that will war that he might have one then, for it's more than he had when he was alive, for granma war a monstrous overbearin woman. The colt would come up in my mind, every time I'd think where I was to git a hoss. 'Git out!' said I at first—*he* never could run, and 'sides if he could, mam rides him now, and he's too old for anything, 'cept totin her and bein called mine. For you see, though he war named Colt, yet for the old lady to call him old would been like the bear 'fecting contempt for the rabbit, on account of the shortness of his tail.

"Well, thought I, it does look sorta unpromisin, but it's colt or none. So I 'termined to put him in trainin the first chance. Last Saturday, who should come ridin up but the new circuit preacher, a long-legged, weakly, never-contented-unless-the-best-on-the-plantation-war-cooked-for-him sort of a man. But I didn't look at him twice. His hoss was the critter that took my eye; for the minute I looked at him I knew him to be the same hoss as Sam Spooner used to win all his splurgin dimes with, the folks said, and what he used to ride past our house so fine on.

"The hoss war a heap the worse for age and change of masters; for preachers, though they're mighty 'ticular 'bout their own comfort, seldom tends to their hosses, for one is private property and t'other generally borrowed. I seed from the way the preacher rid that he didn't know the animal he war straddlin, but I did, and I 'termined I wouldn't lose such a chance of trainin Colt by the side of a hoss what had run real races.

"So that night a'ter prayers and the folks was abed, I and Nigger Bill tuck the hosses and carried them down to the pastur. It war a forty-acre lot, and consequently just a quarter across—for I thought it best to promote Colt, by degrees, to a four miler. When we got there, the preacher's hoss showed he war willin; but Colt, dang him! commenced nibblin a fodder stack over the fence. I nearly cried for vexment, but an idea struck me. I hitched the critter, and told Bill to get on Colt and stick tight when I give the word. Bill got ready, and unbeknownst to him I pulled up a bunch of nettles, and as I clapped them under Colt's tail, yelled 'Go!' Down shut his graceful [tail] like a steel trap, and away he shot so quick and fast that he jumped clean out from under Bill, and got nearly to the end of the quarter 'fore the nigger toch the ground. He lit on his head, and in course warn't hurt—so we cotched Colt and I mounted him.

"The next time I said 'go' he showed that age hadn't sp'iled his legs or his memory. Bill and me 'greed we could run him now, so Bill mounted Preacher and we got ready. There war a narrow part of the track 'tween the oaks; but as it war near the end of the quarter, I 'spected to pass Preacher 'fore we got there, so I warn't afraid of barkin my shins.

"We tuck a fair start, and off we went like a peeled onion, and I soon discovered that it warn't such an easy matter to pass Preacher, though Colt done delightful. We got nigh the trees, and Preacher warn't passed yet, and I 'gan to get scared, for it warn't more than wide enough for a hoss and a half. So I hollered to Bill to hold up, but the impudent nigger turned his ugly pictur and said he'd be cussed if he warn't goin to play his hand out. I gin him to understand he'd better fix for a foot race when we stopped, and tried to hold up Colt, but he wouldn't stop.

"We reached the oaks; Colt tried to pass Preacher; Preacher tried to pass Colt, and cowollop, crash, cachunk! we all come down like 'simmons a'ter frost. Colt got up and won the race; Preacher tried hard to rise, but one hind leg had got through the stirrup and t'other in the head stall, and he had to lay still, doubled up like a long nigger in a short bed. I lit on my feet, but Nigger Bill was gone entire. I looked up in the fork of one of the oaks, and there he war sittin, lookin very composed on surroundin natur. I couldn't git him down till I promised not to hurt him for disobeyin orders, when he slid down. We'd had 'nough racin for that night, so we put up the hosses and went to bed.

"Next morning the folks got ready for church, when it war discovered that the hosses had got out. I and Bill started off to look for them; we found them clear off in the field, tryin to git in the pastur to run the last night's race over, Old Blaze, the revolutionary mule, bein along to act as judge.

"By the time we got to the house, it war nigh on to meetin hour; and dad had started to the preachin, to tell the folks to sing on, as preacher and mam would be 'long bimeby. As the parson war in a hurry, and had been complainin that his creeter war dull, I 'suaded him to put on Uncle Jim's spurs, what he fotch from Mexico. I saddled the parson's hoss, taking 'ticular pains to let the saddle blanket come down low in the flank. By the time these fixins war through, Mom was 'head nigh on to a quarter.

" 'We must ride on, parson,' I said, 'or the folks'll think we is lost.' So I whipped up the mule I rid; the parson chirruped and chucked to make his critter gallop, but the animal didn't mind him a pic. I 'gan to snicker, and the parson 'gan to git vexed. Sudden he thought of his spurs; so he riz up, and drove them *vim* in his hoss's flanks, till they went through his saddle blanket and like to bored his nag to the hollow. By gosh! but it war a quickener—the hoss kicked till the parson had to hug him round the neck to keep from pitchin him over his head. He next jumped 'bout as high as a rail fence, parson holdin on and trying to git his spurs—but they war locked. His britches split plumb across with the strain, and the wearin truck what's next the skin made a monstrous pretty flag as the old hoss, like drunkards to a barbecue, streaked it up the road.

"Mam war ridin slowly along, thinkin how sorry she was, 'cause Chary Dolin, who always led her off, had such a bad cold and wouldn't be able to 'sist her singin today. She war practicin the hymns, and had got as far as 'I have a race to run,' when the parson huv in sight. And in 'bout the dodgin of a didapper, she found there war truth in the words, for the colt, hearin the hoss comin up behind, began to show symptoms of runnin. But when he heard the parson holler 'Whoa! Whoa' to his hoss, he thought it war me shoutin 'Go!' and sure 'nough off they started just as the parson got up even. So it war a fair race.

"Whoop! git out, but it war excitin. The dust flew, and the rail fence appeared straight as a rifle. There war the parson, his legs fast to the critter's flanks, arms locked round his neck, face as pale as a rabbit's belly, and the white flag streamin far behind. And there war Mam, first on one side and then on t'other, her new calico swelled up round her like a bear with the dropsy, the old lady so much surprised she couldn't ride steady, and tryin to stop her colt, but he war too well trained to stop while he heard 'Go!'

"Mam got 'cited at last, and her eyes 'gan to glimmer like she seen her daddy's ghost axin if he ever trained up a child or a race hoss to be 'fraid of a small brush on a Sunday. She commenced ridin beautiful; she braced herself up in the saddle, and began to make calculations how she war to win the race, for it war nose and nose, and she saw the parson spurrin his critter every jump. She tuck off her shoe, and the way a number ten go-to-meetin brogan commenced givin a hoss particular Moses were a caution to hoss flesh, but still it kept nose and nose.

"She found she war carryin too much weight for Colt, so she 'gan to throw off plunder, till nothin was left but her saddle and clothes, and the spurs kept tellin still. The old woman commenced strippin to lighten, till it wouldn't been the clean thing for her to have taken off one dud more, and then when she found it war no use while the spurs lasted, she got cantankerous.

" 'Parson,' said she, 'I'll be cussed if it's fair or gentlemanly for you, a preacher of the gospel, to take advantage of an old woman this way, usin spurs when you know *she* can't wear 'em—'tain't Christian-like, nuther,' and she burst into cryin. "Whoa! Miss Hibbs! Whoa! Stop! Madam! Whoa! Your son!'—he attempted to say, when the old woman tuck him on the back of the head, and fillin his mouth with right smart of the saddle horn, and stoppin the talk, as far as his share went for the present.

"By this time they'd got nigh to the meetin house, and the folks were harkin away on 'Old Hundred,' and wonderin what could have become of the parson and Mam Hibbs. One sister in a long beard axed another brethren in church, if she'd heered anything 'bout that New York preacher runnin way with a woman old enough to be his mother. The brethrens gin a long sigh and groaned, 'It ain't possible! merciful heavens! you don't 'spicion?' when the sound of the hosses comin roused them up like a touch of the aguer, and broke off their serpent-talk.

"Dad run out to see what was to pay, but when he seed the hosses so close together, the parson spurrin and mam ridin like clothes war scarce where she come, he knew her fix in a second, and 'termined to help her. So clinchin a saplin, he hid 'hind a stump 'bout ten steps off, and held on for the hosses.

"On they went in beautiful style, the parson's spurs tellin horrible, and mam's shoe operatin no small pile of punkins—parson stretched out the length of two hosses, while mam sot as straight as a bull yearling in his first fight, hittin her nag, first on one side, next on t'other, and the third for the parson, who had chawed the horn till little of the saddle and less of his teeth war left, and his voice sounded as hollow as a jackass nicker in an old saw mill.

"The hosses war nose and nose, jam up together so close that mam's last coverin and parson's flag had got locked, and 'tween bleached domestic and striped linsey made a beautiful banner for the pious racers.

"On they went like a small earthquake, and it seemed like it war goin to be a drawn race. But dad, when they got to him, let down with all his might on Colt, scarin him so bad that he jumped clean ahead of parson, beatin him by a neck, buttin his own head agin the meetin house, and pitchin mam, like a lamb for the sacrifice, plumb through the window 'mongst the mourners, leavin her only garment flutterin on a nail in the sash. The men shut their eyes and scrambled out'n the house, and the women gin mam so much of their clothes that they like to put themselves in the same fix.

"The parson quit the circuit, and I haven't been home yet."

Johnson Jones Hooper

(1815-1862)

If imitation is the sincerest form of flattery, Mark Twain *paid Hooper's tale about Simon Suggs at a camp meeting a heartfelt compliment.* America's greatest humorist clearly modeled the twentieth chapter of Adventures of Huckleberry Finn *after this narrative, one that he had read during his youth and had recalled shortly before he rewrote it to suit his own purposes. Bernard DeVoto, for one, believed that Twain on this occasion*

falls below his predecessor. . . . Hooper lacks the Olympian detachment of Mark Twain and his sketch therefore exists on a lower level, but its realism is sharper, its intelligence quite as great, and its conviction considerably greater. . . . A high moment in Huckleberry Finn would be better if Mark Twain had adhered to the scene that unquestionably produced it.

Hooper, born in North Carolina, as a young man moved to what then was the frontier state of Alabama. There he became a journalist and a part-time politician whose humorous writings spread his fame far beyond Alabama. Some Adventures of Simon Suggs *(1845), in which the narrative became a chapter, a tongue-in-cheek "campaign biography," tells about the shady career of a tacky confidence man whose motto is "It is good to be shifty in a new country." From his youth, when Simon cheats his father at cards, to his middle age, when he outwits fellow swindlers and becomes a cynical candidate for public office, this comic rascal lives, with varying success, according to his formula. Hooper's ironic life story purports to recommend him to the voters of his county. In some ways, Suggs is a Southwestern counterpart of the rascally Yankee, Birdofredum Sawin, about whom James Russell Lowell would write a few years after Simon was celebrated in Hooper's picaresque novel.*

69

Simon Suggs Attends a Camp Meeting

Simon Suggs

Oddities in Southern Life and Character
(Boston: Houghton, Mifflin, 1883, p. 91).

Captain Suggs found himself as poor at the conclusion of the Creek war as he had been at the beginning. Although no arbitrary, despotic, corrupt and unprincipled judge had fined him a thousand dollars for his proclamation of martial law at Fort Suggs, or the enforcement of its rules in the case of Mrs. Haycock, yet somehow—the thing is alike inexplicable to him and to us—the money which he had contrived by various shifts to obtain, melted away and was gone forever. To a man like the Captain, of intense domestic affections, this state of destitution was most distressing. "He could stand it himself—didn't care a damn for it, no way," he observed, "but the old woman and the children, *that* bothered him."

As he sat one day ruminating upon the unpleasant condition of his financial concerns, Mrs. Suggs informed him that "the sugar and coffee was nigh about out," and that there were not a dozen j'ints and middlins, *all put together*, in the smoke house."

Suggs bounced up on the instant, exclaiming, "Damn it! *somebody* must suffer!" But whether this remark was intended to convey the idea that he and his family were about to experience the want of the necessaries of life; or that some other, and as yet unknown, individual should "suffer" to prevent that prospective exigency, must be left to the commentators, if perchance any of that ingenious class of persons should hereafter see proper to write notes for this history. It is enough for us that we give all the facts in this connection, so that ignorance of the subsequent conduct of Captain Suggs may not lead to an erroneous judgment in respect to his words.

Having uttered the exclamation we have repeated—and perhaps, hurriedly walked once or twice across the room—Captain Suggs drew on his famous old green-blanket overcoat and ordered his horse, and within five minutes was on his way to a camp meeting, then in full blast on Sandy Creek, twenty miles distant, where he hoped to find amusement, at least. When he arrived there, he found the hollow square of the encampment filled with people, listening to the mid-day sermon, and its dozen accompanying exhortations.

A half-dozen preachers were dispensing the word; the one in the pulpit, a meek-faced old man, of great simplicity and benevolence. His voice was weak and cracked, notwithstanding which, however, he contrived to make himself heard occasionally above the din of the exhorting, the singing, and the shouting which were going on around him. The rest were walking to and fro (engaged in the other exercises we have indicated), among the "mourners"—a host of whom occupied the seat set apart for their especial use—or made personal appeals to the mere spectators.

The excitement was intense. Men and women rolled about on the ground, or lay sobbing or shouting in promiscuous heaps. More than all, the Negroes sang and screamed and prayed. Several, under the influence of what is technically called "the jerks," were plunging and pitching about with convulsive energy. The greatest object of all seemed to be, to see who could make the greatest noise.

> "And each—for madness ruled the hour—
> Would try his own expressive power."

"Bless my poor old soul!" screamed the preacher in the pulpit, "if yonder ain't a squad in that corner that we ain't got one out'n yet! It'll never do"—raising his voice—"you must come out'n that! Brother Fant, fetch up that youngster in the blue coat! I see the Lord's a-workin upon him! fetch him along—glory—yes!—hold to him!"

"Keep the thing warm!" roared a sensual seeming man, of stout mould and florid countenance, who was exhorting among a bevy of young women, upon whom he was lavishing caresses. "Keep the thing warm, breethring!—come to the Lord, honey!" he added, as he vigorously hugged one of the damsels he sought to save.

"Oh, I've got him!" said another in exulting tones, as he led up a gawky youth among the mourners. "I've got him—he tried to git off, but—ha! Lord!" shaking his head as much as to say, it took a smart fellow to escape him—"Ha! Lord"—and he wiped the perspiration from his face with one hand, and with the other, patted his neophyte on the shoulder—"he couldn't do it! No! then he tried to argue wi' me—but bless the Lord!—he couldn't do that nuther! Ha! Lord! I tuck him, first in the Old Testament—bless the Lord!—and I argued him all through Kings—then I throwed him into Proverbs—and from that, here we had it up and down, clear down to the New Testament, and then I begun to see it work him! Then we got into Matthew, and from Matthew right straight along to Acts, and *there* I throwed him! Y-e-s—L-o-r-d! assuming the nasal twang and high pitch which are, in some parts, considered the perfection of rhetorical art—"Y-e-s L-o-r-d! and h-e-r-e he is! Now g-i-t down there," addressing the subject, "and s-e-e if the L-o-r-d won't do something f-o-r you!" Having thus deposited his charge among the mourners, he started out summarily to convert another soul.

"Gl-o-*ree*!" yelled a huge, greasy Negro woman, as in a fit of the jerks, she threw herself convulsively from her feet, and fell like a thousand of brick across a diminutive old man in a little round hat, who was speaking consolation to one of the mourners.

"Good Lord, have Mercy!" ejaculated the little man earnestly and unaffectedly, as he strove to crawl from under the sable mass which was crushing him.

In another part of the square a dozen old women were singing. They were in a state of absolute ecstasy, as their shrill pipes gave forth:

> "I rode on the sky,
> Quite undestified I,
> And the moon it was under my feet!"

Near these last, stood a delicate woman in that hysterical condition in which the nerves are uncontrollable, and which is vulgarly—and almost blasphemously—termed the "holy laugh." A hideous grin distorted her mouth and was accompanied with a maniac's chuckle, while every muscle and nerve of the face twitched and jerked in horrible spasms.

Amid all this confusion and excitement Suggs stood unmoved. He viewed the whole affair as a grand deception—a sort of opposition line running against his own—and looked on with a sort of professional jealousy. Sometimes he would mutter running comments upon what passed before him.

"Well, now," said he, as he observed the full-faced brother who was officiating among the women, "that-ere fellow takes *my* eye! There he's been this half-hour, a-figurin among them gals, and 's never said the first word to nobody else. Wonder what's the reason these-here preachers never hugs up the old, ugly women? Never seed one do it in my life—the spirit never moves 'em that way! It's natur, though; and the women, *they* never flocks around one of the old, dried up breethring—bet two to one old splinter legs there"—nodding at one of the ministers—"won't git a chance to say turkey to a good-lookin gal today! Well! who blames 'em? Natur will be natur, the world over; and I judge, if I was a preacher, I should save the purtiest souls first, myself!"

While the Captain was in the midst of his conversation with himself, he caught the attention of the preacher in the pulpit, who inferring from an indescribable something about his appearance that he was a person of some consequence, immediately determined to add him at once to the church if it could be done; and to that end began a vigorous, direct personal attack.

"Breethring," he exclaimed, "I see yonder a man that's a sinner. I *know* he's a sinner! There he stands," pointing at Simon, "a miserable old critter, with his head a-blossomin for the grave! A few more short years, and d-o-w-n he'll go to perdition, lessen the Lord have mer-cy upon him! Come up here you old hoary-headed sinner, a-n-d git down on your knees, a-n-d put up your cry for the Lord to snatch you from the bottomless pit! You're ripe for the devil—you're b-o-u-n-d for hell, and the Lord only knows what'll become on you!"

"Damn it," thought Suggs, "if I only had you down in the crick swamp for a minute or so, *I'd* show you who's *old*! I'd alter your tune *mighty* sudden, you sassy 'ceitful old rascal!" But he judiciously held his tongue and gave no utterance to the thought.

The attention of many having been directed to the Captain by the preacher's remarks, he was soon surrounded by numerous well-meaning, and doubtless very pious persons, each one of whom seemed bent on the application of his own particular recipe for the salvation of souls. For a long time the Captain stood silent, or answered the incessant stream of exhortations only with a sneer; but at length, his countenance began to give token of inward emotion. First his eyelids twitched—then his upper lip quivered—next a transparent drop formed on one of his eye lashes, and a similar one on the tip of his nose—and at last, a sudden bursting of air from nose and mouth told that Captain Suggs was over-powered by his emotions. At the moment of the explosion, he made a feint as if to rush from the crowd, but he was in experienced hands who well knew that the battle was more than half won.

"Hold to him!" said one. "It's a-workin in him as strong as a Dick horse!"

"Pour it into him," said another. "It'll all come right directly!"

"That's the way I love to see 'em do," observed a third. "When you begin to draw the water from their eyes, 'tain't gwine to be long afore you'll have 'em on their knees!"

And so they clung to the Captain manfully, and half dragged, half led him to the mourners' bench; by which he threw himself down, altogether unmanned, and bathed in tears. Great was the rejoicing of the brethren, as they sang, shouted and prayed around him—for by this time it had come to be known that the convicted old man was Captain Simon Suggs, the very chief of sinners in all that region.

The Captain remained grovelling in the dust during the usual time, and gave vent to even more than the requisite number of sobs and groans and heart-piercing cries. At length, when the proper time had arrived, he bounced up, and with a face radiant with joy, commenced a series of vaultings and tumblings, which laid in the shade all previous performances of the sort at that camp meeting. The brethren were in ecstasies at the demonstration of completion of the work; and whenever Suggs shouted "Gloree!" at the top of his lungs, every one of them shouted it back, until the woods rang with echoes.

The effervescence having partially subsided, Suggs was put upon his pins to relate his experience, which he did somewhat in this style—first brushing the tear drops from his eyes, and giving the end of his nose a preparatory wring with his fingers, to free it of the superabundant moisture.

"Friends," he said, "it don't take long to curry a short horse, accordin to the old sayin, and I'll give you the particulars of the way I was brought to a knowledge"—here the Captain wiped his eyes, brushed the tip of his nose and snuffled a little—"in less 'n no time."

"Praise the Lord!" ejaculated a bystander.

"You see I come here full of romancin and devilment, and just to make game of all the proceedins. Well, sure enough, I done so for some time, and was a-thinkin how I should play some trick—"

"Dear soul alive! *Don't* he talk sweet!" cried an old lady in black silk. "Where's John Dobbs? You Sukey!" screaming at a Negro woman on the other side of the square—"if you don't hunt up your Mass John in a minute, and have him here to listen to this 'sperience, I'll tuck you up when I git home and give you a hundred and fifty lashes, madam!—see if I don't! Blessed Lord!"—referring again to the Captain's relation—"ain't it a *precious* 'scourse?"

"I was just a-thinkin how I should play some trick to turn it all into ridicule, when they begun to come round me and talk. Long at first, I didn't mind it, but a'ter a little that brother"—pointing to the reverend gentleman who had so successfully carried the unbeliever through the Old and New Testaments and who Simon was convinced was the "big dog of the tanyard"—"that brother spoke a word that struck me clean to the heart and run all over me, like fire in dry grass—"

"*I-I-I* can bring 'em!" cried the preacher alluded to in a tone of exultation—"Lord thou knows if thy servant can't stir 'em up, nobody else needn't try—but the glory ain't mine! I'm a poor worm of the dust," he added, with ill-managed affectation.

"And so from that I felt something a-pullin me inside—"

"Grace! grace! nothin but grace!" exclaimed one; meaning that "grace" had been operating in the Captain's gastric region.

"And then," continued Suggs, "I wanted to git off, but they hilt me, and bimeby I felt so miserable, I had to go yonder"—pointing to the mourners' seat—"and when I lay down there it got worse and worse, and 'peared like somethin was a-mashin down on my back—"

"That was his load of sin," said one of the brethren—"never mind, it'll tumble off presently, see if it don't!" And he shook his professionally and knowingly.

"And it kept a-gittin heavier and heavier, until it looked like it might be a four year old steer, or a pine log, or somethin of that sort—"

"Glory to my soul!" shouted Mrs. Dobbs. "It's the sweetest talk I *ever* hearn! You Sukey! ain't you got John yit? never mind, my lady, I'll settle wi' you!" Sukey quailed before the finger which her mistress shook at her.

"And a'ter a while," Suggs went on, " 'peared like I fell into a trance, like, and I seed—"

"Now we'll get the good on it!" cried one of the sanctified.

"And I seed the biggest, longest, riproarinest, blackest, scaliest—" Captain Suggs paused, wiped his brow, and ejaculated, "Ah, L-o-r-d!" so as to give full time for curiosity to become impatience to know what he saw.

"*Serpent!* warn't it?" asked one of the preachers.

"No, not a serpent," replied Suggs, blowing his nose.

"Do tell us *what* it war, soul alive!—where *is* John?" said Mrs. Dobbs.

"Alligator!" said the Captain.

"Alligator!" repeated every woman present, and screamed for very life. Mrs. Dobbs' nerves were so shaken by the announcement, that after repeating the horrible word, she screamed to Sukey, "You Sukey, I say, you S-u-u-k-e-ey! if you let John come a-nigh this way where the dreadful alliga—pshaw! what am I thinkin 'bout? 'Twarn't nothin but a vision!"

"Well," said the Captain in continuation, "the alligator kept a-comin and a-comin towards me, with his great long jaws a-gapin open like a ten-foot pair of tailor's shears—"

"Oh! oh! oh! Lord! gracious above!" cried the women.

"Satan!" was the laconic ejaculation of the oldest preacher present, who thus informed the congregation that it was the devil which had attacked Suggs in the shape of an alligator.

"And then I concluded the jig was up, 'thought I could block his game some way; for I seed his idee was to snap off my head—"

The women screamed again.

"So I fixed myself just like I was perfectly willin for him to take my head, and rather he'd do it as not"—here the women shuddered perceptibly—"and so I hilt my head straight out'—the Captain illustrated by elongating his neck—"and when he come up and was a-gwine to shut down on it, I just pitched in a big rock which choked him to death, and that minute I felt the weight slide off, and I had the best feelins—sorta like you'll have from *good* spirits—anybody every had!"

"Didn't I *tell* you so? Didn't I *tell* you so?" asked the brother who had predicted the off-tumbling of the load of sin. "Ha, Lord! fool *who*! I've been *all* along there!—yes, *all along there*! and I know every inch of the way just as good as I do the road home!" And then he turned round and round, and looked at all, to receive a short tribute to his superior penetration.

Captain Suggs was now the lion of the day. Nobody could pray so well, or exhort so movingly, as "Brother Suggs." Nor did his natural modesty prevent the proper performance of appropriate exercises. With the reverend Bela Bugg (him to whom, under providence, he ascribed his conversion) he was a most especial favorite. They walked, sang, and prayed together for hours.

"Come, come up; there's room for all!" cried Brother Bugg in his evening exhortation. "Come to the seat, and if you won't pray yourselves, let *me* pray for you!"

"Yes!" said Simon, by way of assisting his friend. "It's a game that all can win at! Ante up! ante up, boys—friends I mean—don't back out!"

"There ain't a sinner here," said Bugg, "no matter if his soul's black as a nigger, but what there's room for him!"

"No matter what sort of hand you've got," added Simon in the fulness of his benevolence, "take stock! here am *I*, the wickedest and blindest of sinners—has spent my whole life in the service of the devil—has now come in on *ne'er a pair* and won a *pile*!" And the Captain's face beamed with holy pleasure.

"D-o-n-'t be afeared!" cried the preacher. "Come along! The meanest won't be turned away! Humble yourselves and come!"

"No!" said Simon, still indulging in his favorite style of metaphor. "The bluff game ain't played here! No runnin of a body off! Everybody holds four aces, and when you bet, you win!"

And thus the Captain continued, until the services were concluded, to assist in adding to the number at the mourners' seat. And up to the hour of retiring, he exhibited such enthusiasm in the cause that he was unanimously voted to be the most effective addition the church had made during that meeting.

The next morning, when the preacher of the day first entered the pulpit, he announced that "Brother Simon Suggs," mourning over his past iniquities, and desirous of going to work in the cause as speedily as possible, would take up a collection to found a church in his own neighborhood, at which he hoped to make himself useful as soon as he could prepare himself for the ministry, which the preacher didn't doubt would be in a very few weeks, as Brother Suggs was a man of mighty good *judgment* and of a great discourse. The funds were to be collected by "Brother Suggs," and held in trust by Brother Bela Bugg, who was the financial officer of the circuit, until some arrangement could be made to build a suitable house.

"Yes, breethring," said the Captain, rising to his feet, "I want to start a little 'sociation close to me, and I want you all to help. I'm mighty poor myself, as poor as any of you—don't leave, breethring,"—observing that several of the well-to-do were about to go off—"don't leave. If you ain't able to afford anything, just give us your blessin and it'll be all the same!"

This insinuation did the busines, and the sensitive individuals reseated themselves.

"It's mighty little of this world's goods I've got," resumed Suggs, pulling off his hat and holding it before him. "But I'll bury that in the cause anyhow." And he deposited his last five-dollar bill in the hat.

There was a murmur of approbation at the Captain's liberality throughout the assembly.

Suggs now commenced collecting, and very prudently attacked first the gentlemen who had shown a disposition to escape. These, to exculpate themselves from anything like poverty, contributed handsomely.

"Look here, breethring," said the Captain, displaying the bank notes thus received. "Brother Snooks has dropped a five wi' me, and Brother Snodgrass a ten! In course 'tain't expected that you *that ain't as well off as them* will give *as much*, but every one give accordin to their means."

This was another chain shot that raked as it went! Who so low as not to be able to contribute as much as Snooks and Snodgrass?

"Here's all the *small* money I've got about me," said a burly old fellow, ostentatiously handing to Suggs, over the heads of a half dozen, a ten-dollar bill.

"That's what I call magnanimous!" exclaimed the Captain. "That's the way every *rich* man ought to do."

These examples were followed, more or less closely, by almost all present, for Simon had excited the pride of purse in the congregation, and a very handsome sum was collected in a very short time.

The Reverend Mr. Bugg, as soon as he observed that our hero had obtained all that was to be had at that time, went to him and inquired what amount had been collected. The Captain replied that it was still uncounted, but that it couldn't be much under a hundred.

"Well, Brother Suggs, you'd better count it and turn it over to me now. I'm goin to leave presently."

"No!" said Suggs. "Can't do it!"

"Why?—what's the matter?" inquired Bugg.

"It's got to be *prayed over*, first!" said Simon, a heavenly smile illuminating his whole face.

"Well," replied Bugg, "let's go one side and do it!"

"No," said Simon, solemnly.

Mr. Bugg gave a look of inquiry.

"You see that crick swamp?" asked Suggs. "I'm gwine down in *there*, and I'm gwine to lay the money down *so*"—showing how he would place it on the ground—"and I'm gwine to git on these-here knees"—slapping the right one—"and I'm *n-e-v-e-r* gwine to quit the grit until I feel it's got the blessin! And nobody ain't got to be there but me!"

Mr. Bugg greatly admired the Captain's fervent piety, and bidding him God speed, turned off.

Captain Suggs struck for the swamp, sure enough, where his horse was already hitched. "If them fellows ain't done to a cracklin," he muttered to himself as he mounted, "I'll never bet on two pair agin! They're peart at the snap game theyselves, but they're badly lewed this hitch! Well! Live and let live is a good old motto, and it's my sentiments adzactly!" And giving the spur to his horse, off he cantered.

Phillip B. January
(Obe Oilstone)

*V*ery *little is known about Phillip B. January (the dates of his birth and death, for instance) except that he was a planter in Mississippi, quite possibly in the neighborhood of Natchez, and that, beginning in 1838 and well into the 1840s, he contributed to a magazine that did very well by American humor. The magazine was* The Spirit of the Times, *and, like many other contributors, January signed his distinctive yarns with a pseudonym, Obe Oilstone. He was evidently on good terms with other pseudonymous writers for the periodical, for they celebrated him in several anecdotes. "That Big Dog Fight at Myers's," which appeared in 1845, was a very popular story, not only in the Natchez region but elsewhere in the Old Southwest, as frequent references and reprintings testify. Norris W. Yates, the historian of the* Spirit, *calls January one of the liveliest contributors to the periodical and said that this story is a fine example of its author's artistry. "As so often happens," says Yates, "the events of the tale are less important than the life and spirit breathed into the yarn by the narrator, a 'character' of the first water. Uncle Johnny is perversely and slyly digressive, and his language . . . is colorful and pungent." January showed that he thought well of this narrator by having him tell a couple of other tales. "That Big Dog Fight at Myers's," like a good many other tales published in the* Spirit, *is quite masculine in its subject matter and its appeal.*

That Big Dog Fight at Myers's

Well, them was great times, and *men* lived about here them days, too! Not sayin they're all dead, but the settlements is got too thick for 'em to splurge, and they are old. Besides, they're waitin for their boys to do somethin when they gits *men*! I tell you what, if they lived till kingdom come *they* wouldn't be men. I'd like to see one single one of 'em that ever rid his horse up two pair of stairs, jumped him through—"

"Stop, stop, Uncle Johnny! Do tell us about *that big dog fight at Myers's.*"

"Ha, ha, boy! *You* there? Had your bitters yet? Well, well—we'll take 'em together. Liquor *is* better now than it used to was; but people don't drink so much, and that's strange, ain't it? Well, I was talkin to these men about old Greensville, and about them same men, for they was all at that same dog fight. Fayette, the Devil! never be a patchin to what old Greensville was about the times *Old Col* was sheriff! I'll just bet all the liquor I ever *expect* to drink that there ain't no second story in Fayette that's got hoss tracks on the floor and up agin the ceil—"

"I must stop you again, Uncle Johnny. Fayette is yet in its youth, and promises—"

"Youth, Hell! yes, like the *youth* of some of my old friends' sons—upwards of thirty, and they're expectin to make *men* out'n 'em yet! I tell you what, young men in *my* time'd just get in a spree, sorta open their shirt collars, and shuck theirselves with a growl, and come out ready-made men; and most on 'em has *stayed* ready for fifty-one year! I ain't failed now, yet, and—"

"*Uncle* Johnny, for God's sake stick to the dog story; we'll hear all this after—"

"Ah, you boy, you never will let me tell a story *my* way, but here goes: Let me see—yes, yes. Well, it was a great day in Greensville, anyhow. Charle Cox had run old Saltrum agin a hoss from the Red-licks and beat him shameful—run right plumb up the street in Greensville so as everybody might see. Well, a power of liquor was wasted—nighly every house in town rid through—women and children scared out, and every drink we took was a *general* invite, and about night there was *one* general *in town—General Intoxication.* Well, 'bout sundown the old General—God bless him!—called up his troops; some of the same ones who was at Orleans; let's see—there was the high sheriff, Dick, Bat, Jim, old Iron Tooth, and—"

"Iron Tooth! who's he?" suggested I.

"Why, *he's* the man what fit the dog! Ain't you never seen a man here in Fayette, when he gits *high* up, just pulls out his knife, and goes to chawin it as if he'd made a bet he could bite it in two?"

"Yes, yes, go on."

"Well, the General made 'em all mount, formed line, and rid right into the grocery—formed line agin, had a big stirup drink handed to 'em all, and when the General raised *his* hat and said 'the Hero of Orleans,' the yell that went up put a bead on that men's liquor that stayed nighly a month, I hearn. We come a-rearin out'n the grocery—charged up and down two or three times, cleared the streets of all *weak* things, then started out home, all in a breast. Every one of us had a Polk stalk—"

"Hel-lo!—Polk stalks that early?"

"Well, well, hickory sticks—same thing. Out of town we went, chargin everything we see—fences, cattle, ox-teams. And at last we got to old Myers's, fairly squealin to rear over somethin! Old Myers's dog was awful bad—the worst in anybody's knowledge—why people sent fifty miles to git pups from him! Well, he come a-chargin, too, and met us at the gate, lookin like a young hyena.

"Iron Tooth just turned himself round to us, and says he, 'Men, I'll take *this* fight off'n *your* hands.' So down he got, undressed to his shirt, *stock,* and boots—got down on his all-fours in the road, walkin back'ards and forrards, pitchin up the dust and bellerin like a bull! When the dog see him at that sort of work, he *did* sorta stop barkin, but soon as he see *our* animal strut up to the gate, and begin to smell then, like another dog, he got fairly crazy to git through at him—rearin', cavortin, and *tearin* off pickets!

"Our animal was a-takin all this quite easy—smellin through at him, whinin *me-you, me-you, me-you*—struttin back'ards and forrards, h'istin up one leg agin the gate. Well, after a while the dog begin to git sorta tired, and then *our* animal begin to git mad! Snap for snap he gin the dog, and the spit and slobber flew, and soon the dog was worse than he *had* been. There we was settin on our hosses, rollin with laughter and liquor, and thought the thing was rich, as it was; but just then, our animal riz on his hinders, unlatched the gate, and the dog *lunged* for him.

"Ain't you never noticed when one dog bounces at another, he sorta whirls round sideways, to keep him from hittin him a fair lick? Well, just so our animal: he whirled round sideways, to let the dog have a glancin lick, and true to the character, he was goin to allow the dog a dog's chance, and he stuck to his all-fours. The dog didn't make but one lunge, and he stopped—as still as the pictur of the wolf in the spellin book—for you see our animal was right stern-end facin him, his shirt smartly up over his back, and standin mighty high up on his hind legs at that! We all raised the old Indian yell for you never *did* see such a *sight*, and there stood the dog with the awfullest countenance you ever seen a *dog* wear! Our man, sorta thinkin he'd bluffed the dog, now give two or three short goat-pitches back'ards at him! Ha! ha! ha!"

"What did he do? What did he do?"

"Do? why *run*? wouldn't a damned hyena run! The dog had a big block and chain to him, and soon our animal was a'ter him, givin some of the awfullest leaps and yelps—'twarn't but a little square picket yard round the house, and the dog couldn't git out, so round and round he went—at last, turnin a corner, the chain wrapped round a stump, and there the dog *was fast, and he had to fight*! But he did give powerful licks to get loose!

"When he see his enemy right on him agin, and when Iron Tooth seen the dog *was* fast, round and round he'd strut; and such struttin! Ain't you never seen one of these big, long-legged short-tailed baboons struttin round on top of the lion's cage? Well, so he'd go—sorta smellin at the dog (and his tongue hanging out right smart, for he *was* tired), '*me-you! me-you!*' '*Snap!* snap!' the dog would go, and he begin to show fight damned plain agin, for our varmint was a-facin him, and he seen '*twas* a *man* a'ter all!

"But our animal knowed how to come the giraffe over *him*—so round he turns and gives him the stern view agin! *That* fairly broke the dog's heart, and he just *reared* back a-pullin and got loose! One or two goat-pitches back'ards and the dog was flat on his back, playin his fore-paws mighty fast, and perhaps some of the awfullest barks you ever heard a dog gin! Old Iron Tooth he seen he had the dog at about the right p'int, and he give one mortal lunge back'ards, and he lit with both hands on the dog's throat, turned quick as lightnin, div down his head, and fastened his teeth on the dog's ears!

"Such a shakin and howlin! The dog was too scared to fight, and our animal had it all his own way. We hollered to give him *some* in the short ribs, but he only held on and growled at us, playin the dog clean out, I tell you. Well, there they was, rollin and tumblin in the dirt—first one on top, and then t'other—our animal holdin on like pitch to a wagon wheel, the dog never thinkin 'bout fightin once, but makin real honest licks to git loose. At last our varmint's hold broke—the dog riz—made one *tiger* lunge—the chain snapped—he tucked *his* tail, and—but you all know what scared dogs *will* do!

"Nobody ain't got no pups from Myers since—the blood run right out!"

John S. Robb
(Solitaire)

(ca. 1813-1856)

Like Madison Tensas, Solitaire, alias John S. Robb, wrote a very popular story ("Nettle Bottom Ball") about a respectable female who is embarrassed when she inadvertently appears before others un-clothed. When strapping on a cushion where a bustle is customarily worn, rustic Betsy falls from a loft into the midst of a startled group: "I may die, if Betsy, without a thing on earth on her but one of those stearn cushions, didn't drop right through the floor, and sot herself in the pan of mush!" Robb's "The Standing Candidate," a more seemly sketch that was equally popular, reports the comic monologue of an old Missouri character called Sugar.

Born in Philadelphia, Robb became a wandering printer, journalist, and editor. During the 1840s, he worked for the St. Louis Reveille, *a newspaper famous for its humorous sketches. He left St. Louis to cover the gold rush and subsequently worked for several newspapers in the Far West, among them the Stockton* Journal. *In 1846, a number of his sketches, "The Standing Candidate" among them, were collected in* Streaks from Squatter Life, and Far-West Scenes.

The Standing Candidate
(His Reason for Being a Bachelor)

Sugar

Cyclopaedia Of Wit and Humor, (1858, I.222).

At Buffalo Head, Niauga County, State of Missouri, during the canvass of 1844, there was held an extensive political Barbecue, and the several candidates for Congress, legislature, county offices, &c. were all congregated at this southern point for the making of an *immense* demonstration. *Hards, softs,* Whigs and Tylerites were represented, and to hear their several expositions of state and general policy, a vast gathering of the Missouri sovereigns had also assembled. While the important candidates were awaiting the signal to mount the "stump," an odd-looking old man made his appearance at the brow of a small hill bounding the place of meeting.

"Hurrah for Old Sugar!" shouted a hundred voices, while on steadily progressed the object of their cheer.

Sugar, as he was familiarly called, was an old man, apparently about fifty years of age, and was clad in a coarse suit of brown linsey-woolsey.

His pants were patched at each knee, and around the ankles they had worn off into picturesque points. His coat was not of the modern close-fitting cut, but hung in loose and easy folds upon his broad shoulders, while the total absence of buttons upon this garment exhibited the owner's contempt for the storm and the tempest. A coarse shirt, tied at the neck with a piece of twine, completed his body covering. His head was ornamented with an old woolen cap, of divers colors, below which beamed a broad, humorous countenance, flanked by a pair of short, funny little grey whiskers. A few wrinkles marked his brow, but time could not count them as sure chronicles of his progress, for Sugar's hearty, sonorous laugh oft drove them from their hiding place. Across his shoulder was thrown a sack, in each end of which he was bearing to the scene of political action a keg of brand new whiskey, of his own manufacture, and he strode forward on his moccasin-covered feet, encumbered as he was, with all the agility of youth. Sugar had long been the standing candidate of Niauga County for the legislature, and founded his claim to the office upon the face of his being the first squatter in that county—his having killed the first bear there, ever killed by a white man, and, to place his right beyond cavil, he had 'stilled the first keg of whiskey. These were strong claims, which urged in his comic rhyming matter, would have swept the diggins, but Sugar, when the canvass opened, always yielded his claim to some liberal purchaser of his fluid, and duly announced himself as a candidate for the next term.

"Here you air, old fellow!" shouted an acquaintance, "allays on hand 'bout 'lection."

"Well, Nat," said Sugar, "you've just told the truth as easy as if you'd taken some of my mixtur:—

"Where politicians congregate,
I'm allays there, at any rate."

"Set him up! set the old fellow up somewhere, and let us take a universal liquor!" was the general shout.

"Hold on, boys—keep cool and shady," said Old Sugar. "Where's the candidates? None of your splurgin round till I git an appropriation for the spirits. Send them along and we'll negotiate for the fluid, a'ter which I shall gin 'em my instructions, and they may then proceed to

"Talk away like all creation
What they knows about the nation."

The candidates were accordingly summoned up to pay for Sugar's portable grocery, and to please the crowd and gain the good will of the owner, they made up a purse and gathered round him. Sugar had placed his two kegs upon a broad stump and seated himself astride of them, with a small tin cup in his hand and a paper containing brown sugar lying before him—each of his kegs was furnished with a spigot. And as soon as the money for the whole contents was paid in, Sugar commenced addressing the crowd as follows:

"Boys, fellows, and candidates," said he, "I, Sugar, am the first white man ever seed in these-here diggins. I killed the first bear ever a white skinned in this county, and I calculate I have hurt the feelings of his relations some since, as the bear-skin linin of my cabin will testify. 'Sides that, I'm the first manufacturer of whiskey in the range of this district, and powerful mixtur it is, too, as the whole b'ilin of fellows in this crowd will declare—more'n that, I'm a candidate for the legislatur, and intend to gin up my claim *this* term, to the fellow who can talk the prettiest. Now, finally, at the eend, boys, this mixtur of mine will make a fellow talk as oily as goose grease—as sharp as lightnin and as *per*-suadin as a young gal at a quiltin. So don't spare it while it lasts, and the candidates kin drink first, 'cause they've got to do the talkin!"

Having finished his charge, he filled the tin cup full of whiskey, put in a handful of brown sugar, and with his forefinger stirred up the sweetening. Then surveying the candidates he pulled off his cap, remarking as he did so:

"Old age, allays, afore beauty! your daddy first, in course." Then holding up the cup, he offered a toast, as follows:

"Here is to the string that binds the states; may it never be bit apart by political rats!" Then holding up the cup to his head, he had a hearty swig, and passed it to the next oldest looking candidate. While they were tasting it, Sugar kept up a fire of lingo at them:

"Pass it along lively, gentle*men*, but don't spare the fluid. You can't help tellin truth a'ter you've swallowed enough of my mixtur, just for this reason: it's been 'stilled in honesty, rectified in truth, and poured out with wisdom. Take a *leetle* drop more," said he to a fastidious candidate, whose stomach turned at thought of the way the mixtur was mixed. "Why, Mister," said Sugar, coaxingly,

"If you were a baby, just new born,
'Twould do you good, this juicy corn."

"No more, I thank you," said the candidate, drawing back from the proffer.

Sugar winked his eye at some of his cronies, and muttered, "He's got an *a*-ristocracy stomach, and can't go the native liquor."

Then dismissing the candidates, he shouted, "Crowd up, constitu-*ents*, into a circle, and let's begin fair—your daddy first, allays. And mind, no changin places in the circle to git the sugar in the bottom of the cup. I know you're a'ter it, Tom Williams; but none on your Yankeein round to git the sweetnin—it's all syrup, fellows, 'cause Sugar made and mixed it. The gals at the frolics allays git me to prepare the cordials, 'cause they say I make it mighty drinkable. What you, old Ben Dent!—Well, hold your hoss for a minute, and I'll sweeten the tin with a speck more, just because you can calculate the value of the liquor, and do it justice!"

Thus chatted Sugar as he measured out and sweetened up the contents of his kegs, until all who would drink had taken their share, and then the crowd assembled around the speakers. We need not say that the virtues of each political party were duly set forth to the hearers—that follows as a matter of course, candidates dwell upon the strong points of their argument, always. One among them, however, more than his compeers, attracted the attention of our friend Sugar, not because he had highly commended the contents of his kegs, but because he painted with truth and feeling the claims of the western *pioneers*!

Among these he ranked the veteran Col. Johnson and his compatriots, and as he rehearsed their struggles in defense of their firesides, how they had been trained to war by their conflict with the ruthless savage, their homes oft desolated and their children murdered,—yet still, ever foremost in the fight and last to retreat, winning the heritage of these broad valleys for their children, against the opposing arm of the red man, though aided by the civilized power of mighty Britain and her serried cohorts of trained soldiery! We say as he dwelt upon these themes Sugar's eye would fire up, and then, at some touching passage of distress dwelt on by the speaker, tears would course down his rude cheek. When the speaker concluded, he wiped his eyes with his head bowed, and said to those around him:—

"That are true as the yearth! there's suthin like talk in that fellow?—He's the right breed, and his old daddy has told him about them times. So did mine relate 'em to me, how the only sister I ever had, when a baby had her brains dashed out by one of the red-skinned devils. But didn't we pepper them for it? Didn't I help the old man, afore he grew too weak to hold his shooting iron, to send a few on 'em off to rub out the account? Well, I *did!—Hey!*" and shutting his teeth together, he yelled through them the exultation of full vengeance.

The speaking being done, candidates and hearers gathered round old Sugar, to hear his comments upon the speeches and to many inquiries of how he had liked them, the old man answered:—

"They were all pretty good, but that tall fellow they call Tom, from St. Louis; *you*, I mean, stranger," pointing at the same time to the candidate, "you just scairt up my feelins to the right p'int—you just made me feel as when I and old dad were a'ter the red varmints; and now, what'll *you* take? I'm goin to publicly decline in your favor."

Pouring out a tin full of the liquor, and stirring it as before, he stood upright on the stump, with a foot on each side of his kegs, and drawing off his cap, toasted:—

"To the memory of the western pioneers!"

A shout responded to his toast, which echoed far away in the depths of the adjoining forest, and seemed to awaken a response from the spirits of those departed heroes.

"That's the way to sing it out, boys," responded Old Sugar. "Such a yell as that would care an enemy into ague fits, and make the United States Eagle scream, 'Hail, Columby!'"

"While you're up, Sugar, said one of the crowd, "give us a stump speech yourself."

"Agreed, boys," said the old man. "I'll just gin you a few words to wind up with; so keep quiet while your daddy's talkin;

"Some tell it out just like a song,
I'll gin it to you sweet and strong."

"The on'y objection ever made to me in this-ere county, as a legislator, was made by the *women*, 'cause I war a *bachelor*, and I never told you afore why I *re*-mained in the state of number *one*—no fellow stays single *pre*-meditated, and, in course, a handsome fellow like me, who all the gals declare to be as enticin as a jaybird, warn't goin to stay alone, if he could help it.

"I did see a creatur, once, named Sophie Mason, up the Cumberland, nigh onto Nashville, Tenne*see*, that I tuck an awful hankerin a'ter, and I sot in to lookin anxious for matrimony, and gin to go reg'lar to meetin, and tuck to dressin tremendous fancified, just to see if I could win her good opinion. She did git to lookin at me, and one day, comin from meetin, she was takin a look at me kind of shy, just as a hoss does at suthin he's scairt at, when a'ter champin at a distance for a while, I sidled up to her and blarted out a few words about the sermon. She said yes, but cuss me if I know whether that were the right answer or not, and I'm a-thinkin she didn't know then, nuther! Well we laughed and talked a leetle, all the way along to her daddy's, and there I gin her the best bend I had in me, and raised up my brand new hat as peart and polite as a minister, lookin all the time so enticin that I sot the gal tremblin.

"Her old daddy had a powerful numerous lot of healthy niggers, and lived right a'j'inin my place, while on t'other side lived Jake Simpson—a sneakin, cute varmint, who were worser than a miser for stinginess, and no sooner did this cussed serpent see me sidlin up to Sophie than he went to slickin up too, and sot himself to work to cut me out.

"That-ere were a struggle equal to the battle of Orleans. First some new fixup of Jake's would take her eye, and then I'd sport suthin that would outshine him, until Jake at last gin in tryin to outdress me, and sot to thinkin of suthin else. Our farms were just the same number of acres, and we both owned three niggers apiece. Jake knew that Sophie and her dad kept a sharp eye out for the main chance, so he thought he'd clear me out by buyin another nigger; but I just followed suit and bought one the day a'ter he got his, so he had no advantage there. He then got a cow, and so did I, and just about then both on our *purses* gin out.

"This put Jake to his wits' eend, and I war a-wonderin what in the yearth he would try next. We stood so, hip and thigh, for about two weeks, both on us talkin sweet to Sophie, whenever we could git her alone. I thought I seed that Jake, the sneakin cuss, were gettin a mite ahead of me, 'cause his tongue were so iley; however, I didn't let on but kept a top eye on him. One Sunday mornin I were a leetle mite late to meetin, and when I got there the first thing I seed war Jake Simpson sittin close bang up agin Sophie, in the same pew with her daddy! I b'iled a spell with wrath, and then turned sour; I could taste myself! There they were singin *himes* out of the same book. Je-e-mny, fellows, I war so *enormous* mad that the new silk handkercher round my head lost its color.

"A'ter meetin out they walked, linked arms, a-smilin and lookin as pleased as a young couple at their first christenin, and Sophie turned her cold shoulder at me so awful p'inted that I wilted down, and gin up right straight—there were no disputin it! I headed home, with my hands as far in my trousers pocket as I could push 'em, swearin all the way that she were the last one would ever get a chance to rile up my feelins. Passin by Jake's plantation I looked over the fence, and there stood an explanation of the matter, right facin the road, where every one passin could see it—his consarned cow was tied to a stake in the garden, *with a most promisin calf alongside of her*! That *calf* just soured my milk, and made Sophie think, that a fellow who war allays gettin ahead like Jake, were a right smart chance for a lively husband!"

A shout of laughter here drowned Sugar's voice, and as soon as silence was restored, he added, in a solemn tone, with one eye shut, and his forefinger pointing at his auditory: —

"What is a cussed sight worser than his gittin Sophie war the fact, *that he borrowed the calf the night before from Dick Hartley*. A'ter the varmint got Sophie hitched, he told the joke all over the settle*ment*, and the boys never seed me a'terwards that they didn't *b-a-h* at me for lettin a calf cut me out of a gal's affections. I'd a-shot Jake, but thought it war a free country, and the gal had a right to her choice without being made a widow, so I just sold out and traveled! I've allays thought since then, boys, that women were a good deal like liquor: if you love em too hard, they're sure to throw you some way:

> "Then here's to women, then to liquor;
> There's nothin swimmin can be slicker!"

William Tappan Thompson

(1812-1882)

*T*he son of a Virginia-born father, William Tappan Thompson *was born in Ohio and reared in that state and in Pennsylvania. He first worked in the North as a printer's devil, but, after studying law in Florida and serving in the second Seminole war, he became a Southwestern journalist. Looking for a way to popularize the Madison, Georgia,* Southern Miscellany, *of which he was the editor, he remembered an early piece of his that had been unusually well received. He wrote many in the same vein after readers not only in Georgia but elsewhere found some amusing. When collected in* Major Jones's Courtship *(1843),* Chronicles of Pineville *(1845), and* Major Jones's Sketches of Travel *(1848), these enjoyed good sales in several editions, the last of which appeared late in the century. Thompson's most popular character, Major Jones of Pineville, Georgia, was a letter writer and the barely educated owner of a small plantation, naive but skilled as a storyteller and as a commentator. More reputable than most famed humorous frontier characters, the pious major (of the militia) was a bashful suitor, a doting family man, and a keen-eyed observer who told about his misadventures and commented on them in salty dialect. He was a Southwestern version of Yankee Jack Downing or Hosea Biglow.*

"A Coon Hunt in a Fency Country," Thompson's most amusing piece, though it doesn't take the form of a letter from Jones, has as its narrator a man who shares the major's tendency to moralize, his narrative skill, and his flair for amusing vernacular speech. Henry Prentice Miller aptly described the formula Thompson follows in this and in other stories: "A single paragraph of general moralizing or crackerbox philosophizing; a quick sketching of the characters; a few statements about background; a single incident, and finally the point or nub which ties up the initial paragraph."

Mark Twain showed his liking for Thompson by imitating this piece and others, and, no wonder, for some of Thompson's narratives are humorous masterpieces. In the thirteenth chapter of A Tramp Abroad, *Twain writes in the first person about circular wanderings and bewilderments in a dark European bedroom that greatly resemble the experiences of Bill Sweeney and Tom Culpepper in a nighttime Georgia forest. The version of "A Coon Hunt in a Fency Country" reproduced here appeared in an 1872 edition of* Major Jones's Courtship. *The earliest version of the story was published in a magazine in 1847. In "The Hoosier and the Salt Pile" (1848), Thompson's report on a tall tale-telling session provides a firsthand account of a frontier pastime that was important as a source for humor. The version reproduced here, one containing some revisions, appeared in the 1872 volume.*

A Coon Hunt in a
Fency Country

It is really astonishin what a monstrous sight of mischief there is in a bottle of rum. If one of 'em was to be submitted to a analization, as the doctors call it, it would be found to contain all manner of devilment that ever entered the head of man, from cussin and stealin up to murder and whippin his own mother, and nonsense enough to turn all the men in the world out of their senses. If a man's got any badness in him, let him drink whiskey, and it will bring it out just as sassafras tea does the measles; and if he's a good-for-nothin sort of a fellow, without no bad traits in particular, it'll bring out all his foolishness. It affects different people in different ways—it makes some men monstrous brave and full of fight, and some it makes cowards—some it makes rich and happy, and some poor and miserable. And it has different effects on different peoples's eyes— some it makes see double, and some it makes so blind that they can't tell themselves from a side of bacon. One of the worst cases of rum-foolery that I've heard of for a long time tuck place in Pineville last fall.

Bill Sweeney and Tom Culpepper is the two greatest old coveys in our settlement for coon-huntin. The fact is, they don't do much of anything else, and when *they* can't catch coons, it's a sure sign that coons is scarce. Well, one night they had everything ready for a regular hunt, but owin to some extra good fortun, Tom had got a pocket-pistol, as he called it, of genuine old Jamaica rum. After takin a good startin horn, they went out on their hunt, with their lightwood torch a-blazin, and the dogs a-barkin and yelpin like they was crazy.

They struck out into the woods, gwine in the direction of old Starlin Jones's new-ground, a great place for coons. Every now and then they would stop to wait for the dogs, and then they would drink one another's health, until they begun to feel first-rate. On they went, chattin away about one thing and another, takin a nip now and then from Tom's bottle, not mindin much where they was gwine. By and by they come to a fence. Well, over they got without much difficulty.

"Whose fence is this?" says Bill.

" 'T ain't no matter," says Tom. "Let's take a drink."

After takin a pull at the bottle, they went on again, wonderin what upon yea'th had come of the dogs. The next thing they come to was a terrible muddy branch. After gropin their way through the bushes and briars and gittin on t'other side, they tuck another drink. Fixing up their torch and startin on agin, they didn't go but a little ways before they come to another branch, as bad as the first one, and a little further they come to another fence—a monstrous high one this time.

"Where upon yea'th is we got to, Culpepper?" says Bill. "I never seed such a heap of fences and branches in these parts."

"Why," says Tom, "It's old Starlin's doins. You know, he's always building fences and makin infernal improvements, as he calls 'em. But never mind, we's through 'em now."

"The devil we is," says Bill. "Why, here's the all-firedest high fence yit."

Sure enough, there they was right ag'in another fence. By this time they begun to be considerable tired and limber in their j'ints; and it was such a terrible high fence. Tom dropped the last piece of the torch, and there they was in the dark.

"Now you *is* done it!" says Bill.

Tom knowed he had, but he thought it was no use to grieve over what couldn't be helped, so, says he,

"Never mind, old hoss—come ahead, and I'll take you out," and the next minute, kerslash! he went into the water up to his neck.

Bill heard the splash, and he clung to the fence with both hands, like he thought it was slewin round to throw him off.

"Hello, Tom!" says he. "Where in creation has you got to?"

"Here I is!" says Tom, spittin the water out of his mouth, and coughin like he'd swallowed something. "Look out, there's another dratted branch here."

"Name o' sense, where is we?" says Bill. "If this isn't a fency country, dad fetch my buttons!"

"Yes, and a branchy one, too!" says Tom, "and they is the thickest and deepest that I ever seed in all my born days."

After a good deal of cussin and gruntin, Bill got himself loose from the fence.

"Which way is you?" says he.

"Here, right over the branch," says Tom.

The next minute in Bill went, up to his middle in the branch.

"Come ahead," says Tom, "and let's go home."

"Come thunder!" says Bill, "in such a place as this, where a fellow hain't more'n got his coattail unhitched from a fence before he's head and ears in a cussed branch."

Bill made a terrible job of gittin across the branch, which he swore was the deepest one yit. They managed to git together agin after feelin about in the dark a while, and, takin another drink, they sot out for home, cussin the fences and the branches, and helpin one another up now and then when they got their legs tangled in the brush. But they hadn't gone more'n twenty yards before they found themselves in the middle of another branch. After gittin through the branch and gwine about twenty yards they was brung up all standin agin by another ever-lastin fence.

"Dad blame my pictur," says Bill, "if I don't think we's bewitched. Who upon yea'th would go and build fences all over outdoors this way?"

It tuck 'em a long time to climb the fence, but when they got on top of it they found the ground on t'other side without much trouble. This time the bottle was broke, and they come monstrous nigh havin a fight about the catastrophe. But it was a very good thing the liquor was spilt, for after crossin three or four more branches and climbin as many fences, it got to be daylight, when to their great astonishment they found out that they had been climbin the same fence and wadin the same branch all night, not more'n a hundred yards from the place where they first come to 'em.

Bill Sweeney says he can't account for it no other way but that the liquor sorta turned their heads; and he says he really does believe if it hadn't gin out, they'd been climbin that same fence and wadin that same branch till now.

The Hoosier and the Salt Pile

It is very refreshin in these days of progress, after rattlin over the country for days and nights, at the rate of twenty miles a hour in a railroad car—with your mouth full of dust and smoke, and with such a everlastin clatter in your ears that you can't hear yourself think—to git into a good old-fashioned stage-coach. There's something sociable and cosy in stage-coach travelin, so different from the bustle and confusion of a railroad, where people are whirled along slam bang to eternal smash, like they were so many bales and boxes of dry-goods and groceries, without so much as a chance of seein where they're gwine, or of takin any interest in their fellow sufferers. I love to hear the pop of the whip and the interestin conversation between the driver and his horses; and I like the constant variation in the motion of the stage, the rattle of the wheels over the stones, the stillness of the drag through the heavy sand, the lungin and pitchin into the ruts and gullies, the slow pull up the steep hills, the rush down agin, and the splashin of the horses' feet under the wheels in water and mud. And then one has time to see the country he's passin through, to count the rails in the panels of the fences, and the women and children in the doors of the house, to notice the appearance of the crops, and the condition of the stock on the farms, and now and then to say a word to the people on the roadside. All these things is pleasant, after a long voyage on the railroad. But what's still more agreeable about stage-coach travelin is that we have a opportunity of making the acquaintance of our fellow travelers, of conversin with them and studyin their traits of character, which from the strikin contrast they often present, never fail to amuse if they don't interest our mind.

Some years ago I had a tolerably fair specimen of a stage-coach ride from Warrenton to Milledgeville. The road wasn't the best in the world, and didn't run through the most interestin part of Georgia, but we had a good team, a good stage, and a first-rate driver, what could sing like a camp-meetin and whistle like a locomotive, and the company was just about as good a one as could be jumped up for such an occasion. There was nine of us besides the driver, and I don't believe there ever was a crowd of the same number that presented a greater variety of characters. There was a old gentleman in black, with big round spectacles, and a gold-headed cane; a dandy gambler, with a big diamond breast-pin and more gold chains hangin round him than would hang him; a old hardshell preacher, as they call 'em in Georgia, with the biggest mouth and the ugliest teeth I ever seed; a circus clown, whose breath smelled strong enough of whiskey to upset the stage; a cross old maid, as ugly as a tarbucket; a beautiful young school-gal, with rosy cheeks and mischievous bright eyes; a cattle-drover from Indiany, who was gwine to New Orleans to git a army contract for beef; and myself.

For a while after we started from Warrenton nobody didn't have much to say. The young lady put her green veil over her face and leaned her head back in the corner; the old maid, after a row with the driver about her band-boxes, sot up straight in her seat and looked as sharp as a steel trap; the old gentleman with the spectacles drummed his fingers on his cane and looked out of the coach window; the circus man tried to look interestin; the gambler went to sleep; the preacher looked solemn; and the Hoosier stuck his head out of the window on his side to look at the cattle what we passed every now and then.

"This ain't no great stock country," says he to the old gentleman with the specs.

"No, sir," says the old gentleman. "There's very little grazing here. The range in these parts is pretty much worn out."

Then there was nothing said for some time. By and by the Hoosier opened agin.

"It's the damndest place for 'simmon trees and turkey buzzards I ever did see."

The old gentleman didn't say nothin, and the preacher fetched a long groan. The young lady smiled through her veil, and the old maid snapped her eyes and looked sideways at the preacher.

"Don't make much beef down here, I reckon," says the Hoosier.

"No," says the old gentleman.

"Well, I don't see how in the hell they manage to live in a country where there ain't no ranges, and they don't make no beef. A man ain't considered worth a cuss in Indiany what hasn't got his brand on a hundred head or so of cattle."

"Yours is a great beef country, I believe," says the old gentleman.

"Well, sir, it ain't nothing else. A man that's got sense enough to follow his own cow bell, with us, ain't no danger of starvin. I'm gwine down to Orleans to see if I can't git a contract out of Uncle Sam to feed the boys what's been lickin them infernal Mexicans so bad. I s'pose you've seen them cussed lies what's been in the newspapers about the Indiany boys at Buena Vista?"

"I've read some accounts of the battle," says the old gentleman, "that didn't give a very flattering account of the conduct of some of our troops."

With that the Indiany man went into a full explanation of the affair, and gittin warmed up as he went along, began to cuss and swear like he'd been through a dozen campaigns himself.

The old preacher listened to him with evident signs of displeasure, twistin and groanin every time he uttered a big oath until he couldn't stand it no longer.

"My friend," says he, "you must excuse me, but your conversation would be a great deal more interestin to me, and I'm sure it would please the company much better, if you wouldn't swear so terribly. It's very wicked to swear so, and I hope you'll have respect for our religious feelins, if you hain't got no respect for your Maker."

If the Hoosier had been struck with a clap of thunder and lightning he couldn't have been more completely tuck aback. He shut his mouth right in the midst of what he was sayin, and looked at the preacher, while his face got as red as fire.

"Swearin," continued the old hardshell, "is a terrible bad practice, and there ain't no use in it no how. The Bible says 'swear not at all,' and I suppose you know the commandments about taking the Lord's name in vain."

The Hoosier didn't open his mouth.

"I know," says the old preacher, "a great many people swear without thinkin, and that some people don't believe in the Bible."

And then he went on to preach a regular sermon agin, and to quote the Scripture like he knowed the whole Bible by heart. In the course of his arguments he undertook to prove the Scriptures to be true, and told us all about the miracles and prophecies and their fulfillment. The old gentleman with the cane tuck a part in the conversation, and the Hoosier listened without ever once openin his head.

"I've just heard of a gentleman," said the preacher, "what has been to the Holy Land, and went all over the Bible country. It's astonishin what wonderful things he seed there. He was at Sodom and Gomorrah, and seed the place where Lot's wife fell!"

"Ah?" says the old gentleman with the specs.

"Yes," says the preacher. "He went to the very spot, and what's the most remarkablest thing of all, he seed the pillar of salt what she was turned into."

"Is it possible?" says the old gentleman.

The Hoosier's countenance all at once brightened up, and he opened his mouth wide.

"Yes, sir; he seed the salt standin there to this day."

The Hoosier's curiosity was raised to a p'int beyond endurance.

"What!" says he, "real genewine good salt?"

"Yes, sir, a pillar of salt just as it was when that wicked woman was punished for her disobedience."

All but the gambler, who was snoozin in the corner of the coach, looked at the preacher—the Hoosier with an expression of countenance that plainly told that his mind was powerfully convicted of an important fact.

"Standin right out in the open air?" he axed.

"Yes, sir—right out in the open field where she fell."

"Well," says the Hoosier, "all I've got to say, *if she'd dropped in Indiany, the cattle would licked her up long ago!*"

William C. Hall
(Yazoo)

(1819?-1865)

*W*illiam C. Hall, a native of Mississippi, graduated from Transylvania University and became a New Orleans newspaper man. Five sketches signed with Yazoo — the name of the county in which he was born — first came out in the New Orleans Delta and then in other newspapers, some magazines, and some anthologies of humor. They celebrated a character roughly patterned after a cotton planter of Yazoo county: very roughly, since the character, Mike Hooter, though a thoroughly domesticated animal at home, was a profane, tall-talking, guzzling backwoodsman, and his prototype was a well-to-do and pious gentleman. Although the payoff of "How Sally Hooter Got Snake-bit" is obvious long before the story ends, the leisurely buildup charmed the author's contemporaries. Incredibly enough, the piece had another appeal during an era when most writers shied away like frightened animals from any references to sex. Believe it or not, in those days the far-from-graphic depiction of Potter fumbling around in search of the snake's tail was considered pretty racy. And the statement that Potter carried on his search "sorta like he didn't like to do it at first, and then sorta like he did" was positively devilish. Regrettably, Yazoo had a tendency to be unfashionably frank; one of his sketches graphically describing a whorehouse in Natchez, "Under-the-Hill," isn't particularly funny.

How Sally Hooter
Got Snakebit

Our old acquaintance, Mike Hooter, made another visit to town last week, and being, as he supposed, beyond the hearing of his brethren in the church (for be it remembered that Mike is of pious inclining, and a ruling elder in the denomination of Methodists), concluded that he would go on a bust. Having sold his crop of cotton and fobbed the tin, forth sallied Mike with a pocket full of rocks and bent on a bit of a spree.

After patronizing all the groceries and getting rather mellow, he grew garrulous in the extreme, and forthwith began to expatiate on his wonderful exploits. After running through with a number of panther and bear fights, and several wolf disputes, he finally subsided into the recital of events more nearly appertaining to members of his family.

"That Yazoo," said Mike, "is the durndest hole that ever come along. If it ain't the next place to nowhere, you can take my head for a drinkin gourd—you can. And as for that-ere devil's camp ground that they calls Satartia, if this world was a kitchen, it would be the slop hole, and a mighty stinkin one at that! I pledge you my word, it comes closer to bein the jumpin off place than any I ever hearn tell on. Talk about Texas! It ain't nothin to them Yazoo hills. The eternalest out-of-the-way place for bear, and panthers, and wolfs, and possums, and coons, and skeeters, and gnats, and hoss flies, and chiggers, and lizards, and frogs, and mean fellows, and drinkin whiskey, and stealin one-another's hogs, and gittin corned, and swappin horses, and playing hell generally, that ever you did see! Pledge you my word 'nough to sink it.

"And as for snakes! whew! don't talk! I've hearn tell of the Boa Constructor, and the Annagander, and all that kind o' ruptile what swallows a he-goat whole, and don't care a switch of his tail for his horns; and I see the preacher tell 'bout Aaron's walkin stick what turned itself into a serpent, and swallowed up ever-so many other sticks, and rods, and bean poles, and chunks of wood, and was hungry yet—and all that kind a hellerbelloo, but that's all moonshine. Just wait a minute till you've hearn 'bout the snakes what flourishes up 'bout my stompin ground, and how one of 'em come precious nigh chawin up my daughter Sal, and if you don't forgit everything you ever knowed, then Mike Hooter's the durndest liar that ever straddled a fence rail.

"Jeeminy, criminy! Just to see him, one of them-ere great big rusty rattlesnakes, and hear him shake that-ere tail of hisn! I tell you what, if you didn't think all the peas in my corn field was a-spillin in the floor, there ain't no 'simmons! talk about the clouds burstin and the hail rattlin down in a tin pan! Why 'tain't a patchin to it! Cracky! it's worse nor a young earthquake—beats hell!

"Now, I don't value a snake more nor a she bear in suckin time—'specially a rattlesnake, cause you see it's a vermin what always rattles his tail 'fore he strikes, and gives you time to scoot out'n the way, but the women folks and my gal Sally is always, in generally, the scaredest in the world of 'em. I never seed but one woman what wouldn't cut up when a snake was about, and that was old Missus Lemay, and she didn't care a doggone bit for all the serpents that ever come along. That old gal was a hoss! Pledge you my word I b'lieve she was poison—couldn't be no other way. Didn't never hear how that old petticoat bit the snake? Well, I'll tell you.

"She went out one day and was a-squattin down, pickin up chips, and the first thing she knowed she'd got onto the whappinest, biggest, rustiest yellow moccasin that ever you shuck a stick at, and bein as how she was kind-a deaf, she didn't hear him when he gin to puff and blow, and hiss like. The first thing she knowed he bit her, *slap*—the all-firedest, biggest kind o' lick! You oughta seen that old gal, how she fell down, and rolled, and wallowed, and tumbled 'bout and hollered 'nough, and screamed, and prayed, and tried to sing a paslm, and played hell generally! You'd a-thought the very yearth was a-comin to an eend! Then she begin hollerin for help.

"Says she, 'Missus Hooter, come here and kill this here snake!' Well, my wife run out and fotch the old 'oman in the house and gin her some whiskey, and she tuck it like milk. Directly she sorta come to herself, and says my wife to her—says she to Missus Lemay, says she—'Missus Lemay, what hurts you?'

"'Snakebit!' says she.

"'Where 'bouts?' says I.

"'Never mind,' says she—'snakebit!'

"'But, Missus Lemay,' says I, 'tell me where he bit you, so as we may put somethin to it.'

"Says she, lookin kinda glum, and turnin red in the face—says she to me, 'It don't want nothin to it: I'm snakebit, and 'tain't none of your business where!'

"With that I smelt a mice and commenced laughin. You oughta hearn me holler! If I didn't think I'd a-bust my boiler, I wish I may never see Christmas! I ain't laughed so much since the time John Potter got on the bear's back without no knife, and rode him round like a hoss, and was scared to get off! I give you my word I fairly rolled!

"Soon as the old 'oman gin to open her eyes and I see there warn't much the matter with her, my wife she grabbed up the tongs and went out to kill the snake, and I followed. When I see the reptile, says I to my wife, 'Just wait a minute,' says I. ' 'Tain't no use killin him—he's past prayin for!' I pledge my word he was dead as Billy-be-damned!

" 'What made him die?' says my wife to me.

" 'Don't know,' says I—s'pose he couldn't stand it.'

"Directly Mat Read he come up, and, when he hearn what had been goin on, he was so full of laugh his face turned wrong side out'ards, and says he, 'Poisoned, by golly!'

"That old 'oman ain't been scared of a snake since, and goes out huntin 'em regular. I told her one day, says I, 'Missus Lemay,' says I, 'I'll give you the best bunch of hogs' bristles I've got, to brush your teeth with, if you'll tell me how not to git scared of a snake!' She didn't say ne'er a word, but she turned round and took me kerbim right 'tween the eyes! I tell you what, it made me see stars. I ain't said snake to her since.

"Howsever, that ain't tellin you how the serpent kinda chawed up my daughter Sal. I'll tell you how 'twas. You see, there was gwine to be a mighty big camp meetin down at Hickory Grove, and we all fixed up to go down and stay a week, and my wife, she cooked up everything 'bout the house, and all sorts of good things—bacon, and possum fat, and ash cake, and a great big sausenger, 'bout as big as your arm, and long enough to eat a week—'cause, whe said, Parson Dilly loved sausengers the best in the world.

"Well, when we got there I went to the basket what had the vittles in it, to git somethin to eat, but the sausenger wasn't there, and says I to my daughter, says I, 'Sally, gal, what's come of that-ere sausenger?'

"Then she turned red in the face, and says she, 'Never mind—it's all right.'

"I smelt that there war somethin gwine on wrong. For you see the women folks 'bout where I lives is hell for new fashions, and one day one of them-ere all-fired Yankee peddlers come along with a outlandish kind of a jigamaree to make the women's coat sorta stick out in the t'other eend, and the shes, they all put on one, 'cause they s'posed the hes would love to see it. Well, my Sal, she got monstrous tuck up 'bout it, and axed me to give her one. But I told her she had no more use for one nor a settin hen had for a midwife, and I wouldn't do no such a thing 'cause how she was big enough there at first.

"Well, as I were a-sayin, camp meetin day it came, and we was all there, and the she-folks they was fixed up in a inch of their lives, and there she was a fidgitin, and a-twistin, and a wrigglin about with a new calico coat on, all stuck up at the hind eend, and as proud as a he lizard with two tails! Tell you what—she made more fuss nor a settin hen with one chicken! I was 'stonished what to make of that whoppin lump on behind. Howsever, it was 'simmon time, and she'd been eatin a powerful sight of 'em, and I s'posed she was gittin fat—so I shut up my fly trap, and lay low and kept dark!

"Directly the preachin it begin, and Parson James, he was up on a log a-preachin, and a-goin it 'hark from the tomb!' I tell you what, Brother James was loud that day! There he was, with the Bible on a board—stuck in between two saplins—and he was a-comin down on it with his two fists worse nor maulin rails, and a-stompin his feet, and a-slobberin at the mouth and a-cuttin up shines worse nor a bobtail bull in fly time! I tell you what, if he *didn't* go it boots that time, I don't know.

"Directly I spy the heathens they commence takin on, and the spirit it begin to move 'em, for true—for Brother Sturtevant's old nigger Cain, and all of 'em, they gin to kinda groan and whine, and feel about like a cornstalk in a storm, and Brother Gridle, he begin a-rubbin his hands and slappin 'em together, and scramblin 'bout on his knees, and a-cuttin up like mad!

"In about a minute I hearn the all-firedest to-do, down 'mongst the women, that ever come along, and when I kinda cast my eye over that way, I spy my Sal a-rearin and a-pitchin, a-rippin and a-tearin, and a-shoutin like flinders!

"When Brother James he see that, he thought she'd done got good, and he come down off the log, and says he, 'Pray on, sister!' And the shes they all got round her, and cotch hold of her, and tried to make her hold still. But 'twarn't no use. The more they told her to 'don't' the more she hollered.

"Directly I discover she'd done got 'ligious, and I was so glad it kinda lift me off'n the ground, and says I, "Go it, Sal! Them's the licks! Blessed am them what seeks for them's 'em what shall find!"

"The women they all cotch hold of her by the hair, and commence wallowin her 'bout in the straw, and says I, 'That's right, sisters—beat the Devil out'n her!' And they *did* too! I tell you what—the way they did hustle her about 'mongst the straw and shucks was forked! In about a minute I 'gin to get tired and disgustified, and tried to make her shut up, but she wouldn't, but kept a-hollerin worser and worser, and she kinda keeled up like a possum when he makes 'tend he's dead!

"Directly she sorta come to herself so she could talk, and says I, 'Sal, what ails you, gal?'

"The first word she says, says she, 'Snake!'

" 'Whar 'bouts?' says I.

" 'Snake,' says she agin—'serpent! Take it off, or he'll chaw me up be God!'

" 'Well!' says my wife, 'that's cussin!'

" 'Where's any snake?' says I.

" 'Snake!' says she, 'snake! snake!' and then she put her hand on the outside of her coat and cotch hold of somethin and squeezed it tight as a vise.

"When I seed that, I knowed it was a snake sure 'nough, what had crawled up under her coat, and I see she'd put her hand on the outside of her clothes, and cotch it by the head. Soon as I seed that, I knowed he couldn't bite her, for she helt onto him like grim death to a dead nigger, and I 'cluded 'twarn't no use bein in too big a hurry. So I told John Potter not to be scared and go and grab the serpent by the tail and sling him hellwards!

"Well, Potter he went and sorta felt of him on the outside of her coat, and I pledge you my word he was the whoppinest, biggest reptile that ever scooted across a road! I tell you, if he warn't as big as my arm, Mike Hooter is as big a liar as old Dave Lemay—and you know he's a few in that line! Well, when Potter discover that she helt the snake fast, he begin feelin up for the reptile's tail, sorta like he didn't like to do it at first, and then sorta like he did. When it come to that, Sal she kinda turned red in the face and squirmed a bit, but 'twarn't no time for puttin on quality airs then, and she stood it like a hoss! Well, Potter, he kept a-feelin up, and feelin and a-feelin up, sorta easy-like, and directly he felt somethin in his hand.

" 'I've got him,' says Potter. 'Well, I have, by jingo!'

" 'Hold on to him, Sal,' says I, 'and don't you do nothin, Mr. Potter, till I give the word, and when I say, "Go!" then, Sal, you let go of the varmint's head; and Potter—you give the all-firedest kind on a jerk, and sling him to hell and gone!'

"I tell you what, them was squally times! And I 'vise you, the next time you go up to Yazoo, just ax anybody, and if they don't say the snakes up in them parts beats creation, then Mike Hooter'll knock under."

At this point of the narration we ventured to ask Mike what became of the snake.

"As I was a-sayin," continued he, "that was my Sal a-holdin the serpent by the head, and John Potter he had him by the tail, and Sal she was a-hollerin and a-screamin, and all the women, they was all standin round, scared into a fit, and the durndest row you ever hearn.

" 'Hold onto him, Sal,' says I. 'And you, John Potter, don't you move a peg till I give the word, and when I say "Jerk!" then you sling him into the middle of next week.' I tell you what, we had the awfullest time that ever I see! Let's liquor!

"That's the best red eye I've swallowed in a coon's age," said the speaker, after belting a caulker.

"But how did you manage at last?" asked a listener.

"Well, you see," said he, "there was my Sal, and there was all the folks, and there was the snake, and John Potter holdin him by the tail, scared out'n his senses, and hell to pay! I was gettin sorta weak in the knees, I tell you, and brother James's eyes looked like they'd pop out'n his head.

"And says I to John Potter, says I to him, says I, 'John Potter, don't you budge till I say, "Go!" and when I gives the word, then you give him a jerk, and send him kerslap up agin that tree, and perhaps you'll gin him a headache. Now John Potter,' says I, 'is you ready?' says I.

" 'I is,' says he.

" 'Now look at me,' says I, 'And when I drop this handkercher,' says I, 'then you jerk like flujuns,' says I.

" 'Yes,' says he.

"Then I turned round to Miss Lester, and says I, 'Miss Lester, bein as how I ain't got no handkercher, s'pose you let me have that coon-skin cape of yourn.'

"Says she, 'Uncle Mike, you can have anything I is got.'

" 'Bliged to you,' says I. 'And now, John Potter,' says I, 'when I drops this coon-skin cape, then you pull!'

" 'Yes,' says he.

" 'Now,' says I, 'keep your eye skinned, and look me right plumb in the face, and when you see me drop this, then you wallum the serpent out. Is you ready?' says I.

" 'Yes,' says he.

" 'Good,' says I. 'Jerk!' And when I said, 'Jerk!' he gin the *whoppinest* pull, and sent him kerwhop! about a mile and a feet! I pledge you my word, I thought he'd a-pulled the tail of the varmint clean off!"

Here Mike took a quid of tobacco, and proceeded. "I've been in a heap of scrapes, and seem some of the all-firedest cantankerous snakes that ever come along, but that time beats all!"

"What kind of a snake was it?" asked a listener.

"I'll tell you," said he. " 'Twarn't nothin more'n what I 'spected. Sal thought she'd look big like, and when she was shoutin and dancin about, that sausenger what she'd put on for a bustle, got loose round her ankle, and she thought 'twas a snake crawlin up her clothes!"

Mike left in a hurry.

William Penn Brannan

(1825-1866)

*T*his *mock sermon, first published (perhaps) in a New Orleans newspaper in 1855, was reprinted in hundreds of comic journals and newspapers in the 1850s and 1860s, a tremendous hit. During the Civil War, a comic, Alf Burnett, featured it during his appearances before Union troops. First published in 1855 in the* Spirit of the Times *it gave its name in 1858 to an anthology in which it reappeared,* The Harp of a Thousand Strings, Laughter for a Lifetime, *edited by S. P. Avery, and thereafter it was often anthologized. Editor Henry Watterson in* Oddities in Southern Life and Character *(1882) called it one of "the most notable stories which have gone the rounds of the American press the last forty years, . . . thoroughly characteristic, in tone, color, and action, of the era . . . ."*

On the basis of a newspaper article in 1881 and "proofs" offered in a book— The Harp of a Thousand Strings with Waifs of Wit and Pathos *(1907)—this piece, having been claimed by several humorists, was for some time attributed to Henry Taliaferro Lewis (1825-1866). More recently—and believably—it has been assigned to William Penn Brannan, a wandering artist and an engraver who for some years painted portraits and published newspaper sketches in Mississippi River towns. Brannan is known to have written a number of burlesque sermons and to have published under the pseudonyms Bill Easel and Vandyke Brown.*

The Harp of a
Thousand Strings

Baptist Preacher
Cyclopaedia Of Wit and Humor, (1858, I.477).

"I may say to you, my brethering, that I am not an eddicated man, and I am not one of them that believes that eddication is necessary for a gospel minister. For I believe the Lord eddicates his preachers just as he wants 'em to be eddicated. And although I say it that oughtn't to say it, yet in the state of Indiany, where I live, there's no man as gits a bigger congregation nor what I gits.

"There may be some here today, my brethering, as don't know what persuasion I am of. Well, I may say to you, my brethering, that I am a

Hard-Shell Baptist. There's some folks as don't like the Hard-Shell Baptists, but I'd rather have a hard shell as no shell at all. You see me here today, my brethering, dressed up in fine clothes. You mout think I was proud, but I am not proud, my brethering. And although I'm capting of that flat boat that lies at your landing, I'm not proud, my brethering.

"I'm not gwine to tell you edzactly where my text may be found. Suffice it to say, it's in the lids of the Bible, and you'll find it somewhere 'tween the first chapter of the book of Generation and the last chapter of the book of Revolutions. And if you'll go and search the Scriptures, you'll not only find *my* text there, but a great many other *texes* as will do you good to read. And my text, when you shall find it, you shall find it to read thus:

" 'And he played on a harp of a thousand strings—spirits of just men made perfect.'

"My text, bretheren, leads me to speak of spirits. Now there's a great many kind of spirits in the world. In the first place, there's the spirits as some folks call ghosts. Then there's the spirits of turpen*time*. And then there's the spirits as some folks call liquor, and I've got as good article of them kind of spirits on my flatboat as was ever fotched down the Mississippi River. But there's a great many other kind of spirits, for the text says, 'And he played on a harp of a *thou*-sand strings—spirits of just men made perfect.'

"But I'll tell you the kind of spirits as is meant in the text: it's *fire*. That is the kind of spirits as is meant in the text, my brethering. Now there's a great many kinds of fire in the world. In the first place, there's the common sort of fire you light a cigar or a pipe with. And then there's camfire, fire before you're ready to fall back, and many other kinds of fire, for the text says, 'He played on a harp of a *thou*-sand strings— spirits of just men made perfect.'

"But I'll tell you the kind of fire as is meant in the text, my brethering—it's *hell-fire*! And that's the kind of fire as a great many of you will come to if you don't do better nor what you've been doing—for 'He played on a harp of a *thou*-sand strings—spirits of just men made perfect.'

"And the different sorts of fire in the world may be likened unto the different persuasions in the world. In the first place, we have the 'Piscopalians, and they are a high-sailin and highfalutin set. And they may be likened unto a turkey buzzard, that flies up into the air, and he goes up and up till he looks no bigger than your finger nail. And the first thing you know, he comes down and down, and is a-fillin himself on the carcass of a dead horse by the side of the road—and 'He played on a harp of a *thou*-sand strings—spirits of just men made perfect.'

"And then there's the Methodists, and they may be likened unto the squirrel, runnin up into a tree. For the Methodists believes in gwine on from one degree of grace to another, and finally on to perfection. And the squirrel goes up and up, and he jumps from limb to limb, and branch to branch, and the first thing you know, he falls, and down he comes kerflummux. And that's just like the Methodists, for they is alluz falling from grace, ah! And 'He played on a harp of a *thou*-sand strings—spirits of just men made perfect.'

"And then, my brethering, there's the Baptists, ah! And they have been likened unto a possum on a 'simmon tree. And the thunders may roll, and the earth may quake, but that possum clings there still, ah! And you may shake one foot loose, and the other's there. And you may shake all feet loose, and he laps his tail around the limb, and he clings forever—for 'He played on a harp of a thousand strings—spirits of just men made perfect.' "

Harden E. Taliaferro

(1818-1875)

Born in Surry County, North Carolina, Harden Taliaferro worked during his teens in a mill and on a farm and did some part-time preaching. When he was nineteen, he moved to Alabama, where he became a preacher in Talladega and Eufaula, as well as the editor of the Southwestern Baptist. His visit to his native county after a twenty-year absence led him to write Fisher's River Scenes and Characters (1859), which portrays the folk of the area and their ways of living as he had known them during his youth. Although he contributed sketches to the Southern Literary Messenger between 1860 and 1863, he published only one book during his lifetime, and it contained his best writing. Published in New York, it was appreciated for its social history, its characterizations, and the oral tales that it recorded. Memorable characters tell the tales with skill. One such character is mentioned in the framework for the story that follows, Uncle Davy Lane, a hard-drinking and hearty-eating gunsmith who enlarged upon his own hunting feats. Larkin Snow, a more reputable raconteur, tells the "Story of the Eels." It conforms to the definition of a tall tale formulated by Norris W. Yates, a leading authority on the genre: "a fantastic yarn rendered temporarily plausible by the supporting use of realistic detail."

Larkin Snow, the Miller

Larkin Snow was doomed to be a miller. I have ever believed that a man will fill the station for which he was designed by the Sovereign Master Overseer of mankind. Though Providence designs a man for a certain position, natural causes and agencies operate also, and ere he is aware of it, he is fulfilling his destiny. But I will not moralize; my business is with facts.

Larkin Snow was a graduate—an old stager—in milling when I was a mill-boy; and the last time I heard of him, and no doubt at this present time of writing, he is grinding away at somebody's tub-mill, for he never owned a mill—not he. Over a quarter of a century ago I was a jolly, singing, hoop-pee mill-boy, and carried many a grist to William Easley's tub-mill on Little Fishers River, kept by my old friend Larkin Snow. But where am I wandering?

After all, the reader must indulge me a little while I pay a tribute of respect to the numerous tub-mills of my native country, for it does me good to think of them and of my mill-boy days. Who has not been a romping mill-boy?

Well, I love tub-mills, and ever shall, for my grandfather was the father of them in that section.

"But who is your grandfather?"

Never mind. Go and ask Larkin Snow, for he knows every man that ever built a mill, or ever kept one, in that mountain territory. His memory is a perfect genealogy of mills and millers. Uncle Billy Lewis built a tub-mill on nearly every mountain branch (and they were numerous) where he could get two or three customers. Uncle Davy Lane, who figures largely in this volume, had a tub-mill on Moore's Fork, as lazy and slow in its movements as its owner. The truth is, Uncle Dave had the advantage, for serpents could move him to the speed of electricity, but a good head of water made but little difference with his mill. His son Dave kept it (said Dave was his daddy's own son), and he and I used to bake johnny cakes to keep from starving while it was grinding my grist. We ate nearly as fast as it could grind. But my old neighbor, William Easley, had the fastest tub-mill in all that country, on Little Fishers River, and Larkin Snow was his faithful miller.

Every man has ambition of some kind, and Larkin, though nothing but a humble miller who gloried in his calling, had his share, and a good one too, of ambition. His ambition consisted in being the best miller in the land, and in being *number one* in big story-telling. He had several competitors, as may be seen by these sketches, but he held his own with them all, even with Uncle Davy Lane. The reader will judge best, however, when he reads the stories given as samples of Larkin's gift in that line. Larkin must pardon us, should he ever see these pages, for giving but two of his fine stories, that of the eels and the foxdog. These stories will do him ample justice.

Larkin Snow was a patient, kind, forbearing-looking man, of ordinary size. His eyes squinted, and so did his sallow features. His dress was plain: tow and cotton shirt, summer and winter; striped cotton pants in summer and dressed buckskin ones in winter. His hat was wool, turned up all round, gummed up with meal, and so was his entire suit. His looks were wholly unambitious—strange that he should ever strive to excel in big story-telling. But looks sometimes deceive one, and we will let Larkin speak for himself in the

Story of the Eels

"Now, you see, while I were keepin Mr. Easley's mill," said Larkin, squinting his eyes and features, showing the remains of his little round teeth, nearly worn to the gums chewing tobacco, "I planted me a truck patch near the bank of the river, just below the mill-dam. I knowed I could work it at odd spells, while the water were low and the mill ran slow, and I just filled it with all sorts of things and notions. But as all on us—the old Quilt (his wife), childering and all—was mighty fond of peas, I were mighty partic'lar to plant a mighty good share of them, and to make a bully crop of Crowders and all other sorts of peas ever hearn on. I pitched them in the best spot of the little bit of yearth near the river, closte on the bank.

"We, the old Quilt and I, spilt several gallons of human grease workin on 'em, and they growed monstrous nice. We was a-congratterlatin ourselves on the monst'ous crop we'd make, when we seed suthin kept croppin 'em, partic'lar right on the bank of the river. Every mornin it was worse and worse. I soon seen the thing would be out wi' my peas if there warn't a stop put to it, for there wouldn't a-been a Crowder to sweeten our teeth with. I kept watchin and watchin, but couldn't make the least 'scovery. The fence were alluz up good, the gate shut, and not the track of varmints could be seen nor smelt, hair nor hide. I were mighty low down in the mouth, I tell you. Starvation hove in sight; my sallet were meltin away mighty fast.

"I were so mightily taken down 'bout it I couldn't sleep a wink; so I thought I mout as well watch. I sneaked along down to the bank of the river through my pea-patch.

"The moon were shinin mighty bright, and what do you think I seen? I seen 'bout five hundred big maul-bustin eels dart into the river out'n my pea patch. I soon seen through the dreadful 'vastation of my black-eyed Crowders: the pesky eels had done it."

"Dang it, Larkin," said Dick Snow, "where did such a gull-bustin chance of eels come from?"

"Eels, you see," continued Larkin, "if you knowed the natur on 'em, are mighty creeturs to travel, and they'd come up—a host on 'em—far as the mill-dam, and couldn't git no further. They had to live, and they'd cotched every minnow, and had eat up everything in the river about there, and they moseyed out on my pea-patch.

Larkin Snow
Fisher's River
(New York: Harper & Bros., 1859, p. 146).

"Now I warn't far from lettin them eat up my crop, so I put on my studyin cap to find out the best plan to make a smash of the whole b'ilin on 'em. I soon hit the nail on the head, and fixed on the plan.

"You see there were but one place where they could git out'n the river into my patch of Crowders, and that were a narrow place, 'bout three foot wide, that crossed the river. I knowed it warn't worth while to try to hold the creeturs, they was so slickery; so, you see, I sot a big, whoppin barrel near the river where they come out, near that path. I told the old Quilt to fill it full of dry ashes durin the day while I were grindin, which she done, for the old creetur thought a mighty sight of her pea patch.

"Now, when night come on, and a dark one too—a good night for eels to graze—and when I thought all on 'em was out a-grazin, I sneaked along by the bank of the river, mighty sly, I tell you, till I got to the barrel. I then listened, and hearn 'em makin the peas wake; so I just turned the barrel over right smack in their path, and filled it chug full of the dry ashes for ten steps, I reckon. I then went up in the patch above 'em, gin a keen holler, and away they went, scootin for the river. You never hearn such a rippin and clateration afore, I reckon. I knowed I had 'em; so, you see, I called for a torchlight to see my luck. Now when the old Quilt and the childering brought the light, hallelujah! what a sight! Such a pile on 'em, all workin up together in the dry ashes, like maggots in carrion. The ashes were the very thing for 'em, for they soon gin up the ghost.

"I soon, you see, 'cided what to do with 'em. We went to work and tuck out'n the ashes five hundred and forty-nine, some of 'em master eels. All the next day we was a-skinnin, cleanin, and barrelin on 'em up. They'd got fat out'n my peas, but we got good pay out'n 'em for it. The fryin-pan stunk for months with fat eels, and we all got fat and sassy. So I were troubled no more with eels that year; for I think, you see, we shucked out the whole river."

George Washington Harris

(1814-1869)

George Washington Harris, born in Pennsylvania, was carried when five years old to frontier Tennessee, and during most of the rest of his life he lived in Knoxville, Nashville, or the Great Smoky Mountains. Many frontier humorists had varied backgrounds, but Harris outdid any in versatility, working as a metalsmith, a steamboat captain, a farmer, a glassworks superintendent, a sawmill and mine manager, a postmaster, a railway conductor, and a part-time journalist.

An informed contemporary held that Harris's comic stories of the 1840s, 1850s, and 1860s had "a circulation and popularity, throughout the country, which no similar productions, in modern times, have enjoyed." When some of Harris's stories were collected in Sut Lovingood's Yarns in 1867, Mark Twain in a review backed the claim that the stories were very popular "in the West" and announced that "the book abounds in humor, and is said to represent the Tennessee dialect correctly." His guess was that Easterners "will call it coarse and probably taboo it." Some readers must have refused to avoid the book for the suggested reason: it remained constantly in print for more than seven decades.

It was still in print in 1930 when Franklin Meine, a pioneer in the popularization of Southwestern humor, included Harris in his anthology, Tall Tales of the Southwest, and showed marked partiality to him. "For vivid imagination, comic plot, Rabelaisian touch, and sheer fun," wrote Meine, "the Sut Lovingood Yarns surpass anything else in American humor." Many scholars and critics have shared Meine's enthusiasm, and growing numbers of general readers have found Harris's comedy appealing. Not only is Harris well represented in recent collections of Old Southwestern humor (forty-five pages in a 1964 collection), he also has made most anthologies of American humor and many of American literature. Several modern authors, notably Stark Young, Robert Penn Warren, Flannery O'Connor, and William Faulkner have spoken affectionately of Harris and his chief character and storyteller, Sut Lovingood.

115

Faulkner on one occasion placed Sut among literature's great comic characters and on another said:

I like Sut Lovingood from a book written by George Harris about 1840 or '50 in the Tennessee mountains. He had no illusions about himself, did the best he could; at certain times he was a coward and knew it and wasn't ashamed; he never blamed his misfortunes on anyone and never cursed God for them.

The belief that Sut's opera should be rendered readable isn't a new one. Between 1932 and 1941, several scholars who briefly quoted passages, in the words of one of them, "transliterated" some of the dialect "for the protection of the reader." In 1942, Donald Day, author of several articles and a doctoral dissertation on Harris, prepared a "normalization" of the Yarns, which he failed to peddle to a wartime publisher. In 1954, Prof. Brom Weber simplified and modernized a large number of Harris's pieces for readability for an edition published by the Grove Press. Although Faulkner had in his library an 1867 printing that he had inherited, it was Weber's collection that he kept at his bedside until his death.

Rare Ripe Garden Seed

Sut Lovingood

Sut Lovingood's Yarns
(New York: Dick & Fitzgerald, 1867, p. 153).

"I tell you now, I minds my first big scare just as well as rich boys minds their first boots, or seeing the first spotted horse circus. The red top of them boots is still a rich red stripe in their minds, and the burnin red of my first scare has left as deep a scar onto my thinking works.

"Mam had me a-standin atwixt her knees. I can feel the knobs of her j'ints a-rattlin a-past my ribs yet. She didn't have much petticoats to speak of, and I had but one, and hit were calico slit from the nape of my neck to the tail, hilt together at the top with a drawstring, and at the bottom by the hem. Hit were the handiest clothes I ever seed, and would be pow'ful comfortin in summer if hit warn't for the flies. If they was good to run in, I'd wear one yet. They beats pasted shirts, and britches, as bad as a feather bed beats a bag of warnut shells for sleepin on.

"Say, George, wouldn't you like to see me into one, 'bout half faded, slit and a-walkin just so, up the middle street of your city church, a-aimin for your pew pen, and it chock full of your fine city gal friends, just a'ter the people had sot down from the first prayer, and the organ beginnin to groan. What would you do in such a 'mergency? Say, hoss?"

"Why, I'd shoot you dead, Monday morning before eight o'clock," was my reply.

"Well I 'spect you would. But you'd take a real old maid faint first, right among them-ere gals. Lordy! wouldn't you be 'shamed of me! Yet, why not to church in such a suit, when you hasn't got no store clothes?

"Well, as I were sayin, mam were feedin us brats onto mush and milk, without the milk, and as I were the baby then, she hilt me so as to see that I got my share. When there ain't enough food, big childer roots little childer out'n the trough, and gobbles up their part. Just so the yearth over: bishops eats elders, elders eats common people. They eats such cattle as me; I eats possums; possums eats chickens; chickens swallows worms, and worms am content to eat dust, and the dust am the end of hit all. Hit am all as regular as the sounds from the treble down to the bull bass of a fiddle in good chune. And I 'spect hit am right, or hit wouldn't be 'lowed.

" '*The sheriff!*' hissed mam in a keen tremblin whisper. Hit sounded to me like the screech of a hen when she says 'hawk!' to her little round-shouldered, fuzzy, bead-eyed striped-backs.

"I acted just adzackly as they does. I darted on all fours under mam's petticoat-tails, and there I met, face to face, the wooden bowl, and the mush, and the spoon what she slid under from t'other side. I's mad at myself yet, for right there I showed the first flush of the nat'ral born durn fool what I now is. I oughta et hit all up, in justice to my stomach and my growin, while the sheriff was levyin onto the bed and the chairs. To this day, if anybody says 'sheriff,' I feels scare, and if I hears 'constable' mentioned, my legs goes through runnin motions, even if I is asleep. Did you ever watch a dog dreamin of rabbit huntin? Them's the motions, and the feelin am the rabbit's.

"Sheriffs am awful 'spectable people; everybody looks up to 'em. I never adzackly seed the 'spectable part myself. I's too feared of 'em, I reckon, to 'zamine for hit much. One thing I know; no country atwixt here and Tophet can ever 'lect me to sell out widows' plunder or poor men's corn, and the thoughts of hit gins me a good feelin. Hit sort of flashes through my heart when I thinks of hit.

"I axed a parson once, what hit could be, and he pronounced hit to be unregenerate pride, what I ought to squelch in prayer, and in 'tendin church on collection days. I were in hopes it mout be 'ligion, or sense, a-soakin into me. Hit feels good, anyhow, and I don't care if every circuit-rider out'n jail knows hit.

"Sheriffs' shirts alluz has nettle dust or fleas inside of 'em when they lies down to sleep, and I's glad of hit, for they's alluz discomfortin me, durn 'em. I scarcely ever get to drink a horn, or eat a mess in peace. I'll hurt one some day, see if I don't. Show me a sheriff a-steppin softly round, and a-sorta sightin at me, and I'll show you the speed of a express engine, fired up with rich, dry rosiny scares. They don't catch me much, usin only human legs as weapons.

"Old John Dobbin were a 'spectable sheriff, mons'ously so, and had the best scent for poor fugitive devils and women I ever seed. He were sure fire. He toted a warrant for this here skinful of durned fool 'bout that-ere misfortunate nigger meetin business, until he wore hit into six separate square bits, and had wore out much shoe leather a-chasin of me. I'd found a doggery in full milk, and hated pow'ful bad to leave that settlement while hit sucked free. So I sot into sort of try and wean him off from botherin me so much. I succeeded so well that he not only quit racin of me, and women, but he were teetotally sp'iled as a sheriff, and lost the 'spectable section of his character. To make you fool fellows understand how hit were done, I must introduce your minds to one Wat Mastin, a bullet-headed young blacksmith.

"Well, last year—no, hit were the year afore last—in struttin and gobblin time—Wat felt his keepin right warm; so he sot into bellowin and pawin up dust in the neighborhood round the old widow McKildrin's. The more dust he flung up, the worse he got, until at last he just couldn't stand the ticklin sensations another minute. So he put for the county clerk's office, with his hands socked down deep in his britches pockets, like he was feared of pickpockets, his back roached round, and a-chompin his teeth until he splotched his whiskers with foam. Oh! he were yearnest hot, and as restless as a cockroach in a hot skillet."

"What was the matter with this Mr. Mastin? I cannot understand you, Mr. Lovingood. Had he hydrophobia?" remarked a man in a square-tail coat and cloth gaiters, who was obtaining subscribers for some forthcoming Encyclopedia of Useful Knowledge, who had quartered at our camp, uninvited and really unwanted.

"What do you mean by hy-dry-foby?" and Sut looked puzzled.

"A madness produced by being bit by some rabid animal," explained Square-tail, in a pompous manner.

"Yes, hoss, he had hy-dry-foby *awful*, and Mary McKildrin, the widow McKildrin's only daughter, had gin him the complaint. I don't know whether she bit him or not. He might have cotch hit from her breath, and he were now in the roach back chompin stage of the sickness. So he were a'ter the clerk for a ticket to the hospital. Well, the clerk sold him a piece of paper, part printin and part writin, with a picture of two pigs' hearts, what some boy had shot a arrow through and left hit stickin, printed at the top. That paper were a splicin pass—some calls hit a pair of license—and that very night he tuck Mary, for better, for worse, to have and to hold to him, his heirs and—"

"Allow me to interrupt you," said our guest. "You do not quote the marriage ceremony correctly."

"You go to *hell*, mistofer; you bothers me."

This outrageous remark took the stranger all aback, and he sat down.

"Where were I? Oh, yes, he married Mary tight and fast, and next day he were able to be about. His coat, though, and his trousers looked just a scrimption too big and heavy to tote. I axed him if he felt sound. He said yes, but he'd welded a steamboat shafts the day before, and were sort of tired like. There he told a durn lie, for he'd been a-hornin up dirt most of the day, round the widow's garden, and bellowin in the orchard.

"Mary and him sot square into housekeepin, and 'mong other things he bought a lot of *rare ripe garden seed*, from a Yankee peddler. Rare ripe corn, rare ripe peas, rare ripe 'taters, rare ripe everything, and the two young durned fools were dreadfully exercised 'bout hit. Wat said he meant to get him a rare ripe hammer and anvil, and Mary vowed to gracious that she'd have a rare ripe wheel and loom, if money could get 'em.

"Pretty soon a'ter he had made the garden, he tuck a notion to work a spell down to Atlanty, in the railroad shop, as he said he had a sort of ailin in his back, and he thought weldin rail car-tire and engine axletrees were lighter work nor sharpenin plows and puttin lap-links in trace-chains.

"So down he went, and found hit agreed with him, for he didn't come back until the middle of August. The first thing he seed when he landed into his cabin door were a shoe box with rockers under hit. And the next thing he seed were Mary herself, propped up in bed. And the next thing he seed a'ter that were a pair of little rat-eyes a-shinin above the end of the quilt. And the next and last thing he seed were the two little rat-eyes aforesaid, a-turnin into two hundred thousand big green stars, and a-swingin round and round the room, faster and faster, until they mixed into one awful green flash. He drapped into a limber pile on the floor. The durned fool what had welded the steamboat shafts had fainted safe and sound as a gal scared at a mad bull.

"Mary fotch a weak cat-scream, and covered her head, and sot into work on a whifflin dry cry, while little Rat-eyes gin hitself up to suckin. Cryin and suckin both at once ain't fair; must come pow'ful strainin on the wet section of a woman's constitution; yet hit am often done, and more too.

"Old Missis McKildrin, what were a-nursin Mary, just got up from knittin, and flung a big gourd of water square into Wat's face. Then she fotch a glass bottle of swell-skull whiskey out'n the three-cornered cupboard, and stood fornint Wat, a-holdin hit in one hand and the tin cup in t'other, waitin for Wat to come to. She were the piousest lookin old 'oman just then, you ever seed outside of a prayer meetin. After a spell, Wat begun to move, twitchin his fingers and battin his eyes, sorta 'stonished like. That pious-lookin statue said to him:

" 'My son, just take a drap of spirits, honey. You's very sick, dumplin. Don't take on, darlin, if you can help it, ducky, for poor Margaret-Jane am mons'ous ailin, and the least n'ise or takin on will kill the poor sufferin dear, and you'll lose your turkle ducky dove of a sweet wifey, a'ter all she's done gone through for you. My dear son Watty, you must consider her feelins a little.' "

"Says Wat, a-turnin up his eyes at that virtuous old relic sorta sick like — 'I is a-considerin 'em a heap, right now.'

" 'Oh, that's right, my good kind child.'

"Oh damned if old mother-in-laws can't plaster humbug over a fellow, just as soft and easy as they spreads a cambric handkerchief over a three-hour-old baby's face. You don't feel hit at all, but hit am there, a plumb inch thick, and stickin fast as court plaster.

"She raised Wat's head, and sot the edge of the tin cup agin his lower teeth, and turned up the bottom slow and careful, a-winkin at Mary, who were a-peepin over the edge of the coverlid, to see if Wat *tuck the prescription*, for a heap of family comfort depended on that-ere horn of spirits. *One* horn alluz softens a man, the yearth over.

"Wat keep a-battin his eyes. worse nor a owl in daylight. At last he raised hisself onto one elbow, and rested his head in that hand, sort of weak like.

"Says he, mons'ous tremblin and slow: 'Aprile—May—June—July—and 'most—half—of—August,' a-countin the months onto the fingers of t'other hand, with the thumb, a-shakin of his head and lookin at his spread fingers like they warn't hisn, or they were nastied with somethin.

"Then he counted 'em agin, slower: 'Aprile—May—June—July, and 'most half-of-August.' And he run his thumb atwixt his fingers, as meanin 'most half of August, and looked at the p'int of hit, like hit mout be a snake's head. He raised his eyes to the widow's face, who were standin just as steady as a hitchin post, and still a-wearin that pious expression onto her personal featurs, and a flood of soft love for Wat, a-shinin straight from her eyes into hisn.

"Says he, 'That just makes four months, and most a half, don't hit, Missis McKildrin?'

"She never said one word.

"Wat reached for the hearth, and got a dead fire-coal; then he made a mark clean across a floor-plank.

"Says he, 'Aprile,' a-holdin down the coal onto the end of the mark, like he were feared hit mout blow away afore he got hit christened Aprile.

"Says he, 'May'—and he marked across the board agin. Then he counted the marks, one, two, a-dottin at 'em with the coal.

" 'June,' and he marked agin, one, two, three, counted with the p'int of the coal. He scratched his head with the little finger of the hand holdin the charcoal, and he drawed hit slowly across the board agin, peepin under his wrist to see when hit reached the crack, and says he, 'July,' as he lifted the coal; 'one, two, three, four,' countin from left to right and then from right to left.

" 'That hain't but four, no way I can fix hit. Old Pike hisself couldn't make hit five, if he were to cipher onto hit until his legs turned into figure eights.'

"Then he made a mark, half acrost a plank, spit on his finger, and rubbed off a half inch of the end, and says he, ' 'Most half of August.' He looked up at the widow, and there she were, same as ever, still a-holdin her flask agin her bosom, and says he, 'Four months, and 'most a half. *Hain't enough, is hit, mammy?* Hit's just 'bout (lackin a little) *half enough*, hain't it, mammy?'

"Missis McKildrin shuck her head sort of uncertain like, and says she, 'Take a drap more spirits, Watty, my dear pet. Does you mind buyin that-ere rare ripe seed from the peddler?'

"Wat nodded his head, and looked 'what of hit?' but didn't say hit.

"This is what comes of hit, and four months and a half am rare ripe time for babies, adzackly. To be sure, hit lacks a day or two, but Margaret-Jane were alluz a pow'ful enterprisin gal, and a early riser."

"Says Wat, 'How 'bout the 'taters?'

" 'Oh, *we* et 'taters as big as goose-eggs afore old Missis Collins's blossomed.'

" 'How 'bout corn?'

" 'Oh, we shaved down roas'in-ears afore hern tassled.'

" 'And peas?'

" 'Yes, son, we had gobs and lots in three weeks. Everything comes in adzackly half the time that hit takes the old sort, and you *knows*, my darlin son, you planted hit wasteful. I thought then you'd rare ripe everything on the place. You planted *often*, too, didn't you, love, for fear hit wouldn't come up.'

" 'Ye-ye-s-s he-he did,' said Mary, a-cryin.

"Wat studied pow'ful deep a spell, and the widow just waited. Widows alluz wait and alluz win.

"At last, says he, 'Mammy.'

"She looked at Mary and winked these-here words at her, as plain as she could a-talked 'em:

" 'You hearn him call me *mammy twiste*. I's *got him* now. His backbone's a-limberin fast; he'll own the baby yet; see if he don't. Just hold still, my daughter, and let your mammy knead this dough; then you may bake hit as brown as you please.'

" 'Mammy, when I married on the first day of Aprile—'

"The widow looked uneasy. She thought he mout be a-couplin that day, his weddin, and the idea, damn fool, together.

"But he warn't, for he said, 'That day I gin old man Collins my note of hand for a hundred dollars, due in one year a'ter date, the balance on this land. Do you think that seed will change the *time* any, or will hit alter the *amount*?' And Wat looked at her, powerful anxious.

"She raised the whiskey bottle way above her head, with the hand on the mouth, and fotch the bottom down onto her hand, spat!

"Says she, 'Watty, my dear b'loved son, prepare to pay *two* hundred dollars 'bout the first of October. For hit'll be due then, *as* sure as that little black-eyed angel in the bed there am your daughter.'

"Wat dropped his head, and said, '*Then hit's a damn sure thing.*'

"Right here, the baby fotch a rattlin loud squall. (I 'spect Mary were sort of fidgety just then, and hurt hit).

"'Yes,' says Wat, a-wallin a red eye towards the bed. 'My little she— what were hit you called her name, mammy?'

"'I called her a sweet little angel, and she is one, as sure as you're her daddy, my b'loved son.'

"'Well,' says Wat. 'My little sweet, patent rare ripe she angel, if you lives to marryin time, you'll 'stonish some man body out'n his shirt, if you don't rare ripe lose hits virtue a'ter the first planting, that's all.'

"He reared up on end, with his mouth pouched out. He had a pow'ful forehead, far-reachin, bread-funnel, anyhow—could a-bit the eggs out'n a catfish, in two foot water, without wettin his eyebrows. 'Dod durn rare ripe seed, and rare ripe peddlers, and rare ripe notes to the hottest corner of—'

"'Stop, Watty, darlin. Don't swear. 'Member you belongs to meet-ing.'

"'My blacksmith's fire,' ended Wat, and he studied a long spell.

"Says he, 'Did you save any of that infernal double-trigger seed?'

"'Yes,' says the widow. 'There in that bag by the cupboard.'

"Wat got up off'n the floor, took a countin sorta look at the charcoal marks, and reached down the bag. He went to the door and called, 'Sook, muley! Sook, sook, cow! Chick, chick, chickie, chick!'

"'What's you gwine to do now, my dear son?' said Missis McKildrin.

"'I's just gwine to feed this active *smart* trick to the cow and the hens; that's what I's gwine to do. Old muley hain't had a calf in two years, and I'll eat some rare ripe eggs.'

"Mary now ventured to speak. 'Husband, I ain't sure hit'll work on hens. Come and kiss me, my love.'

"'I hain't sure hit'll work on hens, either,' said Wat. 'They's pow'ful uncertain in their ways, well as women,' And he flung out another handful, spiteful like.

"'Takin the rare ripe invention all together, from 'taters and peas to notes of hand, and childer, I can't say I likes hit much.' And he flung out another handful.

" 'Your mam had thirteen the old way, and if this truck stays 'bout the house, you's good for twenty-six, maybe thirty, for you's a pow'ful enterprisin gal, your mam says.' And he flung out another handful, overhanded, as hard as if he were flingin rocks at a stealin sow.

" 'Make your mind easy,' said the widow. 'Hit never works on married folks only the first time.'

" 'Say them words agin,' said Wat. 'I's glad to hear 'em. Is hit the same way with notes of hand?'

" 'I 'spect hit am, answered the widow, with just a taste of strong vinegar in the words, as she sot the flask in the cupboard with a push."

Funny Fellows

Charles Farrar Browne
(Artemus Ward)

(1834-1867)

*C*harles Farrar Browne was probably the first full-time humorist in the United States to make a really good living at his trade. Born in Maine and minimally educated, he worked as a printer and then as a journalist on several publications before he discovered his vocation. In 1858 he wrote a letter to the newspaper for which he was then reporting, the Cleveland Plain Dealer, and signed it Artemus Ward. Ward announced that he was traveling around the country with his wax museum and a bedraggled little menagerie, that he was en route to Cleveland, and that he'd like to line up the editor's help: "Now mr. Editor scratch off few lines and tel me how is the show bisnes in your good city i shal have hanbils printed at your offis you scratch my back i will scratch your back, also git up a grate blow in the paper about my show."

The letter was the first of a number of communications from the showman, drumming up trade and telling about his experiences. From the start, the letters were a big hit. Plain Dealer sales soared. Vanity Fair, a top comic monthly, bought simultaneous rights to the letters and then lured Browne to New York and a full-time job as a comic writer and in time as the managing editor. Books collecting the pieces had huge sales, and Browne traveled widely, giving well-attended comic lectures. Eventually, he sailed to England, where he was immediately employed by Punch and where he gave funny lectures that were the hit of the season. He died in London in 1867, at the height of his fame.

Why the popularity? One reason was that the role he played kidded the most famous showman of the day, P. T. Barnum. Another reason was that Lincoln in the White House let it be known that Artemus Ward was a favorite of his. Also, as the quoted passage shows, Artemus was sensationally bad in spelling, capitalization, and grammar. Beginning in the mid-1850s and lasting for several decades, assaults on respectable styles—with resulting puns, malapropisms, maladroit phrasings, and crippled sentences, in short, solecisms of all kinds—were what a vast *public went for. Why? Because, as Allen Walker Reed suggested, "The common schools had as one of their principal aims the teaching of traditional spelling, and good spelling was a symbol of cultural achievement." So, we might add, were good grammar and an elegant style. Finally, Ward had capabilities as a humorist in addition to the popular ones—a fact that became clear when, in many later works, he normalized his style. Since readers today enjoy distortions of language hardly at all and in fact may be repulsed by them, we have done away with practically all of them but those we hope may continue to amuse. With luck, what was left is a characterization of a disreputable but sharp showman who amusingly talks with the newly elected Abe Lincoln and reports on a visit to the Tower of London.*

Interview with President Lincoln

Artemus Ward and Abraham Lincoln
Vanity Fair
(December 9, 1860).

I have no politics. Ne'er a one. I'm not in the business. If I was, I s'pose I should holler vociferously in the streets at night and go home to Betsy Jane smellin of coal ile and gin, in the mornin. I should go to the polls early. I should stay there all day. I should git carriages to take the cripples, the infirm and the indignant there. I should be on guard agin frauds and such. I should be on the look-out for the infamous lies of the enemy, got up just before election for political effect. When all was over and my candidate was elected, I should move heaven and earth—so to speak—until I got office, which if I didn't git a office I should turn round and abuse the Administration with all my might and main.

But I'm not in the business. I'm in a far more respectful business nor what politics is. I wouldn't give two cents to be a Congresser. The worst insult I ever received was when certain citizens of Baldwinsville axed me to run for the Legislatur. Sez I, "My friends, dostest think I'd stoop to that there?" They turned as white as a sheet. I spoke in my most awfullest tones, and they knowed I wasn't to be trifled with. They slunked out of sight to once.

Therefore, havin no politics, I made bold to visit Old Abe at his homestead in Springfield. I found the old fellow in his parlor, surrounded by a perfect swarm of office-seekers. Knowin he had been capting of a flatboat on the roarin Mississippi, I thought I'd address him in sailor lingo, so says I, "Old Abe, ahoy! Let out your mainsails, reef home the forecastle, and throw your jib-poop overboad! Shiver my timbers, my hearty!" (N.B. This is genuine mariner language. I know, because I've seen sailor plays acted out by them New York theater fellows.) Old Abe looked up quite cross and says, "Send in your petition by and by. I can't possibly look at it now. Indeed, I can't. It's unpossible, sir!"

"Mr. Lincoln, who do you 'spect I air?" said I.

"A office-seeker, to be sure?" said he.

"Well, sir," said I, "you's never more mistaken in your life. You hain't got a office I'd take under no circumstances. I'm A. Ward. Wax figgers is my profession. I'm the father of twins, and they look like me—*both of them*. I come to pay a friendly visit to the President-elect of the United States. If so be you wants me, say so—if not, say so, and I'm off like a jug handle."

"Mr. Ward, sit down. I am glad to see you, sir."

"Repose in Abraham's bosom!" said one of the office-seekers, his idee bein to git off a joke at my expense.

"Well," says I, "if all you fellows repose in that there bosom there'll be mighty poor nursin for some of you!" whereupon Old Abe buttoned his weskit clear up and blushed like a maiden of sweet sixteen. Just at this p'int of the conversation another swarm of office-seekers arrove and come pilin into the parlor. Some wanted postoffices, some wanted collectorships, some wanted foreign missions, and all wanted somethin. I thought Old Abe would go crazy.

He hadn't more than had time to shake hands with 'em before another tremendous crowd come pourin onto his premises. His house and dooryard was now perfectly overflowed with office-seekers, all clamorous for a immediate interview with Old Abe. One man from Ohio, who had about seven inches of corn whiskey into him, mistook me for Old Abe and addressed me as "The Prahayrie Flower of the West." Thinks I *you* want a office pretty bad. Another man with a gold-headed cane and a red nose told Old Abe that he was "a second Washington and the Pride of the Boundless West."

Says I, "Squire, you wouldn't take a small postoffice if you could git it, would you?"

Says he, "A patriot is above them things, sir!"

"There's a pretty big crop of patriots this season, ain't there, Squire?" says I, when *another* crowd of office-seekers poured in. The house, dooryard, barn and woodshed was now all full, and when *another* crowd come I told 'em not to go away for want of room as the hog pen was still empty. One patriot from a small town in Michigan went on top of the house, got into the chimney and slid down into the parlor where Old Abe was endeavorin to keep the hungry pack of office-seekers from chawin him up alive without benefit of clergy. The minute he reached the fireplace he jumped up, brushed the soot out of his eyes, and yelled: "Don't make any 'p'intment at the Spunkville postoffice till you've read my papers. All the respectful men in our town is signers to that there document!"

"Good God!" cried Old Abe, "they come upon me from the skies — down the chimneys, and from the bowels of the yearth!" He hadn't more 'n got them words out of his delicate mouth before two fat office-seekers from Wisconsin, in endeavorin to crawl atween his legs for the purpose of applyin for the tollgateship at Milwaukee, upsot the President-elect and he would have gone sprawlin into the fireplace if I hadn't caught him in these arms. But I hadn't more 'n stood him up straight before another man come crashin down the chimney, his head strikin me vi'lently agin the innards and prostratin my voluptuous form onto the floor. "Mr. Lincoln," shouted the infatuated being, "my papers is signed by every clergyman in our town, and likewise the schoolmaster!"

Says I, "You egregious ass," gittin up and brushin the dust from my eyes, "I'll sign your papers with this bunch of bones, if you don't be a little more careful how you make my breadbasket a depot in the futur. How do you like that-ere perfumery?" says I, shoving my fist under his nose. "Them's the kind of papers I'll give you! Them's the papers *you* want!"

"But I worked hard for the ticket; I toiled night and day! The patriot should be rewarded!"

"Virtue," said I, holdin the infatuated man by the coat collar, "virtue, sir, is its own reward. Look at me!" He did look at me, and quailed before my gaze. "The fact is," I continued, lookin round on the hungry crowd, "there is scarcely a office for every ile lamp carried round durin this campaign. I wish there was. I wish there was foreign missions to be filled on various lonely islands where epidemics rage incessantly, and if I was in Old Abe's place I'd send every mother's son of you to them. What air you here for?" I continued, warmin up considerable. "Can't you give Abe a minute's peace? Don't you see he's worried most to death? Go home, you miserable men, go home and till the s'ile! Go to peddlin tinware — go to choppin wood — go to b'ilin soap — stuff sassengers — black boots — git a clerkship on some respectable manure cart — go round as original Swiss Bell Ringers — become 'original and only' Campbell Minstrels — go to lecturin at fifty dollars a night — embark in the peanut business — *write for the Ledger* — saw off your legs and go round

givin concerts, with touchin appeals to a charitable public, printed on
your handbills—anything for a honest living, but don't come round
here drivin Old Abe crazy by your outrageous cuttings up! Go home.
Stand not upon the order of your goin, but go to once! If in five minutes
from this time," says I, pullin out my new sixteen dollar huntin cased
watch, and brandishin it before their eyes, "If in five minutes from this
time a single soul of you remains on these here premises, I'll go out to
my cage near by, and let my Boy Constrictor loose! and if he gits among
you, you'll think old Solferino has come again and no mistake!" You
ought to have seen them scamper, Mr. Fair. They run off as though Satan
hisself was a'ter them with a red-hot ten-pronged pitchfork. In five minutes the premises was clear.

"How can I ever repay you, Mr. Ward, for your kindness?" said Old
Abe, advancin and shakin me warmly by the hand. "How can I ever
repay you, sir?"

"By givin the whole county a good, sound administration. By pourin
ile upon the troubled waters, North and South. By pursuin a patriotic,
firm, and just course, and then if any state wants to secede, let 'em
sesesh!"

"How 'bout my Cabinet, Mister Ward?" said Abe.

"Fill it up with Showmen, sir! Showmen is devoid of politics. They
hain't got any principles! They know how to cater for the public. They
know what the public wants, North and South. Showmen, sir, is honest
men. If you doubt their literary ability, look at their posters, and see
small bills! If you want a Cabinet as is a Cabinet fill it up with showmen,
but don't call on me. The moral wax figger profession mustn't be per-
mitted to go down while there's a drop of blood in these veins! A.
Lincoln, I wish you well! If Powers or Walcutt was to pick out a model
for a beautiful man, I scarcely think they'd sculp you; but if you do the
fair thing by your country you'll make as pretty a angel as any of us!
Lincoln, use the talents which Nature has put into you judiciously and
firmly, and all will be well! A. Lincoln, adieu!"

He shook me cordially by the hand—we exchanged picters, so we
could gaze upon each other's lineaments when far away from one
another—he at the hellum of the ship of State, and I at the hellum of
the show business—admittance only fifteen cents.

The Tower of London

Mr. Punch, My dear Sir, —

I scarcely need inform you that your excellent Tower is very popular with people from the agricultural districts, and it was chiefly them class which I found waitin at the gates the other mornin.

I saw at once that the Tower was established on a firm basis. In the entire history of firm basises I don't find a basis more firmer than this one.

"You have no Tower in America?" said a man in the crowd, who had somehow detected my denomination.

"Alahs! no," I answered; "we boast of our enterprise and improvements, and yit we are devoid of a Tower. America, O my unhappy country! thou hast not got no Tower! It's a sweet boon."

The gates were opened after a while, and we all purchased tickets and went into a waitin room.

"My friends," said a pale-faced little man, in black clothes, "this is a sad day."

"Inasmuch as to how?" I say.

"I mean it is sad to think that so many people have been killed within these gloomy walls. My friends, let us drop a tear!"

"No," I said, "you must excuse me. Others may drop one if they feel like it; but as for me, I decline. The early managers of this institution were a bad lot, and their crimes were truly awful; but I can't sob for those who died four or five hundred years ago. If they was my own relations I couldn't. It's absurb to shed sobs over things which occurred durin the reign of Henry the Three. Let us be cheerful," I continued. "Look at the festive Warders, in their red flannel jackets. They are cheerful, and why should it not be thusly with us?"

A Warder now took us in charge, and showed us the Traitors' Gate, the armors and things. The Traitors' Gate is wide enough to admit about twenty traitors abreast, I should judge; but beyond this, I couldn't see that it was superior to gates in general.

Traitors, I will here remark, are a unfortunate class of people. If they wasn't they wouldn't be traitors. They conspire to bust up a country— they fail, and they're traitors. They bust her, and they become statesmen and heroes.

Take the case of Gloucester, afterwards Old Dick the Three, who may be seen at the Tower on horseback, in a heavy tin overcoat—take Mr. Gloucester's case. Mr. G. was a conspirator of the basest dye, and if he'd failed, he would have been hung on a sour apple tree. But Mr. G. succeeded, and became great. He was slewed by Col. Richmond, but he lives in history, and his equestrian figger may be seen daily for a sixpence, in conjunction with other em'nent persons, and no extra charge for the Warder's able and beautiful lectur.

There's one king in the room who is mounted onto a foamin steed, his right hand graspin a barber's pole. I didn't learn his name.

The room where the daggers and pistols and other weapons is kept is interestin. Among this collection of choice cutlery I noticed the bow and arrow used at this day by certain tribes of American Injuns, and they shoot 'em off with such a excellent precision that I almost sighed to be a Injun, when I was in the Rocky Mountain region. They are a pleasant lot them Injuns. Mr. Cooper and Dr. Catlin have told us of the red man's wonderful eloquence, and I found it so. Our party was stopped on the plains of Utah by a band of Shoshones, whose chief said:

"Brothers! the pale face is welcome. Brothers! the sun in sinking in the west, and Wa-na-bucky-she will soon cease speakin. Brothers! the poor red man belongs to a race which is fast becomin extinct."

He then whooped in a shrill manner, stole all our blankets and whiskey, and fled to the primeval forest to conceal his emotions.

I will remark here, while on the subject of Injuns, that they are in the main a very shaky set, with even less sense than the Fenians, and when I hear philanthropists bewailin the fact that every year "carries the noble red man nearer the settin sun," I simply have to say I'm glad of it, though it is rough on the settin sun. They call you by the sweet name of Brother one minute and the next they scalp you with their Thomashawks. But I wander. Let us return to the Tower.

At one end of the room where the weapons is kept, is a wax figger of Queen Elizabeth, mounted on a fiery stuffed hoss, whose glass eye flashes with pride, and whose red morocco nostril dilates haughtily, as if conscious of the royal burden he bears. I have associated Elizabeth with the Spanish Armada. She's mixed up with it at the Surrey Theatre, where *True to the Core* is bein acted, and in which a full ballet corps is introduced on board the Spanish Admiral's ship, givin the audience the idee that he intends openin a music hall in Plymouth the moment he conquers that town. But a very interestin drama is *True to the Core*, notwithstandin the eccentric conduct of the Spanish Admiral; and very nice it is in Queen Elizabeth to make Martin Truegold a baronet.

The Warder shows us some instruments of tortur, such as thumbscrews, throat-collars, etc., statin that these was conquered from the Spanish Armada, and addin what a cruel people the Spaniards was in them days — which elicited from a bright-eyed little girl of about twelve summers the remark that she thought it *was* rich to talk about the cruelty of the Spaniards usin thumbscrews when we was in a Tower where so many poor people's heads had been cut off. This made the Warder stammer and turn red.

I was so blessed with the little girl's brightness that I could have kissed the dear child, and I would if she'd been six years older.

I think my companions intended makin a day of it, for they all had sandwiches, sassiges, etc. The sad-lookin man, who had wanted us to drop a tear afore we started to go round, flinged such quantities of sassige into his mouth that I expected to see him choke hisself to death. He said to me, in the Beauchamp Tower, where the poor prisoners writ their unhappy names on the cold walls, "This is a sad sight."

"It is indeed," I answered. "You're black in the face. You shouldn't eat sassige in public without some rehearsals beforehand. You manage it awkwardly."

"No," he said, "I mean this sad room."

Indeed he was quite right. Though so long ago all these dreadful things happened I was very glad to git away from this gloomy room, and go where the rich and sparklin Crown Jewels is kept. I was so pleased with the Queen's Crown, that it occurred to me what a agree'ble surprise it would be to send a sim'lar one home to my wife; and I asked the Warder what was the value of a good, well-constructed Crown like that. He told me, but on cipherin up with a pencil the amount of funds I have in the J'int Stock Bank, I concluded I'd send her a genteel silver watch insted.

And so I left the Tower. It is a solid and commandin edifice, but I deny that it is cheerful. I bid it adieu without a pang.

I was droven to my hotel by the most melancholy driver of a four-wheeler that I ever saw. He heaved a deep sigh as I gave him two shillings. "I'll give you six d's more," I said, "if it hurts you so."

"It isn't that," he said, with a heart-rendin groan. "It's only a way I have. My mind's upset today. I at one time thought I'd drive you into the Thames. I've been reading all the daily papers to try and understand about Governor Eyre, and my mind is totterin. It's really wonderful I didn't drive you into the Thames."

I asked the unhappy man what his number was, so I could readily find him in case I should want him agin, and bade him good-bye. And then I thought what a frolicsome day I'd made of it.

Respectably, etc.,
Artemus Ward

Charles H. Smith (Bill Arp)

(1826-1903)

Charles H. Smith, whose humor appeared under the byline of
Bill Arp, put some of his biography in a newspaper article.

*Born in Gwinnett county, 1826; father a native of Massachusetts, and mother from
South Carolina; father came to Savannah when a youth, taught school and wedded
his pupil, and never returned North. . . . [I] grew up with all the other town boys,
and was about as bad; went to school some and worked some; was brought up a
merchant; went to college at Athens, Ga.; studied law and got married, and when
the war came commenced writing rebellious letters, and continued to write while in
Virginia in the army.*

To continue the story, Smith would have had to add that he also was a
judge, a state senator, a plantation owner, a journalist, and a professional
lecturer and humorist.

In the first "rebellious letter" Smith wrote, he posed, like Charles
Farrar Browne, as a friendly advisor to Lincoln. The president had put
out a proclamation telling the Southern armies to disperse. Assuming
the role of "a good Union man and a law-abiding citizen" named Bill
Arp, the author set forth the claim that he'd like very much to do as he
was told but inadvertently showed that he didn't know what "disperse"
meant. He also had trouble with a bit in the proclamation about "taking
possession of all private property at 'All Hazards.'" "We," he admitted,
"can't find no such a place on the map." It was the first of a number of
letters filled with poorly spelled words, bad grammar, and other signs
that Bill was poorly educated. And, despite Arp's claim that he was sympathetic, the dumb fellow kept saying things that suggested that Lincoln
was a fool and the Union's cause was doomed to failure. The first of the
letters that follows shows Arp in this role. The second letter shows him
as quite a different person, still a Southerner but now sympathetic with
the Confederate cause rather than that of the North.

The second piece was the introduction of a new Arp, one who took

136

over and brought his creator years of success. In Smith's words, this character is closer to his creator, one with "more than his share of common sense, more than his share of ingenuity, and plan and contrivance, . . . mother wit and good humor." Like the original Arp, this fellow is "an humble man and unlettered in books," so he writes bad grammar and spells poorly. In time, however, even this vestige of the original Arp disappeared, or tended to disappear, and the Arp of Smith's later years became a Josh Billings clone who writes more literately.

Bill Arp to Abe Linkhorn

Bill Arp
Bill Arp's Peace Papers
(New York, 1873).

Rome, Ga., Aprile 1861

Mr. Linkhorn—sir:

These are to inform you that we are all well, and hope these lines may find you *in statu quo*. We received your proclamation, and as you have put us on very short notice, a few of us boys have concluded to write you, and ax for a little more time. The fact is, we are most obleeged to have a few more days, for the way things are happening, it is utterly unpossible for us to disperse in twenty days. Old Virginia and Tennessee and North Carolina are continually aggravatin us into tumults and carousements, and a body can't disperse until you put a stop to such unruly conduct on their part. I tried my darndest yesterday to disperse and retire, but it was no go. And besides, your marshal here ain't doing a darned thing—he don't read the riot act, nor remonstrate, nor nothing, and ought to be turned out. If you conclude to do so, I am authorized to recommend to you Col. Gibbons or Mr. McLung, who would attend to the business as well as most anybody.

The fact is, the boys round here want watchin, or they'll take somethin. A few days ago I heard they surrounded two of our best citizens, because they was named Fort and Sumter. Most of 'em are so hot that they fairly siz when you pour water on 'em, and that's the way they make up their military companies here now. When a man applies to j'ine the volunteers, they sprinkle him, and if he sizzes they take him, and if he don't they don't.

Mr. Linkhorn, sir, privately speakin, I'm afeared I'll git in a tight place here among these bloods, and have to slope out of it, and I would like to have your Scotch cap and cloak that you traveled in to Washington. I suppose you wouldn't be likely to use the same disguise agin, when you left, and therefore I would propose to swap. I am five feet five, and could git my plow breeches and coat to you in eight or ten days if you can wait that long.

I want you to write me immedjitly about things generally, and let us know whereabouts you intend to do your fightin. Your proclamation says somethin about takin possession of all the private property at "All Hazards." We can't find no such place on the map. I thought it must be about Charleston, or Savannah, or Harper's Ferry, but they say it ain't anywhere down South. One man said it was a little factory on an island in Lake Champlain, where they make sand bags. My opinion is, that sand bag business won't pay, and it is a great waste of money. Our boys carry their sand in their gizzards, where it keeps better and is always handy.

I'm afeared your Government is givin you and your Kangaroo a great deal of unnecessary trouble, and my humble advice is, if things don't work better soon, you'd better grease it, or trade the darned old thing off. I'd show you a sleight-of-hand trick that would change the whole concern into buttons quick. If you don't trade or do somethin else with it soon, it will sp'ile or die on your hands, certain.

Give my regards to Bill Seward and the other members of the Kangaroo. What's Hannibal doin? I don't hear anything from him nowadays.

Yours, with care,

Bill Arp

P.S. If you can possibly extend that order to thirty days, do so. We have sent you a CHECK at Harper's Ferry (who keeps that darned old ferry now? it's giving us a heap of trouble), but if you positively won't extend, we'll send you a check drawn by Jeff Davis, Beauregard endorser, payable on sight anywhere.

Yours,

B. A.

Bill Arp Addresses Artemus Ward

Rome, Ga., September 1865

Mr. Artemus Ward, *Showman,*

Sir: The reason I write to you in partic'lar is because you are about the only man I know in all "God's Country," *so called.* For some several years we Rebs, *so called,* but now late of said country deceased, have been a-trying mighty hard to do somethin. We didn't quite do it, and now it is very painful, I assure, to dry up all of a sudden and make out like we wasn't there.

My friend, I want to say somethin. I s'pose there is no law agin thinkin, but thinkin don't help me. It don't let down my thermometer. I must explode myself gen'rally, so as to feel better. You see, I am tryin to harmonize. I'm tryin to soften down my feelins. I'm endeavorin to subjugate myself to the level of surroundin circumstances, *so called.* But I can't do it till I am allowed to say somethin. I want to quarrel with somebody and then make friends. I ain't no giant killer. I ain't no Norwegian bear. I ain't no Bo Constrictor, but I'll be hornswoggled if the talkin and the writin and the slanderin have got to be all done on one side any longer. Some of your folks have got to dry up or turn our folks loose. It's a blamed outrage, *so called.* Ain't you editors got nothin else to do but to peck at us, squib at us, and crow over us? Is every man what can write a paragraph to consider us as bears in a cage and be always a-jabbin at us to hear us growl? Now you see, my friend, that's what's disharmonious, and do you tell 'em, once and all, E Pluribus Unum, *so called,* that if they don't stop it at once, or turn us loose to say what we please, why we Rebs, *so called,* have unanimously, and j'intly, and severally resolved to—to—to—think very hard of it—if not harder.

That's the way to talk it. I ain't a-gwine to commit myself. I know when to put on the brakes. I ain't a-gwine to say *all* I think. Ne'er a time. No, sir. But I'll just tell you Artemus, and you may tell it to your show! If we ain't allowed to express our sentiments, we can take it out in *hatin*, and hatin runs heavy in my family, sure. I hated a man so bad once that all the hair come off my head, and the man drowned himself in a hog wallow that night. I could do it agin; but you see I am tryin to harmonize, to acquiesce, to become ca'm and serene.

> "In Dixie's fall
> We sinned all."

But talkin the way I see it, a big fellow and a little fellow, *so called*, got into a fight, and they fout, and fout, and fout a long time, and everybody all around a-hollerin hands off, but kept a-helpin the big fellow, till finally the little fellow caved in and hollered enough. He made a bully fight, I tell you, selah. Well, what did the big fellow do? Take him by the hand and help him up, and brush the dust off'n his clothes? Ne'er a time! No, sir! But he kicked him a'ter he was down, and throwed mud on him, and drug him about and rubbed sand in his eyes and now he's a-gwine about a-huntin up his poor little property. Wants to confiscate it, *so called*. Bless my jacket if it ain't enough to make your head swim.

But I'm a good Union man, *so called*. I ain't a-gwine to fight anymore. *I* shan't vote for the next war. *I* ain't no guerrilla; I've done tuck the oath and I'm gwine to keep it, but as for my bein subjugated and humiliated and amalgamated and enervated, as Mr. Chase says, it ain't so—ne'er a time. I ain't ashamed of nothin, neither—ain't repentin—ain't axin for no one-hoss short-winded pardon. Nobody needn't be a-playin priest about me. I ain't got no twenty thousand dollars. Wish I had; I'd give it to these poor widows and orphans. I'd fatten my own numerous and interestin offspring in about two minutes and a half. They shouldn't eat roots and drink branch water no longer. Poor unfortunate things! To come into this sublunary world at such a time! There's Bull Run Arp and Harper's Ferry Arp and Chickahominy Arp, that never seed the picturs in a spellin book. I tell you, my friend, we are the poorest people on the face of the yearth—but we are poor and proud. We made a bully fight, selah, and the whole American nation ought to feel proud of it. It shows what Americans can be when they think they are imposed on—"*so called*." Didn't our forefathers fight, bleed and die about a little tax on tea, when not one in a thousand drunk it? Because they succeeded, wasn't it glory? But if they hadn't, I s'pose it would have been treason, and they would have been a-bowin and scrapin around King George for pardon. So it goes, Artemus, and to my mind, if the whole thing was stewed down it would make about a half pint of humbug. We had good men, great men, Christian men, who thought we was right, and many of them has gone to the undiscovered country, and have got a pardon that is a pardon. When I die, I am mighty willin to risk myself under the shadow of their wings, whether the climate is hot or cold. So mote it be. Selah!

Well, maybe I've said enough. But I don't feel easy yet. I'm a good Union man, certain and sure. I've had my britches dyed *blue*, and I've bought a *blue* blanket, and I very often feel *blue*, and about twiste in a while I go to the doggery and get *blue*, and then I look up at the *blue* cerulean heavens, and sing the melancholy chorus of the *blue*-tailed fly.

I'm goin my durndest to harmonize, and I think it could succeed if it wasn't for some things. When I see a blackguard a-goin round the streets with a gun on his shoulder, why right then, for a few minutes, I hate the whole Yankee nation. Jerusalem! how my blood b'iles! The institution which were handed down to us by the heavenly kingdom of Massachusetts, now put over us with powder and ball! Harmonize the devil! Ain't we human beins? Hain't we got eyes and ears and feelin and thinkin? Why the whole of Africa have come to town, women and children and boys and baboons and all. A man can tell how far it is to the city better by the smell than the mile post.

They won't work for us, and they won't work for themselves, and they'll perish to death this winter, as sure as the devil is a hog, *so called*. They are now baskin in the summer's sun, a-livin on roastin ears and freedom, with ne'er a idee that winter will come again, or that castor oil and salts cost money. Some of 'em, a hundred years old, are whinin about goin to college.

The truth is, my friend, somebody's badly fooled about this business. Somebody have drawed the elephant in the lottery, and don't know what to do with him. He's just a-throwin his snout around loose, and by and by he'll hurt somebody. These niggers will have to go back to the plantations and work. I ain't a-goin to support ne'er a one of 'em, and when you hear anybody say so, you tell him it's a lie, *so called*. By golly, I ain't got nothin to support myself on. We fout ourselves out of everything exceptin children and land, and I suppose the land are to be turned over to the niggers for graveyards.

Well, my friend, I don't want much. I ain't ambitious, as I used to was. You all have got your shows, and monkeys, and circuses, and brass bands, and organs, and can play on the petroleum and the harp of a thousand strings, and so on, but I've only got one favor to ax of you. I want enough powder to kill a big yellow stump-tailed dog that prowls around my premises at night. 'Pon honor, I won't shoot at anything blue, black or mulatto. Will you send it? Are you and your folks so scared of me and my folks that you won't let us have any ammunition? Are the squirrels and crows and black raccoons to eat up our poor little corn patches? Are the wild turkeys to gobble all around us with impunity? If a mad dog takes the hydrophobia, is the whole community to run itself to death to git out of the way? I golly! It looks like folks had all took the rebelphobia for good, and was never a-gwine to git over it.

See here, my friend, you must send me a little powder and a ticket to your show, and me and you will harmonize certain.

With these remarks I think I feel better, and hope I hain't made nobody fightin mad, for I am not on that line at this time.

I am truly your friend, all present or accounted for.

Bill Arp, *so called*

P.S. Old man Harris wanted to buy my fiddle the other day with Confederate money. He said it would be good agin. He says that Jim Funderbunk told him that Warren's Jack seed a man who had just come from Virginny, and he see a man had told his cousin Mandy that Lee had whipped me *agin*. Old Harris says that a man by the name of Mack C. Millin is a-comin over with a million o' men. But nevertheless, notwithstandin, somehow else, I'm dubious about the money. If you was me, Artemus, would you make the fiddle trade?

B. A.

David Ross Locke
(Petroleum Vesuvius
Nasby)

(1833-1888)

David Ross Locke, born in New York State, was, like his contemporary, Charles Farrar Browne, a printer who became an Ohio journalist, then an editor, and in time a well-known humorist. Beginning in 1861, his satirical letters, signed Petroleum Vesuvius Nasby, were circulated in newspapers throughout the North and were widely read when they were collected in books. Today, their former popularity is puzzling.

That they were greatly enjoyed there can be no question. Late in the nineteenth century, William Mathews, like many a writer before and after him, filled pages with lamentations about the sad state of American humor. But he was able to praise one humorist for rising above his worthless contemporaries.

Who has forgotten the powerful aid rendered to the North in our late civil war by "Petroleum V. Nasby," of the "Confederate Cross-Roads?" Though he assumed the cap and bells, Rabelais was not more terribly in earnest. . . . His rib-tickling irony cheered the patriots, as well as confounded the Copperheads and Rebels. President Lincoln found relief from the weary anxieties of office in reading the letters of this Toledo blade. Grant declared that he "couldn't get through a Sunday without one;" and Secretary Boutwell publicly attributed the overthrow of the Rebels to three great forces, — the Army and Navy, the Republican Party, and the Letters of Petroleum V. Nasby.

Lincoln was even more fulsome in his praise than Secretary of the Treasury Boutwell, saying that if he were given the skill to write satirical letters such as Locke did, he'd be glad to give up the presidency.

Today, even after the abysmally bad spelling has been corrected, Locke's writings are for the most part quite unappealing. The popular comic figure of the 1970s and 1980s most like Nasby, perhaps, is the bigoted Archie Bunker. But Bunker had many far more likable qualities than the rascal Nasby, whom Locke actually labeled "a sort of a nickle-plated son of a bitch." In addition to being a bigot, Nasby was an

144

ignoramus, a hypocrite, a sluggard, an alcoholic, a coward, a bigamist, a thief, a corrupt politician, and a traitor. Locke satirized the opposition by having this repulsive creature join it and do his unsavory but stupid best to further its causes. What evidently made Nasby effective during the Civil War period and for some years thereafter must have been bitterness or partisanship that at this distance we find all but impossible to comprehend, let alone share. The first of the pieces that follow comes close to being amusing because it displays a flaw that readers still find amusing; the third kids political corruption, which hasn't disappeared, and shows a happy office seeker finally landing a cushy job, celebrating his triumph, and starting to enjoy it. The second piece, concerning the assassination of Lincoln, is a literary curiosity.

Why He Should Not Be Drafted*
(Petroleum V. Nasby)

Petroleum V. Nasby
Swingin Round the Cirkle (New York, 1867).

I see in the papers last night the Government has instituted a draft, and that in a few weeks some hundreds of thousands of peaceable citizens will be dragged to the tented field. I know not what others may do, but as for me, I can't go. Upon a rigid examination of my fizzleckle man, I find it would be worse nor madness for me to undertake a campaign, to wit:

    1. I'm bald-headed, and have been obliged to wear a wig these 22 years.

*Locke's note: One of the most surprising results of the conscription was the amount of disease disclosed among men between "eighteen and forty-five," in districts where quotas could not be raised by volunteering.

2. I have dandruff in what scanty hair still hangs around my venerable temples.

3. I have a chronic catarrh.

4. I have lost, since Stanton's orders to draft, the use of one eye entirely, and have chronic inflammation in the other.

5. My teeth is all unsound; my palate ain't exactly right, and I have had bronchitis 31 years last June. At present I have a cough, the paroxysms of which is frightful to behold.

6. I'm hollow-chested, short-winded, and have alluz had pains in my back and side.

7. I am afflicted with chronic diarrhea and costiveness. The money I have paid (or promised to pay) for Jaynes's carminative balsam and pills would astonish almost anybody.

8. I am ruptured in nine places and am entirely enveloped with trusses.

9. I have varicose veins, have a white swelling on one leg and a fever sore on the other. Also one leg is shorter than t'other, though I handle it so expert that nobody never noticed it.

10. I have corns and bunions on both feet, which would prevent me from marchin.

I don't suppose that my political opinions, which are aginst the prosecution of this unconstooshnel war, would have any weight, with a draft officer. But the above reasons why I can't go, will, I make no doubt, be sufficient.

The Assassination

Saint's Rest
Which Is in the State of New Jersey
April the 20th, 1865

The nation mourns. The hand of the vile assassin has been raised agin the Goril—the head of the nation, and the people's Father has fallen beneath the hand of a patr—vile assassin.

While Abraham Lincoln was a-livin, I need not say that I did not love him. Blessed with a mind of no ordinary dimensions, endowed with all the goodness of Washington, I alluz b'lieved him guilty of all the crimes of a Nero.

No man in New Jersey laments his untimely death more than the undersigned. I commenced weepin the minute I discovered a squad of returned soldiers comin round the corner, who was a-forcin constooshnal Democrats to hang out mournin.

True, he didn't agree with me, but I can overlook that—it was his misfortune. True, he hung unoffendin men, in Kentucky, whose only crime was in bein loyal to what *they* deemed *their* goverment, as though a man in this free country couldn't choose which goverment he'd live under. True, he made cold-blooded war, in the most fiendish manner, on the brave men of the South, who was only assertin the heaven-born right of rulin theirselves. True, he levied armies, made up of pimps, whose chiefest delight was in ravishin the wives and daughters of the South, and a miscellaneous burnin their houses. True, he kept into office just such men as would second him in his hell-begotten schemes, and dismissed any man who refused to become as depraved as he was. True, he would read of these scenes of blood and carnage, and in high glee tell filthy anecdotes; likewise would he ride over the field of battle, and as the wheels of his gorgeous carriage crushed into the shudderin earth the bodies of the fallen braves, sing African melodies.

148

Yet I, in common with all true Democrats, weep! We weep! We wish it to be distinctly understood, we weep! There was that in him that instinctively forces us to weep over his death, and to loathe the foul assassin who so suddenly removed so much loveliness of character. He had ended the war of oppression; he had subjugated a free and brave people, who were strugglin for their rights, and had them under his feet; but I, in common with all Democrats, mourn his death!

Had it happened in 1862, when it would have been of some use to us, we would not be so bowed down with woe and anguish. It would have throwed the goverment into confusion, and probably have secured the independence of the South.

But alas! the tragedy came at the wrong time.

Now we are saddled with the damnin crime, when it will produce no results. The war was over. The game was up when Richmond was evacuated. Why kill Lincoln then? For revenge? Revenge is a costly luxury—a party so near bankrupt as the Democracy cannot afford to indulge in it. The wise man has no such word as revenge in his dictionary, the fool barters his hope for it.

Didst think that Lincoln's death would help the South? Lincoln's hand was velvet—Johnson's may be to the eye, but to the feel it will be found iron. Where Lincoln switched, Johnson will flay; where Lincoln banished, Johnson will hang.

Davis was shocked when he heard it—so was I, and in common with all true Democrats, I weep.

> Petroleum V. Nasby
> Late Pastor of the Church of the New
> Dispensation

The Reward of Virtue

Confederate X Roads
Which Is in the State of Kentucky
August 12, 1866

At last I have it! Finally it come! After five weary trips to Washington, after much weary waitin and much travail, I have got it. I am now Postmaster at Confederate X Roads, and am duly installed in my new position. If I ever had any doubts as to A. Johnson bein a better man than Paul the Apostle, a look at my commission removes it. If I catch myself a-feeling that he deserted us unnecessarily five years ago, another look, and my resentment softens into pity. If I doubt his Democracy, I look at that blessed commission and am reassured, for a President who could turn out a wounded Federal soldier, and appoint such a man as ME, must be above suspicion.

I felt it was coming two weeks ago. I received a circ'lar from Randall, now my superior in office, propoundin these questions:

1. Do you have the most implicit faith in Andrew Johnson, in all that he has done, all that he is doin, and all he may hereafter do?

2. Do you b'lieve that the Philadelphia Convocation will be a convocation of saints, all actuated by pure motives, and devoted to the salvation of our once happy but now distracted country?

3. Do you b'lieve that, next to A. Johnson, Seward, Doolittle, Cowan and Randall are the four greatest, and purest, and bestest, and self-sacrificinest, and honestest, and righteousest men that this country has ever produced?

4. Do you b'lieve that there is a particularly hot place reserved in the next world for Trumbull, a hotter for Wade, and the hottest for Sumner and Thad Stevens?

5. Do you approve of the canin of Grinnell by Rousseau?

6. Do you consider the keepin out of Congress eleven sovereign states

a unconstooshnal and unwarranted assumption of power by a sectional Congress?

7. Do you b'lieve the present Congress a rump, and that (eleven states bein unrepresented) all their acts are unconstooshnal and illegal, 'ceptin them which provides for payin salaries?

8. Do you b'lieve that the Memphis and New Orleans unpleasantnesses was brought about by the unholy machinations of them Radical agitators, actin in conjunction with ignorant and besotted niggers, to wreak their spite on the now loyal citizens of these properly reconstructed states?

9. Are you not satisfied that the African citizens of American descent can be safely trusted to the operations of the universal law which governs labor and capital?

10. Are you willin to contribute a reasonable percent of your salary to a fund to be used for the defeat of objectionable Congressmen in the disloyal states North?

To these inquiries I not only answered yes, but went afore a Justice of the Peace, and took an affidavit to 'em, forwarded it back, and my commission was forthwith sent to me.

There was a jubilee the night it arriv. The news spread rapidly through the four groceries of the town, and such another spontaneous outburst of joy I never witnessed.

The bells rung, and for an hour or two the Corners was in the wildest state of excitement. The citizens congratulated each other on the certainty of the accession of the President to the Democracy, and in their enthusiasm four nigger families was cleaned out; two of 'em, one a male and the other a female, was killed. Then a procession was organized as follows:

Two grocery keepers with bottles.

Deacon Pogram.

ME, with my commission pinned onto a banner, and under it written, "in This Sign We Conquer."

Wagon with tableau onto it: a nigger on the bottom boards; Basom, the grocery keeper, with one foot onto him, holdin a banner inscribed, "The Nigger where he oughta be."

Citizen with bottle.

Deacon Pogram's daughter Mirandy in a attitude of wallopin a wench. Banner: "We've Regained our Rites."

Two citizens with bottles, trying to keep in procession.

Two more citizens, which had emptied their bottles, fallin out by the wayside.

Citizens, two and two, with bottles.

Wagon, loaded with the books and furniture of a nigger school, in a state of wreck, with a dead nigger layin on top of it, which had been captured within the hour. Banner: "My Policy."

The procession moved to the meetin house, and Deacon Pogram takin the chair, a meetin was to once organized.

The Deacon remarked that this was the proudest moment of his life. He was gratified at the appointment of his esteemed friend, because he appreciated the noble qualities which was so conspicuous into him, and because his arduous service in the cause of Democracy entitled him to the position. All these was aside of and entirely disconnected from the fact that there would be a probability of his gittin back a little matter of nine dollars and sixty-two cents ("Hear!-hear!") which he had loaned him about eighteen months ago, afore he had knowed him well or larned to love him. But there was another reason why he met to rejoice tonight. It showed that A. Johnson meant business, that A. Johnson was true to the Democracy, and that he had finally made up his mind to hurl the bolts of official thunder which he held in his Presidential hands at his enemies, and to make fight in earnest, that he was goin to reward his friends—them as he could trust. Our venerable friend's bein put in condition to pay the confidin residents of the Corners the little sums he owes them is a good thing ("Hear! Hear! True! True!" with singular unanimity from every man in the buildin), but what was such considerations when compared to the great moral effect of the decisive movement? ("A damned sight!" shouted one grocery keeper, and "We don't want no moral effect!" cried another.) My friends, when the news of this bold step goes forth to the South, the price of Confederate scrip will go up, and the shootin of niggers will cease; for the redemption of the first I consider assured, and the reducin of the latter to their normal condition I count as good as done.

Squire Gavitt remarked that he was too much overpowered with emotion to speak. For four years, nearly five, the only newspaper which come to that office had passed through the polluted hands of a Abolitionist. He had no partic'lar objection to the misguided man, but he was a symbol of tyranny, and so long as he sot there, he reminded 'em that they were wearin chains. Thank the Lord, that day is over! The Corners is redeemed, the second Jackson has risen, and struck off the shackles. He would not allude to the trifle of twelve dollars and a half that he loaned the app'intee some months ago, knowin that it would be paid out of the first money—

Bascom, the principal grocery keeper, rose, and called the Squire to order. He wanted to know if it was fair play to talk such talk. No man could feel a more heart-felt satisfaction at the appointment of our honored friend than him, showin, as it did, that the President had cut loose from Ab'litionism, which he despised, but he protested agin the Squire undertakin to git in his bill afore the rest had a chance. Who furnished him his liquor for eight months, and who has the best right for the first dig at the proceeds of the postion? He would never—

The other three grocery keepers rose, when Deacon Pogram ruled 'em all out of order, and offered the followin resolutions: —

Whereas, the President has, in a strictly constooshnal manner, relieved this community of an offensive Abolitionist, app'inted by that abhorred tyrant Lincoln, and app'inted in his place a sound constooshnal Democrat — one whom to know is to love; therefore, be it

Resolved, that we greet the President, and assure him of our continued support and confidence.

Resolved, that we now consider the work of Reconstruction, so far as this community is concerned, completed, and we feel that we are once more restored to our proper relations with the Federal government.

Resolved, that the glorious defence made by the loyal Democracy of New Orleans agin the combined conventioners and niggers, showed that freemen cannot be conquered, and that white men shall rule America.

Resolved, that on this happy occasion, we forgive the Government for what we did, and cherish ne'er a resentment agin anybody.

The resolutions was adopted, and the meetin adjourned with three cheers for Johnson and his policy.

Then came a scene. Every last one of 'em had come there with a note made out for the amount I owed him at three months. Kindness of heart is a weakness of mine, and I signed 'em all, feelin that if the mere fact of writin my name would do 'em any good, it would be cruel in me to object to the little labor required. Bless their innocent souls! They went away happy.

The next mornin I took possession of the office.

"Am I awake, or am I dreamin?" thought I. No, no! It is no dream. Here is the stamps, here is the blanks, and here is the commission. It is true! It is true!

I heerd a child, across the way, singin:

> "I'd like to be a angel
> and with the angels stand."

I wouldn't, thought I. I wouldn't trade places with an angel, even up. A Office with but little to do, with four groceries within a stone's throw, is as much happiness as my b'ilers will stand without bustin. A angel forsooth!

Petroleum V. Nasby, PM
(Which is Postmaster)

Henry Wheeler Shaw (Josh Billings)

(1818-1885)

*B*orn *and brought up in Massachusetts, enrolled in Hamilton College but booted out after a year, Henry Wheeler Shaw had several careers before he became a full-time humorist. These included exploring the West, farming, river boating, auctioneering, and selling real estate. Those who prize experience as a teacher may well claim that these wide experiences outfitted Shaw well for homespun philosophizing, his specialty.*

The start of his final career shows how fashionable assaults on spelling and grammar were for a time. He was a realtor in Poughkeepsie, New York, when he came upon some "letters" to newspapers by Artemus Ward that were making a hit. Remembering a piece of his that had attracted little attention, he dug it out and rewrote it in a style similar to Ward's. "Essa on the Muel," signed with the pen name Josh Billings, was peddled and attracted attention that lead Shaw to say, "I think I've struck oil." He wrote similar pieces, sold them, too, clipped them, and carried them to New York. There, Ward's creator, Charles Farrar Browne, persuaded his publisher to collect them in a book. Josh Billings, His Sayings (1865) was the first of ten successful books, all full of bad spelling, afflicted grammar, and peculiar sentences. Annual Josh Billings Farmer's Allminaxes added to Shaw's fame, as did pieces in newspapers and comic lectures.

Shaw's strongest hold wasn't in telling stories but in writing aphoristic essays. "With me," he wrote, "everything has to be put in two or three lines." The lines, often toiled over for hours, formed horse-sensible, witty sayings. No less an authority on aphorisms than Abraham Lincoln placed Billings second only to Shakespeare as a judge of human nature. The typical Billings essa gathered together a series of such insights, organized more or less, to deal with a specific subject. "Live Yankees" is typical.

Live Yankees

Honesty haz a short kreed, and branes haz no pedigree at all.—J. B.

JOSH BILLINGS
Struggling with his Great Burlo-Comic Lecture

THE PROBABILITIES OF LIFE
Perhaps rain—Perhaps not.

Live Yankees are chuck full of character and sizzling hot with enterprise and curiosity.

In build we find them as lean as a hunter's dog, with a parched countenance, ready for a grin, or for a sorrow; of elastic step; thoughtful, but not abstracted; patient, because cunnin; ever watchful; slow to anger; avoiding a fight; but resolute at bay.

In dress always slick, but not stuck up; their harness always betrays them wherever they go.

The oil of their language is their desire to please, and their greasy words foreshadow a profit.

They are nat'ral mechanics; the history of man's necessities is the history of their inventions.

The Live Yankee has no home. His love of inventions breeds a love of change, and wherever a human trail shows itself we find him pantin on the track.

He never gets sick at the stomach in a foreign land or grows sentimental. The beauty of a river to him is its capacity for a steamboat; its sloping banks checker into buildin lots, and its poetry waters might do the drudgery of a cotton mill.

He looks at a marble pyramid, guesses at its height, calculates the stone by the perch, and sells the magnificent relic in Boston at a profit.

He climbs the Alpine heights, crossed by conquerin heroes, and is struck with the propriety of tunneling it.

He sits, cross-legged, beneath the sheltering vine and listens to the uneasy sea, sees the warm promise of the grape, and forgettin the holy memories of the land of song, grinds the smilin vintage into wine and makes a happy bargain.

You can meet him in Constantinople, makin up in grimace what he lacks in language, spreadin a plaster with his tongue, for the man of Mahomet.

Go where you will, from the numb palsied North to the sweating limberness of the South, from the top of earth's morning to half past eleven at night, and the everlastin Yankee you will find, either vehement in an argue, or persuasive in a swap.

His religion is practical; he mourns over the heathen, and is ready to save them by the job.

He loves liberty with a red pepper enthusiasm, and fully believes New England can whip the universe.

If the phlegmatic Englishman brags about roast beef and his ancestors, Jonathan has a pumpkin pie and a grandpop to match them.

If the Frenchman grows crazy over a fricasee of frogs' hind legs, Jonathan pulls out a doughnut and a Rhode Island greening.

If the dusky Italian talks about the mad vomits of Vesuvius, Jonathan turns in the water power of Niagara.

In argument always earnest, and in reasoning always specious, this progressive phenomena tramps the world with the skeleton of a patent right in his carpet bag, and in his ever open hand and face a pleasant "How air you?"

If you would save your pride from being sandpapered, risk it not in a dicker with Jonathan.

His razor is the true Damascus, strapped on the wand of Midas for a golden harvest. His sanctity is often shrewdness, and his sweet savor is often the reflected halo of the common shillin.

Constitutionally and by education honest, he is always ready to cry for the deeds done in the body. His hospitalities and charities are ceremonial duties. And if his religion is sometimes only the severities of a Sabbath, it is because his bias is the thirsting impulse of a creating genius chained to the more sordid passion for lucre.

Finley Peter Dunne

(1867-1936)

*F*inley Peter Dunne's father, brought from Ireland to the New
World when he was six years old, settled in Chicago, married Ellen Finley
from County Kilkenny, did well in carpentry and lumber, and fathered
four sons and four daughters. Peter, the only son to go to high school,
on graduating got a job as an office boy on a Chicago newspaper. In
time, he became a reporter, moved from one paper to another, and as a
sideline developed skill as a writer of Irish dialect. During the 1890s, he
created saloon keeper Martin Dooley and had him comment on local
and national affairs in talks with—and for the most part at—a far less
canny friend, Mr. Hennessy. His talks about the Spanish-American War
particularly enlarged his fame and helped win for him a national audience.

In his first collection of Dooley's monologues, Mr. Dooley in Peace
and War *(1898)*, Dunne described his enchanting conversationalist as a

traveller, archeologist, historian, social observer, saloon-keeper, economist, and philosopher. . . . He reads the newspapers with solemn care, heartily hates them, and
accepts all they print for the sake of drowning Hennessy's rising protests. . . . His
impressions are transferred to the desensitized plate of Mr. Hennessy's mind. . . .
He is opulent in good advice, as becomes a man of his station [who] owns his own
house and furniture, and is only slightly behind on his license . . . .

Mr. Dooley is one satirist of politics and other follies whose comments
often outlive their timeliness. His perceptiveness; his awareness of backgrounds and human ways; his cynicism; his detachment born of his age,
his bachelorhood, and his membership in an ethnic and a religious mi-
nority; and his compassion all contribute to his charm. Unlike most of
America's horse-sensible commentators, the man has a keen sense of
humor that allows him to be ironic and witty on purpose, although he
often pretends that, like his predecessors, he is being funny without
knowing he is. Despite barriers presented by his rather thick brogue,
Martin Dooley managed from the late 1890s until the late 1920s—and

157

for decades beyond — to justify the title of the second book about him — Mr. Dooley in the Hearts of His Countrymen *(1899)*.

In "On the Victorian Era," spurred by the British queen's Diamond Jubilee and, simultaneously, by his own in 1897, Mr. Dooley peers back at the important occurrences of six decades. His mingling of world-shaking events with happenings that were equally important to him juxtaposes wild incongruities preparatory to his sharing of the credit with her royal majesty. Comic though it is, this dooleyfication of history, as he bluntly points out, really is justifiable. "On Reform Candidates" satirizes the gap between the Willie Boys and the Finnegans — the oblivious do-gooders and the practical bread-and-butter politicians. "On Charity" sets forth the sage's cynical beliefs and then in an endearing sequel shows him acting in a way quite inconsistent with his preachments. All three selections are from Mr. Dooley in Peace and in War *(1898)*.

On the Victorian Era

Mr. Dooley

"Are ye going to celebrate the queen's jubilee?" asked Mr. Dooley.

"What's that?" demanded Mr. Hennessy, with a violent start.

"Today," said Mr. Dooley, "her gracious Majesty Victoria, Queen of Great Britain and that part of Ireland north of Sligo, has reigned for sixty long and tiresome years."

"I don't care if she has snowed for sixty years," said Mr. Hennessy. "I'll not celebrate it. She may be a good woman for all I know, but damn her politics."

"Ye needn't be pro-fane about it," said Mr. Dooley. "I on'y asked ye a civil question. For meself, I have no feelin on the subject. I am not with the queen, and I am not again her. At the same time I cordially agree with me friend Captain Finerty, who's put his newspaper in mournin for the event. I won't march in the parade, and I won't put any dynamite under them that does. I don't say marchers and dynamiters aren't both right. 'Tis purely a question of taste, and as

159

the executive says when both candidates are members of the camp, 'Patriots will use their own discretion.'

"The good woman never done me no harm; and beyond throwin a rock or two into an Orangey's procession and subscribin to ten dollars' worth of Fenian bonds, I've treated her like a lady. Any grudge I ever had again her I buried long ago. We're both well on in years, and 'tis no use carrying hard feelins to the grave. About the time the lord chamberlain went to tell her she was queen and she came out in her nighty to hear the good news, I was announced into this world of sin and sorrow. So you see, we've reigned about the same lenth of time, and I ought to be celebratin me diamond jubilee. I would, too, if I had any diamonds. Do ye run down to Alderman O'Brien's and borrow twenty or thirty for me.

"Great happenins have me and Queen Victoria seen in these sixty years. Durin our beneficent presence on earth, the nations have grown rich and prosperous. Great Britain has extended her domain until the sun never sets on it. No more do the original owners of the s'ile, they bein kept movin be the police. While she was lookin on in England, I was lookin on in this country. I have seen America spread out from the Atlantic to the Pacific, with a branch office of the Standard Oil Company in every hamlet. I've seen the shackles dropped from the slave, so's he could be lynched in Ohio. I've seen this great city destroyed by fire from De Koven Street to the Lake View pumpin station, and then rise felix-like from its ashes, all but the West side, which was not burned. I've seen Jim Mace beat Mike McCool, and Tom Allen beat Jim Mace, and somebody beat Tom Allen, and John Sullivan beat him, and Corbett beat Sullivan, and Fitz beat Corbett. And if I live to celebrate my gold-watch-and-chain jubilee, I may see someone put it all over Fitz.

"Oh what things I've seen in me day and Victoria's! Think of that grand procession of lit'ry men—Tennyson and Longfellow and Bill Nye and Ella Wheeler Wilcox and Tim Scanlan and—I can't name them all: they're too many. And the brave generals—Von Moltke and Bismarck and U. S. Grant and gallant Phil Sheridan and Coxey. Think of them durin me reign.

"And th'inventions: the steam engine and the printin press and the cotton gin and the gin sour and the bicycle and the flyin machine and the nickel-in-the-slot machine and the Croker machine and the soda machine and—crownin work of our civilization—the cash register. What great advances has science made in my time and Victoria's! For when we entered public life, it took three men to watch the bar-keep, while today we can tell within eight dollars an hour what he's took in.

"Glory be! When I look back from this day of general rejoicin in me rhinestone jubilee, and see what changes has taken place, and how many people have died, and how much better off the world is, I'm proud of meself. War and pestilence and famine have occurred in me time, but I count them light compared with the benefits that have fallen to the race since I came on th'earth."

"What are ye talkin about?" cried Mr. Hennessy in deep disgust. "All this time ye've been standin behind this bar, ladlin out disturbance to the Sixth Ward, and ye haven't been as far east as Michigan Avenue in twenty years. What have ye had to do with all these things?"

"Well," said Mr. Dooley, "I had as much to do with them as the queen."

On Reform Candidates

That friend of yours, Dugan, is an intelligent man," said Mr. Dooley. "All he needs is an index and a few illustrations to make him a bicyclopedia of useless information."

"Well," said Mr. Hennessy, judiciously, "he ain't no Socrates, and he ain't no answers to questions column, but he's a good man that goes to his duty, and as handy with his pick as some people are with a cocktail spoon. What's he doin again ye?"

"Nawthin," said Mr. Dooley, "but he was in here Tuesday. 'Did ye vote?' says I. 'I did,' says he.

"'Which one of the distinguished bunko steerers got your invaluable suffrage?' says I.

"'I didn't have none with me,' says he, 'but I voted for Charter Haitch,' says he. 'I've been with him in six elections,' says he, 'and he's a good man,' he says.

"'D'ye think ye're votin for the best?' says I. 'Why, man alive!' I says. 'Charter Haitch was assassinated three years ago,' I says.

"'Was he?' says Dugan. 'Ah, well, he's lived it down by this time. He was a good man,' he says.

"Ye see, that's what them reform lads went up again. If I liked reformers, Hennessy, and wanted for to see them win out once in their lifetime, I'd buy them each a suit of chilled steel, arm them with repeatin rifles, and take them east of State Street and south of Jackson Boulevard. At present the opinion that prevails in the ranks of the glorious army of reform is there ain't anything worth seein in this large and commodious desert but the pest house and the bridewell. Me friend William J. O'Brien is no reformer. But William J. understands that there's a few hundreds of thousands of people livin in a part of town that looks like nawthin but smoke from the roof of the Onion League Club that have only two pleasures in life, to work and to vote, both of which they do at the uniform rate of one dollar and a half a day. That's why William J. is now a senator and will be an alderman after next Thursday, and it's why other people are sending him flowers.

"This is the way a reform candidate is elected. The boys down town has heerd that things ain't goin right somehow. Franchises is bein handed out to none of them; and once in a while a member of the Club, comin home a little late and tryin to reconcile a pair of round feet with an embroidered sidewalk, meets a strong-arm boy that pushes in his face and takes away all his marbles. It begins to be talked that the time has come for good citizens for to brace up and do somethin, and they agree to nominate a candidate for alderman.

" 'Who'll we put up?' says they.

" 'How's Clarence Doolittle?' says one.

" 'He's laid up with a coupon thumb, and can't run.'

" 'And how about Arthur Doheny?'

" 'I swore an oath when I came out of college I'd never vote for a man that wore a made tie.'

" 'Well, then, let's try Willie Boye.'

" 'Good,' says the committee, 'he's just the man for our money.'

"And Willie Boye, after thinkin it over, goes to his tailor and orders three dozen pairs of pants, and decides for to be the standard bearer of the people. Musin over his fried oysters and asparagus and his champagne, he bets a polo pony again a box of golf balls he'll be elected unanimous, and all the good citizens make a vow for to set th' alarm clock for half past three on the afternoon of election day, so's to be up in time to vote for the representative of pure govermint.

" 'T is some time before they comprehend that there are other candidates in the field. But th' other candidates know it. The strongest of them, his name is Flannigan, and he's a re-tail dealer in wines and spirits, and he lives over his establishment. Flannigan was nominated enthusiastically at a primary held in his barn, and before Willie Boye had picked out pants that would match the color of the Australian ballot, this-here Flannigan had put a man on the day watch, told him to speak gently to any registered voter that went to sleep behind the stove, and was out that night visitin his friends. Who was it judged the cake walk? Flannigan. Who was it carried the pall? Flannigan. Who was it stood up at the christening? Flannigan. Whose cards did the grievin widow and the blushin bridegroom or the happy father find in the hack? Flannigan's. Ye bet your life. Ye see, Flannigan wasn't out for the good of the community. Flannigan was out for Flannigan and the stuff.

"Well, election day come around, and all the eminent friends of good govermint had special wires strung into the Club, and waited for the returns. The first precin't showed twenty-eight votes for Willie Boye to fourteen for Flannigan.

" 'That's my precin't,' says Willie Boye. 'I wonder who voted them fourteen?'

" 'Coachmen,' says Clarence Doolittle.

" 'There are thirty-five precin'ts in this ward,' says the leader of the reform element. 'At this rate, I'm sure of 440 majority. Gossoon,' he says, 'put a keg of sherry wine on th' ice,' he says. 'Well,' he says, 'at last the community is relieved from misrule,' he says. 'Tomorrow I will start in arrangin amendments to the tariff schedule and th' arbitration treaty,' he says. 'We must be up and doin,' he says.

" 'Hold on there,' says one of the committee. 'There must be some mistake in this from the sixth precin't,' he says.

" 'Where's the sixth precin't?' says Clarence.

" 'Over be the dumps,' says Willie. 'I told me footman to see to that. He lives at the corner of Desplaines and Blue Island Avenue on Goose's Island,' he says. 'What does it show?'

" 'Flannigan, three hundred and eighty-five; Hansen, forty-eight; Schwartz, twenty; O'Malley, seventeen; Casey, ten; O'Day, eight; Larsen, five; O'Rourke, three; Mulcahy, two; Schmitt, two; Maloney, two; Riordan, two; O'Malley, two; Willie Boye, one.''

" 'Gentlemen,' says Willie Boye, arisin with a stern look in his eye, 'the rascal has betrayed me. Waiter, take the sherry wine off th' ice. They's no hope for sound financial legislation this year. I'm goin home.'

"And, as he goes down the street, he hears a band play and sees a procession headed by a calcium light, and in a carriage, with his plug hat in his hand, and his diamond makin the calcium light look like a piece of punk in a smokehouse, is Flannigan, payin his first visit this side of the tracks.''

On Charity

"Br-r-r!" cried Mr. McKenna entering stiffly, and spreading his hands over the potbellied stove. "It's cold."

"Where?" asked Mr. Dooley. "Not here."

"It's cold outside," said Mr. McKenna. "It was ten below at Shannahan's grocery when I went by, and the wind blowing like all possessed. Lord love us, but I pity them that's got to be out tonight."

"Save your pity," said Mr. Dooley, comfortably. "It ain't cold in here. There's frost on the window, 't is true for ye; and the wheels has been singin the livelong day. But what's that to us? Here I am and there ye are, the stove between us and the kettle hummin. In a minute it'll bile, and then I'll give ye a taste of what'll make a king of ye.

"Well, to be sure, 'tis tryin to be drivin a coal wagon or a street car; but 't is all in a lifetime. The difference between me and the man that sets up in the seat thumpin his chest and rubbin his hands is no more than the difference between him and the poor devil that walks along behind the wagon with his shovel on his shoulder, and 'll thank the saints for the first chance to put ten ton of hard coal into a cellar for a quarter of a dollar. The lad afoot envies the driver, and the driver envies me, and I might envy big Cleveland if it wasn't for the heavenly smell of thishere noggin. And who does Cleveland envy? Sure, it'd be sacrilege for me to say.

"Me old father, who was as full of sayins as an almanac, used to sink his spoon into the stirabout and say. 'Well, lads, this ain't bacon and greens and porter, but it'll be anything ye like if ye'll only think of the Cassidys.'

"The Cassidys was the poorest family in the parish. They waked th' oldest son in small beer, and was little thought of. Did me father ever ask them to share the stirabout? Not him. And he was the kindest man in the world. He had a heart in him as big as a lump of turf, but he'd say, 'When ye grow up, take no man's sorrow to yourself,' he says. 'Tis the wise man that goes through life thinkin of himself, fills his own stomach and takes away what he can't eat in his pocket.'

"And he was right, John. We have troubles enough of our own. The world goes on just the same, and ye can find fifty men to say the litany for ye to one that'll give ye what'll relieve a fastin spit. The dead are always popular. I knowed a society once to vote a monument to a man and refuse to help his family, all in one night. 'T is cold outside the door, ye say, but 'tis warm in here, and I'm gettin in me old age to think that the difference between heaven and hell is no broader."

Mr. Dooley's remarks were cut short by a cry from the back room. It was unmistakably a baby's cry. Mr. McKenna turned suddenly in amazement as Mr. Dooley bolted.

"Well, in the name of the saints, what's all this?" he cried, following his friend into the back room. He found the philosopher, with an expression of the utmost sternness, sitting on the side of his bed, with a little girl of two or three in his arms. The philosopher was singing:

> "Ar-rah rock-a-bye babby, on the tree top.
> When the wind blo-ows, the cradle will rock.
> And a-when the bough breaks, the cradle'll fall.
> And a-down 'll come babby, cradle and all."

Then he sang:

> "In the town of Kilkenny there dwelt a fair maid;
> In the town of Kilkenny there dwelt a fair maid.
> She had cheeks like the roses and hair of the same,
> And a mouth like rare strawberries buried in crame."

He rocked the child to and fro, and its crying ceased while he sang:

> "Chip, chip, a little horse.
> Chip, chip, again, sir.
> How many miles to Dublin?
> Three score and ten, sir."

The little girl went to sleep on Mr. Dooley's white apron. He lifted her tenderly and carried her over to his bed. Then he tiptoed out with an apprehensive face, and whispered, "It's John Donahue's kid that wandered away from home, and went to sleep on my doorstep. I sent the Dorsey boy to tell the mother, but he's a long time gone. Do ye run over, John, and leave them know."

Local Colorists

Harriet Beecher Stowe

(1811-1896)

In her early twenties, Harriet Beecher moved with her family *from her native New England to Cincinnati. There she taught school, married Prof. Calvin Stowe, and began to publish sketches of New England life to help support her growing family. After returning to the East, where her husband had a teaching appointment, she wrote several anti-slavery works, including the famous* Uncle Tom's Cabin *(1852), before again cultivating what James Russell Lowell called her true literary ground in* The Minister's Wooing *(1859),* The Pearl of Orr's Island *(1862),* Oldtown Folks *(1869),* Oldtown Fireside Stories *(1872), and* Poganuc People *(1878). These books established her as a leader in the local color movement.*

She took seriously her mission to give what she called "my résumé of the whole spirit and body of New England." "I have tried," she wrote, "to make my mind as still and passive as a looking-glass . . . and then to give you merely the image reflected there. I desire that you should see the characteristics of those [past] times and hear them talk."

Because Stowe was looking fondly back into a past era, her mirror failed to catch many unpleasant details. Although this fact diminished the historical accuracy of her work, it helped her create genial comedy, as did her chief talker, Sam Lawson, "a tall, shambling, loose-jointed man, with a long, thin visage, prominent watery blue eyes, . . . first do-nothing-in-ordinary in our village of Oldtown, . . . a man who wouldn't be hurried, and won't work, and will take his ease in his own way . . . ." In the selection that follows, Sam displays his great skill as a storyteller. He is shrewdly observant and sympathetic, but he is also keenly alive to the quirks and qualities of the pawky Yankees he pictures, and has a wonderful command of rustic speech.

The Minister's Housekeeper

Scene: The shady side of a blueberry pasture. Sam Lawson with the boys, picking blueberries.

Sam *loq.*

"Well, you see, boys, 'twas just here. Parson Carryl's wife she died along in the fore part of March: my cousin Huldy she undertook to keep house for him. The way on't was, that Huldy she went to take care of Mis' Carryl in the first on't, when she first took sick. Huldy was a tailoress by trade, but then she was one of these-here facultised persons that has a gift for most anything, and that was how Mis' Carryl came to set such store by her, that, when she was sick, nothin would do for her but she must have Huldy round all the time, and the minister, he said he'd make

Sam Lawson

Harriet Beecher Stowe, *Oldtown Fireside Stories*
(Boston: Osgood, 1872, frontispiece).

it good to her all the same, and she shouldn't lose nothin by it. And so Huldy, she stayed with Mis' Carryl full three months afore she died, and got to seein to everything pretty much around the place.

"Well, a'ter Mis' Carryl died, Parson Carryl he'd got so kinda used to havin on her round, takin care o' things, that he wanted her to stay along a spell. And so Huldy, she stayed along a spell, and poured out his tea, and mended his clothes, and made pies and cakes, and cooked and washed and ironed, and kept everything as neat as a pin. Huldy was a dreadful chipper sort of gal; and work sorta rolled off from her like water from a duck's back. There warn't no gal in Sherburne that could put such a sight of work through as Huldy, and yet, Sunday mornin, she always come out in the singers' seat like one of these here June roses, lookin so fresh and smilin,and her voice was just as clear and sweet as a meadow-lark's. Lordy massy! I 'member how she used to sing some o' them-ere places where the treble and counter used to go together; her voice kinda trembled a little, and it sorta went through and through a fellow! Tuck him right where he lived!"

Here Sam leaned contemplatively back with his head in a clump of sweet fern, and refreshed himself with a chew of young wintergreen. "This-here young wintergreen, boys, is just like a fellow's thoughts o' things that happened when he was young: it comes up just so fresh and tender every year, the longest time you have to live; and you can't help chawin on it, though 'tis sorta stingin. I don't never get over likin young wintergreen."

"But about Huldah, Sam?"

"Oh, yes! about Huldy. Lordy massy! When a fellow is Indianin round, these here pleasant summer days, a fellow's thoughts gits like a flock of young partridges: they's up and down and everywhere, 'cause one place is just about as good as another, when they's all so kinda comfortable and nice. Well, about Huldy, as I was a-sayin. She was just as handsome a gal to look at as a fellow could have; and I think a nice, well-behaved young gal in the singers' seat of a Sunday is a means of grace; it's sorta drawin to the unregenerate, you know. Why, boys, in them days I've walked over ten miles over to Sherburne of a Sunday mornin, just to play the bass violin in the same singers' seat with Huldy.

"She was very much respected, Huldy was; and when she went out to tailorin, she was alluz bespoke six months ahead, and sent for in wagons up and down for miles around. For the young fellows was alluz 'mazin anxious to be sent after Huldy, and was quite free to offer to go for her. Well, after Mis' Carryl died, Huldy got to be sorta housekeeper at the minister's, and saw to everything and did everything, so that there wa'n't a pin out of the way.

"But you know how 'tis in parishes: there alluz is women that thinks the minister's affairs belongs to them, and they ought to have the rulin and guidin of 'em. And if a minister's wife dies, there's folks that alluz has their eyes open on providence, lookin out who's to be the next one.

"Now there was Mis' Amaziah Pipperidge, a widow with snappin black eyes, and a hook nose, kinda like a hawk. And she was one o' them up-

and-down commandin sort of women, that feel they have a call to be seein to everything that goes on in the parish, and 'specially to the minister.

"Folks did say that Mis' Pipperidge sorta sot her eye on the Parson for herself; well, that-ere might a-been or it might not. Some folks thought that it was a very suitable connection. You see, she had a good property of her own, right nigh to the minister's lot, and was alluz kinda active and busy. So, takin one thing with another, I shouldn't wonder if Mis' Pipperidge should a-thought that Providence p'inted that way. At any rate, she went up to Deacon Blodgett's wife, and they two sorta put their heads together a-mournin and condolin about the way things was likely to go on at the minister's now Mis' Carryl was dead.

"Ye see, the parson's wife, she was one of them women who had their eyes everywhere and on everything. She was a little thin woman, but tough as India rubber,and smart as a steel trap and there wa'n't a hen laid an egg or cackled, but Mis' Carryl was right there to see about it. And she had the garden made in the spring and the meadows mowed in the summer, and the cider made, and the corn husked, and the apples got in the fall. And the doctor, he hadn't nothin to do but just sit stock still a-meditatin on Jerusalem and Jericho, and them things that ministers think about. But Lordy massy! he didn't know nothin about where anything he eat or drunk or wore come from or went to; his wife just led him round in temporal things and took care on him like a baby.

"Well, to be sure, Mis' Carryl looked up to him in spirituals and thought all the world on him, for there wa'n't a smarter minister no-where round. Why, when he preached on decrees and election, they used to come clear over from South Parish, and West Sherburne, and Old Town to hear him; and there was such a row o' wagons tied along by the meetin-house that the stables was all full, and all the hitchin posts was full clean up to the tavern, so that folks said the doctor made the town look like a general-tradin day a Sunday.

"He was great on texts, the doctor was. When he had a p'int to prove, he'd just go through the Bible and drive all the texts ahead of him like a flock o' sheep. And then, if there was a text that seemed agin him, why he'd come out with his Greek and Hebrew, and kinda chase it round a spell, just as you see a fellow chase a contrary bell-wether, and make him jump the fence a'ter the rest. I tell you, there wa'n't no text in the Bible that could stand agin the doctor when his blood was up.

"The year a'ter the doctor was app'inted to preach the 'lection ser-mon in Boston, he made such a figger that the Brattle Street Church sent a committee right down to see if they couldn't get him to Boston; and then the Sherburne folks they up and raised his salary; you see there ain't nothin wakes folks up like somebody else's wantin what you've got. Well, that fall they made him a Doctor o' Divinity at Cambridge College, and so they sot more by him than ever.

"Well, you see, the doctor, of course he felt kinda lonesome and afflicted when Mis' Carryl was gone, but really and truly, Huldy was so up to everything about house, that the doctor didn't miss nothin in a temporal way. His shirt bosoms was pleated finer then they ever was, and them ruffles round his wrists was kept like the driven snow; and there wa'n't a brack in his silk stockins, and his shoe buckles was kept polished up and his coats brushed. And there wa'n't no bread and biscuits like Huldy's, and her butter was like solid lumps o' gold; and there wa'n't no pies to equal hers; and so the doctor never felt the loss o' Mis' Carryl at table. Then there was Huldy alluz opposite to him, with her blue eyes and her cheeks like two fresh peaches. She was kinda pleasant to look at; and the more the doctor looked at her the better he liked her. And so things seemed to be goin on quite quiet and comfortable if it hadn't been that Mis' Pipperidge and Mis' Deacon Blodgett and Mis' Sawin got their heads together a-talking about things.

" 'Poor man,' says Mis' Pipperidge, 'what can that child that he's got there do towards takin the care of all that place? It takes a mature woman,' she says, 'to tread in Mis' Carryl's shoes.'

" 'That it does,' said Mis' Blodgett, 'and when things get to runnin down hill, there ain't no stoppin on 'em,' says she.

"Then Mis' Sawin she took it up. (Ye see, Mis' Sawin used to go out to dress-makin, and was sorta jealous, 'cause folks sot more by Huldy than they did by her.) 'Well,' says she, 'Huldy Peters is well enough at her trade. I never denied that, though I do say I never did believe in her way of makin buttonholes. And I must say, if 'twas the dearest friend I had, that I thought Huldy tryin to fit Mis' Kittridge's plum-colored silk was a piece of presumption. The silk was just sp'iled, so 'twa'n't fit to come into the meetin house. I must say, Huldy's a gal that's always too ventersome about takin 'sponsibilities she don't know nothin about.'

" 'Of course she don't,' said Mis' Deacon Blodgett. 'What does she know about all the lookin and seein to that ought to be in guidin the minister's house? Huldy's well meanin, and she's good at her work, and good in the singers' seat, but Lordy massy! she hain't got no experience. Parson Carryl ought to have an experienced woman to keep house for him. There's the spring house-cleanin and the fall house-cleanin to be seen to, and the things to be put away from the moths; and then the gettin ready for the Association and all the ministers' meetins; and the makin the soap and the candles, and settin the hens and turkeys, watchin the calves, and seein after the hired men and the garden. And that-ere blessed man just sets there at home as serene, and has nobody around but that-ere gal, and don't even know how things must be a-runnin to waste!'

"Well, the upshot on't was, they fussed and fuzzled and wuzzled till they'd drinked up all the tea in the teapot. And then they went down and called on the parson, and wuzzled him all up talkin about this, that and t'other that wanted lookin to, and that it was no way to leave everything to a young chit like Huldy, and that he ought to be lookin about for an experienced woman. The parson he thanked 'em kindly, and said he believed their motives was good, but he didn't go no further. He didn't ask Mis' Pipperidge to come and stay there and help him, nor nuthin of that kind, but he said he'd attend to matters himself. The fact was, the parson had got such a likin for havin Huldy round, that he couldn't think o' such a thing as swappin her off for the widow Pipperidge.

"But he thought to himself, 'Huldy is a good girl; but I oughtn't to be a-leavin everything to her—it's too hard on her. I ought to be instructin and guidin and helpin of her; 'cause 'tain't everybody could be expected to know and do what Mis' Carryl did.'

"And so at it he went; and Lordy massy! didn't Huldy have a time on't when the minister began to come outa his study, and want to tew round and see to things? Huldy, you see, thought all the world of the minister, and she was 'most afraid to laugh. But she told me, she couldn't for the life of her help it when his back was turned, for he wuzzled things up in the most singular way. But Huldy she'd just say, 'Yes, sir,' and get him off into his study, and go on her own way.

" 'Huldy,' says the minister one day, 'you ain't experienced outdoors; and when you want to know anything, you must come to me.'

" 'Yes, sir,' says Huldy.

" 'Now, Huldy,' says the parson, 'you must be sure to save the turkey eggs, so that we can have a lot of turkeys for Thanksgiving.'

" 'Yes, sir,' says Huldy, and showed him a nice dishful she'd been a-savin up. Well, the very next day the parson's hen-turkey was found killed up to Old Jim Scroggs's barn. Folks said Scroggs killed it; though Scroggs, he stuck to it he didn't. At any rate, the Scroggses, they made a meal on't; and Huldy, she felt bad about it, 'cause she'd set her heart on raisin the turkeys, and says she, 'Oh, dear! I don't know what I shall do. I was just ready to set her.'

" 'Do, Huldy?' says the parson. 'Why there's the other turkey out there by the door, and a fine bird, too, he is.'

"Sure enough, there was the old tom turkey, a-struttin and a-sidlin and a-quitterin and a-floatin his tail feathers in the sun, like a lively young widower, all ready to begin life over agin.

" 'But,' says Huldy, 'you know *he* can't set on eggs.'

" 'He can't? I'd like to know why,' said the parson. 'He shall set on eggs, and hatch 'em too.'

" 'Oh doctor!' says Huldy, all in a tremble; 'cause, you know, she didn't want to contradict the minister, and she was afraid she should laugh,—'I never heard that a tom turkey would set on eggs.'

" 'Why they ought to,' said the parson, getting quite earnest. 'What else be they good for? You just bring out the eggs, now, and put 'em in the nest, and I'll make him set on 'em.'

"So Huldy she thought there weren't no way to convince him but to let him try; so she tuck the eggs out and fixed 'em all nice in the nest. And then she come back and found old Tom a-skirmishing with the parson pretty lively, I tell you. You see, old Tom he didn't take the idea at all; and he flapped and gobbled and fit the parson. And the parson's wig got round so that his queue stuck straight out over his ear, but he'd got his blood up. You see, the old doctor was used to carryin his p'ints o' doctrine; and he hadn't fit the Arminians and Socinians to be beat by a tom turkey. So finally he made a dive, and ketched him by the neck in spite o' his flappin, and stroked him down, and put Huldy's apron round him.

" 'There, Huldy,' he says, quite red in the face, 'we've got him now.' And he traveled off to the barn with him as lively as a cricket.

"Huldy came behind, just chokin with laugh, and afraid the minister would look round and see her.

" 'Now, Huldy, we'll crook his legs and set him down,' says the parson, when they got him to the nest. 'You see he is getting quiet, and he'll set there all right.'

"And the parson he sot him down. And old Tom he sot there solemn enough, and held his head down all droopin lookin like a real pious old cock, as long as the parson sot by him.

" 'There! you see how still he sets,' says the parson to Huldy.

"Huldy was most dyin for fear she should laugh. 'I'm afraid he'll get up,' says she, 'when you do.'

" 'Oh, no he won't!' says the parson, quite confident. 'There, there,' says he, layin his hands on him, as if pronouncin a blessin. But when the parson riz up, old Tom he riz up too, and began to march over the eggs.

" 'Stop, now!' says the parson. 'I'll make him get down agin; hand me that corn basket; we'll put that over him.'

"So he crooked old Tom's legs, and got him down agin, and they put the corn basket over him, and they both stood and waited.

" 'That'll do the thing, Huldy,' said the parson.

" 'I don't know about it,' says Huldy.

" 'Oh, yes, it will, child! I understand,' says he.

"Just as he spoke, the basket riz right up and stood, and they could see old Tom's legs.

" 'I'll make him stay down, confound him,' says the parson, for, you see, parsons is men, like the rest on us, and the doctor had got his spunk up.

" 'You just hold him a minute, and I'll get something that'll make him stay, I guess.' And out he went to the fence, and brought in a long, thin, flat stone, and laid in on old Tom's back.

"Old Tom he wilted down considerable under this, and looked really as if he was goin to give in. He stayed still there a good long spell, and the minister and Huldy left him there and come into the house. But they hadn't more than got in the door before they see old Tom a-hippin along, as high steppin as ever, sayin, 'Talk! talk!' and 'Quitter! quitter!' and struttin and gobblin as if he'd come through the Red Sea and got the victory.

"'Oh, my eggs!' says Huldy. 'I'm afraid he's smashed 'em.'

"And sure enough, there they was, smashed flat enough under the stone.

"'I'll have him killed,' said the parson. 'We won't have such a critter round.'

"But the parson he slept on't, and then he didn't do it. He only come out next Sunday with a tip-top sermon on the 'Riginal Cuss' that was pronounced on things in general, when Adam fell, and showed how everything was allowed to go contrary ever since. There was pigweed, and purslane, and Canada thistles, cut worms, and bag-worms, and canker-worms, to say nothin of rattlesnakes. The doctor made it very impressive and sorta improvin. But Huldy she told me, goin home, that she hardly could keep from laughin two or three times in the sermon when she thought of old Tom a-standin up with the corn basket on his back.

"Well, next week Huldy she just borrowed the minister's horse and side-saddle, and rode over to South Parish to her Aunt Bascome's—Widow Bascome's, you know, that lives there by the trout brook—and got a lot o' turkey eggs of her, and come back and set a hen on 'em, and said nothin. And in good time there was as nice a lot o' turkey chicks as ever you see.

"Huldy never said a word to the minister about his experiment, and he never said a word to her. But he sorta kept more to his books, and didn't take it on him to advise so much.

"But not long a'ter he took it into his head that Huldy ought to have a pig to be a-fattin with the buttermilk. Mis' Pipperidge set him up to it. And just then old Tim Bigelow, out to Juniper Hill, told him if he'd call over he'd give him a little pig.

"So he sent for a man, and told him to build a pigpen out by the well, and have it all ready when he came home with the pig.

"Huldy she said she wished he might put a curb round the well out there, because in the dark, sometimes, a body might stumble into it, and the parson, he told him he might do it.

"Well, old Aikin, the carpenter, he didn't come till most the middle of the a'ternoon. And then he sorta idled, so that he didn't get up the well-curb till sundown. And then he went off and said he'd come and do the pigpen next day.

"Well, a'ter dark, Parson Carryl he driv into the yard, full chisel, with his pig. He'd tied up his mouth to keep him from squealin; and he see what he thought was the pigpen—and so he ran and threw piggy over; and down he dropped into the water, and the minister put out his horse and pranced off into the house quite delighted.

" 'There, Huldy, I've got you a nice little pig.'

" 'Oh, dear me!' says Huldy. 'Where have you put him?'

" 'Why, out there in the pigpen, to be sure.'

" 'Oh, dear me!' says Huldy. 'That's the well-curb. There ain't no pig-pen built,' says she.

" 'Lordy massy!' says the parson. 'Then I've thrown the pig in the well.'

"Well, Huldy she worked and worked, and finally she fished piggy out in the bucket, but he was dead as a door nail. And she got him outa the way quietly, and didn't say much. And the parson, he took to a great Hebrew book in his study; and says he, 'Huldy, I ain't much in temporals,' says he.

"Huldy says she kinda felt her heart go out to him, he was so sorta meek and helpless and larned. And says she, 'Well, Parson Carryl, don't trouble your head no more about it. I'll see to things.' And sure enough, a week a'ter there was a nice pen, all ship-shape, and two little white pigs that Huldy bought with the money for the butter she sold at the store.

" 'Well, Huldy,' said the parson, 'you are a most amazin child. You don't say nothin but you do more than most folks.'

"A'ter that the parson set such store by Huldy that he come to her and asked her about everything, and it was amazin how everything she put her hand to prospered. Huldy planted marigolds and larkspurs, pinks and carnations, all up and down the path to the front door, and trained up mornin-glories and scarlet runners round the windows. And she was always a-gettin a root here, and a sprig there and a seed from somebody else; for Huldy was one o' them that has the gift, so that if you just give 'em the leastest sprig of anything, they make a great bush out of it right away; so that in six months Huldy had roses and gerani-ums and lilies, such as it would a-took a gardener to raise. The parson he took no notice at first; but when the yard was all ablaze with flowers, he used to come and stand in a kind o' maze at the front door, and say, 'Beautiful, beautiful! Why, Huldy, I never see anything like it.'

"And then when her work was done a'ternoons, Huldy would sit with her sewin in the porch, and sing and trill away till she'd draw the meadowlarks and the bobolinks and the orioles to answer her, and the great big elm tree overhead would get perfectly rackety with the birds. And the parson, settin there in his study, would get to kinda dreamin about the angels, and golden harps, and the New Jerusalem, but he wouldn't speak a word, 'cause Huldy she was just like the wood thrushes, she never could sing so well when she thought folks was hearin. Folks noticed, about this time, that the parson's sermons got to be like Aaron's rod, that budded and blossomed; there was things in 'em about flowers and birds, and more special about the music o' heaven. And Huldy she noticed that if there was a hymn run in her head while she was round a-workin, the minister was sure to give it out next Sunday. You see, Huldy was just like a bee: she always sung when she was workin, and you could hear her trilling now down in the corn patch, while she was pickin the corn; and now in the buttery, while she was workin the butter; and now she'd go singin down cellar, and then she'd be singin up overhead, so that she seemed to fill a house chock full o' music.

"Huldy was so sorta chipper and fair spoken that she got the hired men all under her thumb; they come to her and took her orders just as meek as so many calves. And she traded at the store, and kept the accounts, and she had her eyes everywhere, and tied up all the ends so tight that there wa'n't no gettin round her. She wouldn't let nobody put nothin off on Parson Carryl 'cause he was a minister. Huldy was alluz up to anybody that wanted to make a hard bargain; and afore he knew just what he was about, she'd get the best end of it, and everybody said that Huldy was the most capable gal they'd ever traded with.

"Well, come to the meetin of the Association, Mis' Deacon Blodgett and Mis' Pipperidge come callin up to the parson's, all in a stew, and offerin their services to get the house ready. But the doctor he just thanked 'em quite quiet, and turned 'em over to Huldy. And Huldy she told 'em that she'd got everything ready, and showed 'em her pantries and her cakes and her pies and her puddins, and took 'em all over the house. And they went peekin and pokin, openin cupboard doors and lookin into drawers, and they couldn't find so much as a thread out o' the way, from garret to cellar, and so they went off quite discontented. A'ter that the women set new trouble a-brewin. Then they begun to talk that it was a year now since Mis' Carryl died; and it really wasn't proper such a young gal to be stayin there, who everybody could see was a-settin her cap for the minister.

"Mis' Pipperidge said, that, so long as she looked on Huldy as the hired gal, she hadn't thought much about it; but Huldy was really takin on airs as an equal, and appearin as mistress o' the house in a way that would make talk if it went on. And Mis' Pipperidge she driv round up to Deacon Abner Snow's, and down to Mis' Lijah Perry's, and asked them if they wasn't afraid that the way the parson and Huldy was a-goin on might make talk. And they said they hadn't thought on't before, but now, come to think on't, they was sure it would, and they all went and talked with sombody else, and asked them if they didn't think it would make talk. So come Sunday, between meetins there wa'n't nothin else talked about; and Huldy saw folks a-noddin' and a-winkin, and a-lookin a'ter her, and she begun to feel dreadful sorta disagreeable.

"Finally, Mis' Sawin she says to her, 'My dear, didn't you never think folks would talk about you and the minister?'

" 'No, why should they?' says Huldy, quite innocent.

" 'Well, dear,' says she, 'I think it's a shame; but they say you're tryin to catch him, and that it's so bold and improper for you to be courtin him right in his own house—you know folks will talk—I thought I'd tell you 'cause I think so much of you,' says she.

"Huldy was a gal of spirit, and she despised the talk, but it made her dreadful uncomfortable; and when she got home at night, she sat down in the mornin-glory porch, quite quiet, and didn't sing a word.

"The minister he had heard the same thing from one of his deacons that day; and when he saw Huldy so kinda silent, he says to her, 'Why don't you sing, my child?'

"He had a pleasant sort of way with him, the minister had, and Huldy had got to likin to be with him, and it all come over her that perhaps she ought to go away. And her throat kinda filled up so she couldn't hardly speak; and says she, 'I can't sing tonight.'

"Says he, 'You don't know how much good your singin has done me, nor how much good you have done me in all ways, Huldy. I wish I knew how to show my gratitude.'

" 'O sir!' says Huldy, '*is* it improper for me to be here?'

" 'No, dear,' says the minister, 'but ill natered folks will talk. But there is one way we can stop it, Huldy—if you will marry me. You'll make me very happy, and I'll do all I can to make you happy. Will you?'

"Well, Huldy never told me just what she said to the minister—gals never does give you the particulars of them-ere things just as you'd like 'em—only I knew the upshot and the whole on't was that Huldy she did a consid'able lot o' clear starchin and ironin the next two days. And the Friday o' last week the minister and she rode over together to Dr. Lothrop's in Old Town; and the doctor, he just made 'em man and wife, 'spite of envy of the Jews,' as the hymn says.

"Well, you'd better believe there was a-starin and a-wonderin next Sunday mornin when the second bell was a-tollin, and the minister walked up the broad aisle with Huldy, all in white, arm in arm with him, and he opened the minister's pew, and handed her in as if she was a princess; for, you see, Parson Carryl come of a good family, and was a born gentleman, and had a sorta grand way of bein polite to women-folks. Well, I guess there was a rustlin among the bonnets. Mis' Pipperidge give a great bounce, like corn poppin on a shovel, and her eyes glared through her glasses at Huldy as if they'd a-sot her afire, and everybody in the meetin house was a-starin, I tell *you*. But they couldn't none of them say nothin agin Huldy's looks; for there wa'n't a crimp or a frill about her that wa'n't just *so*. And her frock was white as the driven snow, and she had her bonnet all trimmed up with white ribbons. And all the fellows said the old doctor had stole a march, and got the handsomest gal in the parish.

"Well, a'ter meetin they all come round the parson and Huldy at the door, shakin hands and laughin; for by that time they was about agreed that they'd got to let pretty well alone.

" 'Why, parson Carryl,' says Mrs. Deacon Blodgett, 'how you've come it over us.'

" 'Yes,' said the parson, with a kind o' twinkle in his eye. 'I thought,' says he, 'as folks wanted so much to talk about Huldy and me, I'd give 'em somethin worth talkin about.' "

George Washington Cable

(1844-1925)

George Washington Cable was born in New Orleans in 1844, the son of a native Virginian and a native New England Puritan mother. Except for a period of service during the Civil War, he lived and worked in New Orleans during the first forty-one years of his life, first at odd jobs, later as a clerk and bookkeeper. During his leisure hours, he read many old records and histories, collecting so much promising material that he decided to use some of it in writings. His first published story, which appeared when he was twenty-nine, plus some others that followed, made up his first book, Old Creole Days (1879). He worked the historical vein further in The Grandissimes (1880), Madame Delphine (1881), Dr. Sevier (1885), and a number of other fictional works that firmly established him as the pioneer local colorist for the region.

As such, he caught the exotic qualities of Louisiana in works combining romance and realism and in works often touched with humor and satire. "Posson [i.e., Parson] Jone'" typically rich in localized detail, plays with incongruities between Creole culture—that of French and Spanish whites—and Protestant Anglo-Saxon culture. The highly individualized dialect is unique among samplings in the present collection in that its English is modified by French pronunciations, constructions, and wordings.

Cable's work was more admired in the North than in the South of his day, partly because many Southerners felt that his characterizations of Creoles and Cajuns, and his representations of their dialect, maligned them. Another irritant was his zealous advocacy of reforms in race relations, notably in The Silent South (1885). The year that book came out, he moved to Northampton, Massachusetts, which was to be his home during the latter half of his life.

"Posson Jone' "

To Jules St. -Ange—elegant little heathen—there yet remained at manhood a remembrance of having been to school, and of having been taught by a strong-headed Capuchin that the world is round—for example, like a cheese. This round world is a cheese to be eaten through, and Jules had nibbled quite into his cheese world already at twenty-two. He realized this as he idled about one Sunday morning where the intersection of Royal and Conti streets some seventy years ago formed a central corner of New Orleans. Yes, yes, the trouble was he had been wasteful and honest. He discussed the matter with that faithful friend and confidant, Baptiste, his yellow body-servant. They concluded that, papa's patience and *tante*'s pin-money having been gnawed away quite to the rind, there were left open only these few easily-enumerated resorts: to go to work—they shuddered; to join Major Innerarity's filibustering expedition; or else—why not?—to try some games of confidence. At twenty-two one must begin to be something. Nothing else tempted; could that avail? One could but try. It is noble to try; and besides, they were hungry. If one could make the friendship of some person from the country, for instance, with money, not expert at cards and dice but as one would say, willing to learn, one might find cause to say some "Hail Marys."

The sun broke through a clearing sky, and Baptiste pronounced it good for luck. There had been a hurricane in the night. The weed-grown tile roofs were still dripping, and from lofty brick and low adobe walls a rising steam responded to the summer sunlight. Up-street, and across the Rue du Canal, one could get glimpses of the gardens in Faubourg Ste. -Marie standing in silent wretchedness, so many tearful Lucretias, tattered victims of the storm. Short remnants of the wind now and then came down the narrow street in erratic puffs heavily laden with odors of broken boughs and torn flowers, skimmed the little pools of rainwater in the deep ruts of the unpaved street, and suddenly went away to nothing, like a juggler's butterflies or a young man's money.

It was very picturesque, the Rue Royale. The rich and poor met together. The locksmith's swinging key creaked next door to the bank; across the way, crouching, mendicant-like, in the shadow of a great importing house, was the mud laboratory of the mender of broken combs. Light balconies overhung the rows of shiny showy shops and stores open for trade this Sunday morning, and pretty Latin faces of the higher class glanced over their savagely pronged railings upon the passers below. At some windows hung lace curtains, flannel duds at some, and at others only the scraping and sighing one-hinged shutter groaning toward Paris after its neglectful master.

M. St. -Ange stood looking up and down the street for nearly an hour. But few ladies, only the inveterate mass-goers, were out. About the entrance of the frequent *cafés* the masculine gentility stood leaning on canes, with which now one and now another beckoned to Jules, some even adding pantomimic hints of the social cup.

M. St. -Ange remarked to his servant without turning his head that somehow he felt sure he should soon return those *bons* that the mulatto had lent him.

"What will you do with them?"

"Me!" said Baptiste quickly; "I will go and see the bullfight in the Place Congo."

"There is to be a bullfight? But where is M. Cayetano?"

"Ah, got all his affairs wet in the tornado. Instead of his circus, they are to have a bullfight—not an ordinary bullfight with sick horses, but a buffalo-and-tiger fight. I would not miss it—."

Two or three persons ran to the opposite corner, and commenced striking at something with their canes. Others followed. Can M. St. -Ange and servant, who hasten forward—can the Creoles, Cubans, Spaniards, San Domingo refugees and other loungers—can they hope it is a fight? They hurry forward. Is a man in a fit? The crowd pours in from the side streets. Have they killed a so-long snake? Bare-headed shopmen leave their wives, who stand upon chairs. The crowd huddles and packs. Those on the outside make little leaps into the air, trying to be tall.

"What is the matter?"

"Have they caught a real live rat?"

"Who is hurt?" asks someone in English.

"Personne," replies a shopkeeper. "A man's hat blow in the gutter, but he has it now. Jules pick it. See, that is the man, head and shoulders on top the rest."

"He in the homespun?" asks a second shopkeeper. "Phumph! an *Américain*—a West Floridian; bah!"

"But wait! 'st! he is speaking, listen!"

"To who is he speak?"

"Sh-sh-sh! to Jules."

"Jules who?"

"Silence, you! To Jules St. -Ange what ho' me a bill since long time. Sh-sh-sh!"

Then the voice was heard.

Its owner was a man of giant stature, with a slight stoop in his shoulders, as if he was making a constant, good-natured attempt to accommodate himself to ordinary doors and ceilings. His bones were those of an ox. His face was marked more by weather than age, and his narrow brow was bald and smooth. He had instantaneously formed an opinion of Jules St. -Ange, and the multitude of words, most of them lingual curiosities, with which he was rasping the wide-open ears of his listeners, signified, in short, that as sure as his name was Parson Jones, the little Creole was a "plum gentleman."

M. St. -Ange bowed and smiled, and was about to call attention, in both gesture and speech, to a singular object on top of the still uncovered head, when the nervous action of the *Américain* anticipated him, as throwing up an immense hand, he drew down a large roll of banknotes. The crowd laughed, the West Floridian joining, and began to disperse.

"Why, that money belongs to Smyrny Church," said the giant.

"You are very dangerous to make your money expose like that, Misty Posson Jone," said St. -Ange, counting it with his eyes.

The countryman gave a start and smile of surprise.

"How d'd you know my name was Jones?" he asked, but, without pausing for the Creole's answer, furnished in his reckless way some further specimens of West Floridian English; and the conciseness with which he presented full intelligence of his home, family, calling, lodging house, and present and future plans, might have passed for consummate art, had it not been the most run-wild nature. "And I've done been to Mobile, you know, on business for Bethesdy Church. It's the on'yest time I ever been from home; now you wouldn't't've believed that, would you? But I admire to have saw you, that's so. You've got to come and eat with me. Me and my boy ain't been fed yet. What might you call your name? Jules? Come on, Jules. Come on, Colossus. That's my nigger—his name's Colossus of Rhodes. Is that your yellow boy, Jules? Fetch him along, Colossus. It seems like a special provi*dence*. Jules, do you believe in a special provi*dence*?"

Jules said that he did.

The new-made friends moved briskly off, followed by Baptiste and a short, square old Negro, very black and grotesque, who had introduced himself to the mulatto, with many glittering and cavernous smiles, as "d'body-servant of d'Rev'n Mr. Jones."

Both pairs enlivened their walk with conversation. Parson Jones descanted upon the doctrine he had mentioned, and concluded that there would always be "a special provi*dence* again cotton until folks quit a-pressin of it and haulin of it on Sundays!"

"*Je dis*," said St.-Ange in response. "I think you is just right. I believe, me, strong-strong in the improvidence, yes. You know my papa he hoan a sugar plantation, you know. 'Jules, me son,' he say one time to me, I goin to make one barrel sugar to fetch the most high price in New Orleans.' Well, he take his best barrel sugar—I never see a so careful man like me papa always to make a so beautiful sugar *et sirop*. 'Jules, go at Father Pierre and get this li'l pitcher fill with holy water, and tell him send his tin bucket and I will make it fill with *quitte*.' I get the holy water, my papa sprinkle it over the barrel, and make one cross on the 'ead of the barrel."

"Why, Jules, said Parson Jones, "that didn't do no good."

"Didn't do no good! It brought the so great value! You can strike me dead if that barrel sugar didn't fetch the more high cost than any other in the city. *Parce-que*, the man who buy that barrel sugar he make a mistake of one hundred pound"—falling back—"*mais* certainlee!"

"And you think that was growin out of the holy water?" asked the parson.

"*Mais*, what could make it else? It could not be the *quitte*, because my papa keep the bucket and forget to send the *quitte* to Father Pierre."

Parson Jones was disappointed.

"Well, now, Jules, you know, I don't think that was right. I reckon you must be a plum Catholic."

M. St.-Ange shrugged. He would not deny his faith.

"I am a *Catholique, mais*"—brightening as he hoped to recommend himself anew—"not a good one."

"Well, you know," said Jones—"where's Colossus? Oh, all right. Colossus strayed off a minute in Mobile, and I plum lost him for two days. Here's the place; come in. Colossus and this boy can go to the kitchen—Now, Colossus, what *air* you a-beckonin at me for?"

He let his servant draw him aside and address him in a whisper.

"Oh, go way!" said the parson, with a jerk. "Who's goin to throw me? What? Speak louder. Why, Colossus, you shain't talk so, sir. 'Pon my soul you're the mightiest fool I ever taken up with. Just you go down that alley-way with this yellow boy, and don't show your face until you called."

The Negro begged; the master wrathily insisted.

"Colossus, will you do as I tell you, or shall I have to strike you, sir?"

"O Marse Jimmy, I—I's gwine, but "—he ventured nearer—"don't on no account drink nothin, Marse Jimmy."

Such was the Negro's earnestness that he put one foot in the gutter, and fell heavily against his master. The parson threw him off angrily.

"There, now! Why, Colossus, you must have been doseted with somethin; you plum crazy—Humph, come on, Jules, let's cut! Humph! to tell me that when I never taken a drop, exceptin for chills, in my life— which he knows as well as me."

The two masters began to ascend a stair.

"*Mais*, he is a sassy; I would sell him, me," said the young Creole.

"No, I wouldn't do that," replied the parson, "though there is people in Bethesdy who says he is a rascal. He's a powerful smart fool. Why, that boy's got money, Jules, more money than religion, I reckon. I'm sure he fallen into mighty bad company"—they passed beyond earshot.

Baptiste and Colossus, instead of going to the tavern kitchen, passed to the next door, and entered the dark rear corner of a low grocery, where, the law notwithstanding, liquor was covertly sold to slaves. There, in the quiet company of Baptiste and the grocer, the colloquial powers of Colossus, which were simply prodigious, began very soon to show themselves.

"For whilst," said he, "Marse Jimmy has eddication, you know— whilst he has eddication, I has 'scretion. He has eddication and I has 'scretion, and so we gits along."

He drew a black bottle down the counter, and laying half his length on the damp board, continued:

"As a p'inciple I discredits the imbimin of awjus liquors. The imbimin of awjus liquors, the wiolation of the Sabbath, the playin of the fiddle and usin of by-words, they is the four sins of the conscience, and if any man sin the four sins of the conscience, the devil done sharp his fork for that man.—Ain't that so, boss?"

The grocer was sure it was so.

"Nevertheless, mind you"—here the orator brimmed his class from the bottle and swallowed the contents with a dry eye—"mind you, a righteous man, such as ministers of the gospel and their body-servants, can take a leetle for the weak stomach."

But the fascinations of Colossus's eloquence must not mislead us; this is the story of a true Christian: to wit, Parson Jones.

The parson and his new friend ate. But the coffee M. St.-Ange declared he could not touch; it was too wretchedly bad. At the French Market, near by, there was some noble coffee. This, however, would have to be bought, and Parson Jones had scruples.

"You see, Jules, every man has his conscience to guide him, which it does so it—"

"Oh, yes!" cried St.-Ange, "conscience, that is the best, Posson Jone. Certainly! I am a *Catholique*; you is a *schismatique*; you think it is wrong to drink some coffee—well, then, it *is* wrong; you think it is wrong to make the sugar to get the so large price—well, then, it *is* wrong. I think it is right—well, then it *is* right; it is all 'abit, *c'est tout*. What a man think is right *is* right; 'tis all 'abit. A man must not go again his conscience. My faith! do you think I would go again my conscience? *Mais allons*, let us go and get some coffee."

"Jules."

"What?"

"Jules, it ain't the drinkin of coffee but the buyin of it on a Sabbath. You must really excuse me, Jules, it's again conscience, you know."

"Ah!" said St. -Ange, "*c'est* very true. For you it would be a sin, *mais* for me it is only 'abit. Religion is a very strange; I know a man one time, he think it was wrong to go to cockfight Sunday evening. I think it is all 'abit. *Mais*, come, Posson Jone; I have got one friend, Miguel; let us go at his home and get some coffee. Come! Miguel have no familie; only him and Joe—always like to see friend; *allons*, let us come yonder."

"Why, Jules, my dear friend, you know," said the shame-faced parson, "I never visit on Sundays."

"Never what?" asked the astounded Creole.

"No," said Jones, smiling awkwardly.

"Never *visite*?"

"Exceptin sometimes amongst church members," said Parson Jones.

"*Mais*," said the seductive St. -Ange, "Miguel and Joe is church member—certainly! They love to talk about religion. Come at Miguel and talk about some religion. I am nearly expire for me coffee."

"Jules," said the weak giant, "I ought to be in church right now."

"*Mais*, the church is right yonder at Miguel, yes. Ah!" continued St. -Ange as they descended the stairs, "I think every man must have the religion he like the best—me, I like the *Catholique* religion the best—for me it *is* the best. Every man will sure go to heaven if he like his religion the best."

"Jules," said the West Floridian, laying his great hand tenderly upon the Creole's shoulders as they stepped out upon the *banquette*, "do you think you have any sure hopes of heaven?"

"Ye-es!" replied St. -Ange; "I am sure-sure. I think everybody will go to heaven. I think you will go, *et* I think Miguel will go, *et* Joe—everybody, I think, *mais*, hof course, not if they have not been christen. Even I think some nigger will go."

"Jules," said the parson, stopping in his walk—"Jules, I don't want to lose my nigger."

"You'll not loose him. With Baptiste he *cannot* get loose."

But Colossus's master was not reassured.

"Now," said he, still tarrying, "this is just the way. Had I of gone to church—"

"Posson Jone," said Jules.

"What?"

"I tell you. We goin to church."

"Will you?" asked Jones joyfully.

"*Allons*, come along," said Jules, taking his elbow.

They walked down the Rue Chartres, passed several corners, and by and by turned into a cross street. The parson stopped an instant as they were turning, and looked back up the street.

"What you lookin?" asked his companion.

"I thought I saw Colossus," answered the parson with an anxious face. "I reckon twa'n't him, though."

And they went on.

The street they now entered was a very quiet one. The eye of any chance passer-by would have been at once drawn to a broad, heavy, white brick edifice on the lower side of the way, with a flagpole standing out like a bowsprit from one of its great windows, and a pair of lamps hanging before a large closed entrance. It was a theater, honeycombed with gambling dens. At this morning hour all was still, and the only sign of life was a knot of little barefoot girls gathered within its narrow shade, and each carrying an infant relative. Into this place the parson and M. St. -Ange entered, the little nurses jumping up from the sills to let them pass in.

A half hour may have passed. At the end of that time the whole juvenile company were laying alternate eyes and ears to the chinks, to gather what they could of an interesting quarrel going on within.

"I did not, sir! I gave you no cause of offense, sir! Mister Jules simply mistaken the house, thinkin it was a Sabbath school! No such thing, sir! I ain't bound to bet! Yes, I can git out! Yes, without bettin! I have a right to my opinion; I reckon I am a *white man*, sir! No, sir! I on'y said I didn't think you could get the game on them cards. 'S no such thing, sir! I do *not* know how to play! I wouldn't have a rascal's money if I should win it! Shoot, if you dare! you can kill me, but you cain't scare me! No, I shain't bet! I'll die first! Yes, sir; Mr. Jules can bet for me if he admires to; I ain't his master."

Here the speaker seemed to direct his words to St. -Ange.

"Sir, I don't understand you, sir. I never said I'd loan you money to bet for me. I didn't suspicion this from you, sir. No, I won't take any more lemonade; it's the most notorious stuff I every drank, sir:"

M. St. -Ange's replies were in falsetto, and not without effect; for presently the parson's indignation and anger began to melt. "Don't ask me, Jules; I can't help you. It's no use; it's a matter of conscience with me, Jules."

"*Mais oui*! 'tis a matter of conscience with me, the same."

"But, Jules, the money's none of mine, nohow; it belongs to Smyrny, you know."

"If I could make just one bet," said the persuasive St. -Ange, "I would leave this place fast-fast, yes. If I had think—*mais* I did not suspicion this from you, Posson Jone—"

"Don't, Jules, don't!"

"No! Posson Jone—"

"You're bound to win?" said the parson, wavering.

"*Mais certainement!* But it is not to win that I want. 'Tis me conscience—me honor!"

"Well, Jules, I hope I'm not a-doin no wrong. I'll loan you some of this money if you say you'll come right out 'thout takin your winnins."

All was still. The peeping children could see the parson as he lifted his hand to his breast pocket. There it paused a moment in bewilderment, then plunged to the bottom. It came back empty, and fell lifelessly at his side. His head dropped upon his breast, his eyes were for a moment closed, his broad palms were lifted and pressed against his forehead, a tremor seized him, and he fell all in a lump on the floor. The children ran off with their infant loads, leaving Jules St. -Ange swearing by all his deceased relatives, first to Miguel and Joe, and then to the lifted parson, that he did not know what had become of the money, " 'cept if" the black man had got it.

In the rear of ancient New Orleans, beyond the sites of the old rampart, a trio of Spanish forts, where the town has since sprung up and grown old, green with the luxuriance of the wild Creole summer, lay the Congo Plains. Here stretched the canvas of the historic Cayetano, who Sunday after Sunday sowed the sawdust for his circus ring.

But today the great showman had fallen short of his printed promise. The hurricane had come by night, and with one fell swash had made an irretrievable sop of everything. The circus trailed away its bedraggled magnificence, and the ring was cleared for the bull.

Then the sun seemed to come out and work for the people. "See," said the Spaniards, looking up at the sky with its great, white fleets drawn off upon the horizon—"see—heaven smiles upon the bullfight!"

In the high upper seats of the rude amphitheatre sat the gaily decked wives and daughters of the Gascons, from the *métairie* along the Ridge, and the chattering Spanish women of the Market, their shining hair unbonneted to the sun. Next below were their husbands and lovers in Sunday blouses, milkmen, butchers, bakers, black-bearded fishermen, Sicilian fruiterers, swarthy Portuguese sailors, in little woolen caps, and strangers of the graver sort: mariners of England, Germany and Holland. The lowest seats were full of trappers, smugglers, Canadian *voyageurs*, drinking and singing; *Américains*, too—more's the shame—from the upper rivers—who will not keep their seats—who ply the bottle and who will get home by and by and tell how wicked Sodom is; broad-brimmed, silver-braided Mexicans, too, with their copper cheeks and bat's eyes, and their tinkling spurred heels. Yonder, in the quieter section, are the quadroon women in their black lace shawls—and there is Baptiste; and below them are the turbaned black women, and there is—but he vanishes—Colossus.

The afternoon is advancing, yet the sport, though loudly demanded, does not begin. The *Américains* grow derisive and find pastime in gibes and raillery. They mock the various Latins with their national inflections, and answer their scowls with laughter. Some of the more aggressive shout pretty French greetings to the women of Gascony, and one barge-man, amid peals of applause, stands on a seat and hurls a kiss to the quadroons. The mariners of England, Germany and Holland, as specta-tors, like the fun, while the Spaniards look black and cast defiant impre-cations upon their persecutors. Some Gascons, with timely caution, pick their women out and depart, running a terrible fire of gallantries.

In hope of a truce, a new call is raised for the bull: "The bull, the bull!—hush!"

In a tier near the ground a man is standing and calling—standing head and shoulders above the rest—calling in the *Américaine* tongue. Another man, big and red, named Joe, and a handsome little Creole in elegant dress and full of laughter, wish to stop him, but the flat-boatmen, ha-ha-ing and cheering, will not suffer it. Ah, through some shameful knavery of the men into whose hands he has fallen, he is drunk! Even the women can see that; and now he throws his arms wildly and raises his voice until the whole great circle hears it. He is preaching!

Ah! Kind Lord, for a special providence now! The men of his own nation—men from the land of the open English Bible and temperance cup and song—are cheering him on to mad disgrace. And now another call for the appointed sport is drowned by the flat-boatmen singing the ancient tune of Mear. You can hear the words:

"Old Grimes is dead, that good old soul"

—from ribald lips and throats turned brazen with laughter, from singers who toss their hats aloft and roll in their seats; the chorus swells to the accompaniment of a thousand brogans—

"He used to wear an old gray coat
All buttoned down before."

A ribboned man in the arena is trying to be heard, and the Latins raise one mighty cry for silence. The big red man gets a hand over the parson's mouth and the ribboned man seizes his moment.

"They have been endeavoring for hours," he says, "to draw the terrible animals from their dens, but such is their strength and fierceness that—"

His voice is drowned. Enough has been heard to warrant the inference that the beasts cannot be whipped out of the storm-drenched cages to which menagerie life and long starvation have attached them, and from the roar of indignation the man of ribbons flees. The noise increases. Men are standing up by hundreds, and women are imploring to be let out of the turmoil. All at once, like the bursting of a dam, the whole mass pours down into the ring. They sweep across the arena and over the showman's barriers. Miguel gets a frightful trampling. Who cares for gates or doors? They tear the beasts' houses bar from bar, and, laying hold of the gaunt buffalo, drag him forth by feet, ears, and tail; and in the midst of the *mêlée*, still head and shoulders above all, wilder, with the cup of the wicked, than any beast, is the man of God from the Florida parishes!

In his arms he bore—and all the people shouted at once when they saw it—the tiger. He had lifted it high up with its back to his breast, his arms clasped under its shoulders; the wretched brute had curled up caterpillar-wise, with its long tail against its belly, and through its filed teeth grinned a fixed and impotent wrath. And Parson Jones was shouting:

"The tiger and the buffler *shall* lay down together! You dare to say they shain't, and I'll comb you with this varmint from head to foot! The tiger and the buffler *shall* lay down together! They shall! Now, you, Joe! behold! I am here to see it done. The lion and the buffler *shall* lay down together!"

Mouthing these words again and again, the parson forced his way through the surge in the wake of the buffalo. This creature the Latins had secured by a lariat over its head, and were dragging across the old rampart and into a street of the city.

The northern races were trying to prevent, and there was pommeling and knocking down, cursing and knife-drawing, until Jules St. -Ange was quite carried away with the fun, laughed, clapped his hands, and swore with delight, and ever kept close to the gallant parson.

Joe, contrariwise, counted all this child's play and interruption. He had come to find Colossus and the money. In an unholy moment he made bold to lay hold of the parson, but a piece of the broken barriers in the hands of a flat-boatmen felled him to the sod, the terrible crowd swept over him, the lariat was cut, and the giant parson hurled the tiger upon the buffalo's back. In another instant both brutes were dead at the hands of the mob; Jones was lifted from his feet, and prating of Scripture and the millennium, of Paul at Ephesus and Daniel in the "buffler's" den, was borne aloft upon the shoulders of the huzzaing *Américains*. Half an hour later he was sleeping heavily on the floor of a cell in the *calaboza*.

When Parson Jones awoke, a bell was somewhere tolling for midnight. Somebody was at the door of his cell with a key. The lock grated, the door swung, the turnkey looked in and stepped back, and a ray of moonlight fell upon M. Jules St. -Ange. The prisoner sat upon the empty shackles and ring-bolt in the center of the floor.

"Misty Posson Jone," said the visitor, softly.

"O Jules!"

"*Mais*, what the matter, Posson Jone?"

"My sins, Jules, my sins!"

"Ah! Posson Jone, is that something to cry, because a man get sometime a litt' bit intoxicate? *Mais*, if a man keep *all the time* intoxicate, I think that is again the conscience."

"Jules, Jules, your eyes is darkened—oh! Jules, where's my poor old nigger?"

"Posson Jone, never mind; he is with Baptiste."

"Where?"

"I don't know where—*mais*, he is with Baptiste. Baptiste is a beautiful to take care of somebody."

"Is he as good as you, Jules?" asked Parson Jones, sincerely.

Jules was slightly staggered.

"You know, Posson Jone, you know, a nigger cannot be good as a white man—*mais* Baptiste is a good nigger."

The parson moaned and clapped his chin into his hands.

"I was to've left for home tomorrow, sunup, on the *Isabella* schooner. Poor Smyrny!" He deeply sighed.

"Posson Jone," said Jules, leaning against the wall and smiling, "I swear you is the most funny man I ever see. If I was you I would say, me, 'Ah! 'ow I am lucky! the money I lost, it was not mine anyhow!' My faith, shall a man make hisse'f to be the more sorry because the money he lost is not his? Me, I would say, 'It is a specious providence.'

"Ah! Misty Posson Jone," he continued, "you make a so droll sermon at the bull ring. Ha, ha! I swear I think you can make money to preach that sermon many time at the theatre St. Philippe. Hah! you is the most brave that I never see, *mais* at the same time the most religious man. Where I'm goin to find one priest to make like that? *Mais*, why can't you cheer up and be 'appy? Me, if I should be miserable like that I would kill mesel."

The countryman only shook his head.

"*Bien*, Posson Jone, I have the so good news for you."

The prisoner looked up with eager inquiry.

"Last evening when they lock you, I come right off at M. Deblanc's house to get you let out of the calaboose. M. DeBlanc he is the judge. So soon I was entering—'Ah! Jules, me boy, just the man to make complete the game!' Posson Jone, it was a specious providence! I win in t'ree hours more than six hundred dollar! Look!" He produced a mass of banknotes, *bons* and due bills.

"And you got the pass?" asked the parson, regarding the money with a sadness incomprehensible to Jules.

"It is here; it takes the effect so soon the daylight."

"Jules, my friend, your kindness is in vain."

The Creole's face became a perfect blank.

"Because," said the parson, "for two reasons: firstly, I have broken the laws, and ought to stand the penalty; and secondly—you must really excuse me, Jules, you know, but the pass has been got unfairly, I'm afeared. You told the judge I was innocent, and in neither case it don't become a Christian (which I hope I can still say I am one) to 'do evil that good may come.' I must stay."

M. St. -Ange stood up aghast, and for a moment speechless, at this exhibition of moral heroism; but an artifice was presently hit upon. "*Mais*, Posson Jone!"—in his old falsetto—"the order—you cannot read it, it is in French—compel you to go hout, sir!"

"Is that so?" cried the parson, bounding up with radiant face—"is that so, Jules?"

The young man nodded, smiling; but though he smiled, the fountain of his tenderness was opened. He made the sign of the cross as the parson knelt in prayer, and even whispered "Hail, Mary," etc., quite through, twice over.

Morning broke in summer glory upon a cluster of villas behind the city, nestled under live oaks and magnolias on the banks of a deep bayou, and known as Suburb St. -Jean.

With the first beam came the West Floridian and the Creole out upon the bank below the village. Upon the parson's arm hung a pair of antique saddlebags. Baptiste limped wearily behind; both his eyes were encircled with broad, blue rings, and one cheekbone bore the official impress of every knuckle of Colossus's left hand. The "beautiful to take care of somebody" had lost his charge. At mention of the Negro he became wild, and, half in English, half in the gumbo dialect, said murderous things. Intimidated by Jules to coolness, he became confident on one point: he could, would and did swear that Colossus had gone home to the Florida parishes: he was almost certain; he thought so.

There was a clicking of pulleys as the three appeared upon the bayou's margin, and Baptiste pointed out, in the deep shadow of a great oak, the *Isabella*, moored among the bulrushes, and just spreading her sails for departure. Moving down to where she lay, the parson and his friend paused on the bank, loath to say farewell.

"O Jules!" said the parson, "suppose Colossus ain't gone home! O Jules, if you'll look him out for me, I'll never forget you—I'll never forget you, nohow, Jules. No, Jules, I never will believe he taken that money. Yes, I know all niggers will steal"—he set foot upon the gangplank—"but Colossus wouldn't steal from me. Good-bye!"

"Misty Posson Jone," said St. -Ange, putting his hand on the parson's arm with genuine affection, "hold on. You see this money—what I win last night? Well, I win it by a specious providence, ain't it?"

"There's no tellin," said the humbled Jones. "Providence

'Moves in a mysterious way
His wonders to perform.' "

"Ah!" cried the Creole, "*c'est* very true. I get this money in the mysterious way. *Mais*, if I keep this money, you know where it goin tonight?"

"I really can't say," replied the parson.

"Goin to the dev'," said the sweetly smiling young man.

The schooner captain, leaning against the shrouds, and even Baptiste, laughed outright.

"O Jules, you mustn't!"

"Well, then, what shall I do with *it*?"

"Anything!" answered the parson. "Better donate it to some poor man—"

"Ah! Misty Posson Jone, that is what I want. You lost five hundred dollar—'twas me fault."

"No, it wa'n't, Jules."

"*Mais*, it was!"

"No!"

"It was me fault! I *swear* it was me fault! *Mais*, here is five hundred dollar; I wish you shall take it. Here, I don't got no use for money—O, my faith! Posson Jone, you must not begin to cry some more."

Parson Jones was choked with tears. When he found voice, he said:

"O Jules, Jules, Jules! my poor, noble, dear, misguidened friend! if you had've had a Christian raisin! May the Lord show you your errors, better than I can, and bless you for your good intentions—oh, no! I cain't touch that money with a ten-foot pole; it wa'n't rightly got; you must really excuse me, my dear friend, but I cain't touch it."

St. -Ange was petrified.

"Good-bye, dear Jules," continued the parson. "I'm in the Lord's hands, and He's very merciful, which I hope and trust you'll find it out. Good-bye!"—the schooner swung slowly off before the breeze—"Good-bye!"

St. -Ange raised himself.

"Posson Jone! make me anyhow *this* promise: you never, never, *never* will come back to New Orleans."

"Ah, Jules, the Lord willin, I'll never leave home again!"

"All right!" said the Creole. "I think He's willin. Adieu, Posson Jone. My faith! you are the so fighting and most religious man as I never saw. Adieu! Adieu!"

Baptiste uttered a cry and presently ran by his master toward the schooner, his hands full of clods.

St. -Ange looked just in time to see the sable form of Colossus of Rhodes emerge from the vessel's hold, and the pastor of Smyrna and Bethesda seize him in his embrace.

"O Colossus!" you outlandish old nigger! Thank the Lord! Thank the Lord!"

The little Creole almost wept. He ran down the towpath, laughing and swearing, and making confused allusion to the entire personnel and furniture of the lower regions.

By odd fortune, at the moment that St. -Ange further demonstrated his delight by tripping his mulatto into a bog, the schooner came brushing along the reedy bank with a graceful curve; the sails flapped, and the crew fell to poling her slowly along.

Parson Jones was on the deck, kneeling once more in prayer. His hat had fallen before him; behind him knelt his slave. In thundering tones he was confessing himself "a plum fool" from whom "the conceit had been jolted out," and who had been made to see that even "his nigger had the longest head of the two."

Colossus clasped his hands and groaned.

The parson prayed for a contrite heart.

"Oh, yes!" cried Colossus.

The master acknowledged countless mercies.

"That's so!" cried the slave.

The master prayed that they might still be "piled on."

"Glory!" cried the black man, clapping his hands. "Pile on!"

"And now," continued the parson, "bring this poor, backslidin jackass of a parson and this poor old fool nigger back to their home in peace!"

"Pray for the money!" called Colossus.

But the parson prayed for Jules.

"Pray for the *money*!" repeated the Negro.

"And oh, give thy servant back that there lost money!"

Colossus rose stealthily, and tiptoed by his still shouting master. St. -Ange, the captain, the crew, gazed in silent wonder at the strategist. Pausing but an instant over the master's hat to grin an acknowledgment of his beholders' speechless interest, he softly placed in it the faithfully-mourned and honestly-prayed-for Smyrna fund; then, saluted by the gesticulated, silent applause of St. -Ange and the schoonermen, he resumed his first attitude behind his roaring master.

"Amen!" cried Colossus, meaning to bring him to a close.

"Unworthy though I be—" cried Jones.

"*Amen*!" reiterated the Negro.

"A-a-men!" said Parson Jones.

He rose to his feet, and, stooping to take up his hat, beheld the well-known roll. As one stunned, he gazed for a moment upon his slave, who still knelt with clasped hands and rolling eyeballs; but when he became aware of the laughter and cheers that greeted him from both deck and shore, he lifted hands and eyes to heaven and cried like the veriest babe. And when he looked at the roll again and hugged and kissed it, St. -Ange tried to raise a second shout, but choked, and the crew fell to their poles.

And now up runs Baptiste, covered with slime, and prepares to cast his projectiles. The first one fell wide of the mark; the schooner swung round into a long reach of water, where the breeze was in her favor; another shout of laughter drowned the malediction of the muddy man; the sails filled; Colossus of Rhodes, smiling and bowing as hero of the moment, ducked as the main boom swept round, and the schooner, leaning slightly to the pleasant influence, rustled a moment over the bulrushes, and then sped far away down the rippling bayou.

M. Jules St. -Ange stood long, gazing at the receding vessel as it now disappeared, now reappeared beyond the tops of the high undergrowth; but when an arm of the forest hid it finally from sight, he turned townward, followed by that fagged-out spaniel, his servant, saying, as he turned, "Baptiste."

"*Miché?*"

"You know what I goin to do with this money?"

"*Non, m'sieur.*"

"Well, you can strike me dead, if I don't goin to pay hall my debts! *Allons!*"

He began a merry little song to the effect that his sweetheart was a wine bottle, and master and man, leaving care behind, returned to the picturesque Rue Royale. The ways of Providence are indeed strange. In all Parson Jones's after life, amid the many painful reminiscences of his visit to the City of Light, the sweet knowledge was withheld from him that by the light of the Christian virtue that shone from him even in his great fall, Jules St. -Ange arose, and went to his father, an honest man.

Joel Chandler Harris

(1848-1908)

*W*hen Uncle Remus: His Songs and Sayings *was published in 1880, Joel Chandler Harris was immediately hailed as a fine portrayer of Uncle Remus and a master reteller of blacks' folktales.* The characterization of old Uncle Remus is achieved in Cable's third-person accounts of the storytelling sessions with a boyish listener: *these catch the slave's physical aspects, his gestures, and details about his biography. Uncle Remus's monologues in dialect add insights into his ways of thinking and looking at things. The poetic speech—rhythmic, vivid, and imaginative—also makes him known.*

In addition, the stories reveal the qualities of the people who localized, enriched, and preserved them. Their world, of course, is a fantasy world in which the hero, as Harris says, is "the weakest and most harmless of all animals," *and yet that hero, Br' Rabbit, is* "victorious in contests with the bear, the wolf, and the fox. It is not virtue that triumphs, but helplessness; it is not malice, but mischievousness." *As John Herbert Nelson says in* The Negro Character in American Literature, *the anthropomorphosis that the animal characters undergo is very illuminating.*

The ideals of the animals are the Negro's; their prying dispositions, their neighborliness, their company manners, their petty thefts, their amusements. . . . Brer Rabbit likes the same kind of food, the same brand of fun, as his interpreter does; he has the same outlook on life. Even the hopeless incongruity of this animal world— the rabbit and the fox owning cows, and hurting their "hands," and feeling an elementary kind of responsibility for their families—is part and parcel of the Negro spirit. It is a product of his outlook on life, of a poetical feeling that takes no account of the hard logic of consistency.

So the animals "had their camp-meetin times and their barbecues when the weather was agreeable" and Br' Rabbit, leaving Miss Meadows and the girls after a social call, "paid 'em his 'specks and tip his beaver, and march off, he did, just as stiff and as stuck up as a fire-stick."

The Wonderful Tar-Baby Story," the best known of the narratives, was preceded in the 1880 collection by "Uncle Remus Initiates the Little Boy." This story introduces the aged storyteller in his cabin, with the seven-year-old son of a Georgia plantation family as his audience: "His head rested against the old man's arm, and he was gazing with an expression of the most intense interest into the rough, weather-beaten face that beamed so kindly upon him." After Br' Fox had been doing his best to catch Br' Rabbit, and Br' Rabbit had been doing all he could to keep him from it, in this story, the former makes two more attempts. The first fails when the little Rabbits, playing in the family's backyard, see Mr. Fox a-coming, warn their parents, and hide with them in the house. The second fails when Br' Rabbit refuses to join Br' Fox at his house for dinner.

The Wonderful Tar-Baby Story

Uncle Remus

Mark Twain's Library of Humor, (p. 131).

"Didn't the fox *never* catch the rabbit, Uncle Remus?" asked the little boy the next evening.

"He come mighty nigh it, honey, sure's you born—Br' Fox did. One day a'ter Br' Rabbit fool him with that calamus root, Br' Fox went to work and got him some tar, and mix it with some turkentime, and fix up a contraption what he call a Tar-Baby, and he tuck this-here Tar-Baby and he sot her in the big road, and then he lay off in the bushes for to see what the news was gwine to be.

"And he didn't have to wait long, nother, cause by and by here come Br' Rabbit pacin down the road—lippity-clippity, clippity-lippity—just as sassy as a jaybird. Br' Fox, he lay low. Br' Rabbit come prancin 'long till he spy the Tar-Baby; and then he fotch up on his behind legs like he was 'stonished. The Tar-Baby, she sot there, she did, and Br' Fox, he lay low.

"'Mornin!' says Br' Rabbit, says he. 'Nice weather this mornin,' says he.

199

"Tar-Baby ain't sayin nothin; and Br' Fox, he lay low.

" 'How does symptoms seem to segashuate?' says Br' Rabbit, says he.

"Br' Fox, he wink his eye slow, and lay low, and the Tar-Baby, she ain't sayin nothin.

" 'How you come on, then? Is you deaf?' says Br' Rabbit. 'Cause if you is I can holler louder,' says he.

"Tar-Baby stay still; and Br' Fox, he lay low.

" 'You're stuck up, that's what you is,' says Br' Rabbit, says he. 'And I'm gwine to cure you, that's what I'm a-gwine to do,' says he.

"Br' Fox, he sort of chuckle in his stomach, he did, but Tar-Baby ain't sayin nothin.

" 'I'm gwine to larn you how to talk to 'spectable folks if hits the last act,' say Br' Rabbit, says he. 'If you don't take off that hat and tell me howdy, I'm gwine to bust you wide open.'

"Tar-Baby stay still, and Br' Fox, he lay low.

"Br' Rabbit keep on axin him; and the Tar-Baby she keep on sayin nothin, till present'y Br' Rabbit draw back with his fist, he did, and blip! he tuck her side of the head. Right there's where he broke his molasses jug. His fist stuck, and he can't pull loose. The tar hilt him. But Tar-Baby, she ain't sayin nothin; and Br' Fox, he lay low.

" 'Turn me loose, 'fore I kick the nat'al stuffin out'n you,' says Br' Rabbit, says he.

"But the Tar-Baby, she ain't sayin nothin. She just hilt on, and then Br' Rabbit lose the use of his feet in the same way. Then Br' Rabbit squall out that if the Tar-Baby don't turn him loose, he butt her cranksided. And then he butted, and his head got stuck. Then Br' Fox, he sa'ntered forth, lookin just as innocent as one of your mammy's mockin birds.

" 'Howdy, Br' Rabbit,' says Br' Fox, says he. 'You look sorta stuck up this mornin,' says he. And then he rolled on the ground and laughed and laughed till he couldn't laugh no more. 'I 'speck you'll take dinner with me this time, Br' Rabbit. I done laid in some calamus root, and I ain't gwine to take no 'skuse,' says Br' Fox, says he."

Here Uncle Remus paused, and drew a two-pound yam out of the ashes.

"Did the Fox eat the rabbit?" asked the little boy to whom the tale had been told.

"That's all the fur' the tale goes," replied the old man. "He mout, and then agin he moutn't. Some say Judge Bear come 'long and loosed him; some say he didn't. I hear Miss Sally callin. You better run 'long."

How Mr. Rabbit Was Too Sharp for Mr. Fox

"Uncle Remus," said the little boy one evening, when he had found the old man with little or nothing to do, "did the fox kill and eat the rabbit when he caught him with the Tar-Baby?"

"Law, honey, ain't I tell you 'bout that?" replied the old darky, chuckling slyly. "I 'clare to gracious I oughta told you that. But Old Man Nod was ridin on my eyelids till a little more and I'd've dis'membered my own name. And then onto that, here come your mammy hollerin a'ter you.

"What I tell you when I first begin? I told you Br' Rabbit was a monst'ous soon beast. Leastways, that's what I laid out for to tell you. Well, then, honey, don't you go and make no other calculations, cause in them days Br' Rabbit and his family was at the head of the gang when any racket was on hand, and there he stayed. 'Fore you begins for to wipe your eyes 'bout Br' Rabbit, you wait and see where 'bouts Br' Rabbit gwine to fetch up at. But that's neither here nor there.

"When Br' Fox find Br' Rabbit mixed up with the Tar-Baby, he feel mighty good, and he roll on the ground and laugh. By-and-by he up and say, says he:

"'Well, I 'spect I got you this time, Br' Rabbit,' says he. 'Maybe I ain't, but I 'spect I is. You been runnin round here sassin a'ter me a mighty long time, but I 'spect you done come to the end of the row. You been cuttin up your capers and boundin round in the neighborhood until you come to b'lieve yourself the boss of the whole gang. And then you're alluz some'eres where you got no business,' says Br' Fox, says he.

"'Who ax you for to come and strike up a 'quaintance with this-here Tar-Baby? And who stuck you up there where you is? Nobody in the round world. You just tuck and jam yourself on that Tar-Baby without waitin for any invite,' says he. 'And there you is, and there you'll stay till I fixes up a brush-pile and fires her up, cause I'm gwine to barbecue you this day, sure,' says Br' Fox, says he.

"Then Br' Rabbit talk mighty humble.

"'I don't care what you do with me, says he, 'so you don't fling me in that brier patch. "Roast me,' says he, 'but don't fling me in that brier patch,' says he.

"'Hit's so much trouble for to kindle a fire,' says Br' Fox, says he, 'that I 'spect I'll ha' to hang you,' says he.

"'Hang me just as high as you please, Br' Fox,' says he, 'but do for the Lord's sake don't fling me in that brier patch,' says he.

"'I ain't got no string,' says Br' Fox, says he. 'And now I 'spect I'll ha' to drown you,' says he.

"'Drown me as deep as you please, Br' Fox,' says Br' Rabbit, says he. 'But don't fling me in that brier patch,' says he.

"'They ain't no water nigh,' says Br' Fox, says he. 'And now I 'spect I'll ha' to skin you,' says he.

"'Skin me, Br' Fox,' says Br' Rabbit, says he. 'Snatch out my eyeballs, tear out my years by the roots, and cut off my legs,' says he. 'But do, please, Br' Fox, don't fling me in that brier patch,' says he.

"Course Br' Fox want to hurt Br' Rabbit as bad as he can. So he cotch him by the behind legs and slung him right in the middle of the brier patch. There was a considerable flutter where Br' Rabbit struck the bushes, and Br' Fox sorta hung around for to see what was gwine to happen. By and by he hear somebody call him, and way up the hill he see Br' Rabbit settin cross-legged on a chinquapin log, combin the pitch out'n his hair with a chip. Then Br' Fox know that he been swap off mighty bad. Br' Rabbit was bleedzed for to fling back some of his sass, and he holler out:

"'Bred and born in a brier patch, Br' Fox—bred and born in a brier patch!' and with that he skip out just as lively as a cricket in the embers."

F. Hopkinson Smith

(1838-1915)

*F*rancis Hopkinson Smith became a writer, full-time at any rate, late in life. Born in Baltimore, he became a resident of New York, where, as a friend put it, he was "a well known water color artist, civil engineer, architect, designer of railway bridges," and "jack-of-all-trades" before he made literature his chief interest. In addition to travel books (which he himself illustrated), he wrote a number of local color stories, the best known dealing with Colonel Carter, a proud old-time Virginian who, after a decline in his fortunes, was expatriated to New York City.

"Ginger and the Goose" was a story that he heard in Virginia and often retold orally before he wrote it out in 1882 and published it in Harper's New Monthly Magazine.

Unbeknownst to Smith, versions of this story had surfaced over the years in at least nine countries in many parts of the world. One version is in Boccaccio's Decameron, "Chichibio, Currado Gianfigliazzi's Cook, Turns His Master's Wrath to Laughter by a Ready Excuse, and Avoids the Punishment in Store for Him." Contrasts between Smith's version and Boccaccio's show that the nineteenth-century American local color story differed in interesting ways from the fourteenth-century Italian telling. Ginger, the American narrator, is much more of an individual than the Italian narrator. His account fully reveals a way of life and complex—and amusing—characters and family relationships that have no counterparts in Neifile's telling in the Decameron. Tastes, of course, differ; but, for these reasons, most Americans are likely to agree with Mark Twain's claim that Smith's version is much better than Boccaccio's.

Ginger and the Goose

Well, I didn't b'long to the last generation, and now I comes to think of it, I didn't b'long to any generation at all, for the war fixed that when I was three year old, and this here only happened lately wise.

You see, Old Miss was mighty sot in her ways, and when Marse Ned marry, his wife she was mighty sot in her ways. And so old Miss kinda drew in, and the young people didn't have the nicest sort of a time. It war pretty dull in the old house, and after a while the old gentleman he say as how he and old Miss would take a little turn to the island, being as how it were springtime, and the eggs at the freshest, and there was a heap of talk, 'cep' from the old gentleman. He war naturally kind of still, but when he make up he mind to do a thing, why you could have bet at once that it were done.

When it war all settled, old Miss call in Aunt Daphne, and they two war closeted in a long time. For, you see, Aunt Daphne come into the family with the first marriage, and she war certainly on old Miss side all the time, whether in peace or war. But whatever they settle between them, no one have any idey of till the time come.

Well, the old lady been hardly turn the corner of the street when Marse Ned wife—Miss Carrie, that is—sweep dowm 'pon those lock closet that she never before have git her eye in. I ain't see it myself, but I hear Aunt Daphne a-talking all round the kitchen consarning it, only there war only the dressers and the pots to hear her. But Lor' Miss Carrie she didn't care nothing 'bout Aunt Daphne's grumblin. In half a day she had all them chiney things that the old man's pa brung from the outside Indies range 'long the room, and all the glass and all the silver and everything that had been store away for nigh fifty year. She have them all spread out, sure's you live, and then she have them wash and clean and rub. I didn't feel good in my mind, either, and when I come 'cross Aunt Daphne with her check apron over her head, a-rushin backards and forrards in the stable yard, and a-prayin again the wrath that war a-comin', I thought I would speak to Marse Ned.

Well, I was mercifully save that, for the next day Marse Ned he send for me, and he say, "Ginger," he say. "Miss Carrie thinks she would like to give a dinner party, and I would like it too, for she have had a very quiet time since she marry me."

And I say, "Yess, Marse Ned, that so!"

And he dig him cane in the gravel where we war a-standin, and he say, sort of shame like, "Aunt Daphne, she thinks your old Miss mightn't want that dinner."

And I say, "In course Aunt Daphne must have her oar in, but that don't 'mount to a row of pins."

And then he poke he cane down deeper, and he says, "But Aunt Daphne say she won't cook that dinner. Ginger," he go on, "don't you think you could cook that dinner for Miss Carrie?"

I say, "Marse Ned, I is ready and willing to help you and Miss Carrie any ways I can." And then come the day, and Miss Carrie she say I must take my market basket and go with Marse Ned and must make him buy everything good that I see.

And directly we come to a big fat goose, and I turn Marse Ned's 'tention that way, and he say, "Ginger, that goose is never goin' in the market basket. Is he a good goose?"

And I say, "Marse Ned, if he can't go in the market basket, he can string round my neck. And as for goodness, he be young and fat and thick." And so we buy him.

When the day come for the dinner, sure 'nough, Aunt Daphne gone off to a funeral, and I have the kitchen all to myself. The dinner table was that loaden with chiney and glass and silver that, have old Miss been dead in her coffin, she would have turn. And then the grass and the flowers war a show.

After I see that all war right, I gone back to the kitchen and send up the dinner to the white people, all but the goose. For the goose war the last course.

Well, he war a pictur when I tuck him out'n the roaster. He war fat and he war round, and he war a splendid brown, and he war a-settin on the kitchen table, ready to go up, when Dolly she come in.

Now Dolly, you know, is the gal I love, and when she come in the kitchen she hold up her nose, and she say, with a long sniff: "He-e-e-e, what that smell so good?"

And I say, "G'long, gal—g'long. What make you so triflin? What you got to do with that smell?"

And she say, "Ginger, that be the nicest smell I ever have had. What is that?"

And I say, "G'long, gal, what you got to do with the white folks' goose."

And Dolly come close to me and look over my shoulder, and she say, "That is a splendid goose. Oh, Ginger, but that goose smell nice."

And I say, "You get 'way from that goose. You see, while you has been a-fooling here, the goose have got cold."

And Dolly say, "That don't count. You just put him in the oven for a minute and hot him again."

And so I did, but that gal kept a-triflin till, when I take him out, why he foot war that burnt that I didn't dare to dish him up.

Then Dolly she come in with her tongue, after makin all the mischief, and she say, "You just make a rich gravy and turn the goose on that side, and pour the gravy all over him, and sure's you live, Marse Ned he'll never miss that foot."

Well, I did just do that thing, and Dolly in course she eat the burn foot. And I bein a kind of uneasy in my mind, I slip on my best coat and take up the goose myself.

Now it all might have been right, 'ceppin that Miss Carrie have asked little Miss Susan, who was her bridesmaid, and the dinner, I has since hearn, was given to she and her sweetheart, Marse William Gibbons. So in course whatever Miss Susan eat, why Marse William he must have the same. So Marse Ned he say, "Well, Susan, what part of the goose will you have?"

And she say, "The leg, if you please."

And then he ask, "And what part will you have, William?" And in course he must have the other leg.

When he say that, the sweat fairly pour down my back, and Marse Ned he turn the goose over, and he give me one look, and that fairly send me clean out of that room. And how that dinner was got through, I couldn't tell to my dying day.

Well, the sun was a-settin before the company done gone. And I was a-standin in the barnyard when Marse Ned come a-whistlin 'long.

"Ginger," he say; but I just pretend that I didn't hear. "Ginger," he call again, and he come right up. "I wouldn't a-believed," he say, "that a 'spectable man like you would have done such a low-down trick."

"Why, what's that, Marse Ned?" I says, 'stonished like.

"I'd like to know," he say, "where that other leg of the goose have gone." And he look straight in my face.

Now it war time that our gooses war a-restin, and I look round and see them all a-standin on their one leg. And so I take Marse Ned by the arm, and I p'int to them all.

"What's you a-meanin, Marse Ned?" I say. "Does you see any of them geeses with more'n one leg that you 'cuse me of such a thing?"

And Marse Ned he just raise up he hand, and he holler, "Shoo shoo!" And then in course the gooses put down the other leg, and they all run.

And then I turn right round at Marse Ned, and I say solemnlike, and I say him loud and say him strong and look him straight in the whites of his eyes—I say, "Marse Ned, when you see that goose on the table in front of you with but one leg, afore the company, did you 'member to say 'shoo!' to that goose? I just ask you that!" And Marse Ned never have one word to say.

Mary E. Wilkins Freeman

(1852-1930)

*U*nlike a number of local colorists who wrote about sections of the country after brief acquaintances with them, Mary E. Wilkins Freeman based her fictions about an area—New England—on a long residence. She was born in Randolph, Massachusetts, not far from Boston, was reared in Vermont, and was educated for a year at Mount Holyoke College. Only after her marriage—to Dr. Charles M. Freeman—in 1902, after she had published her best fictional works, did she leave the area about which she had been writing and move to Metuchen, New Jersey. Her finest creations were included in two collections of short stories, A Humble Romance *(1887)* and A New England Nun and Other Stories *(1891)*. "Gentian" was included in the earlier volume.

The flintiest of the New England local colorists, Mrs. Freeman used a laconic style traditionally associated with Yankees in both her narrative passages and quoted speeches. The style is appropriate for the frugal, pious, repressed, but often quietly comic men and women whose stories are told. Even the rebellions of the women folk are undemonstrative, though rather effective. In "The Revolt of Mother," for instance, Sarah Penn, after forty submissive years of marriage, quietly moves into a newly built barn raised in place of the new house she has wanted. "'We've got jest as good a right to live here as new horses and cows,' she says." He gives in: "'Why mother,' he said, hoarsely, 'I hadn't no idea you was so set on it as all this comes to.'" Similarly, in "Gentian," Lucy Tollet in the end triumphs in a battle of wills with her husband. In both subtly comic stories, Freeman is, it seems, a kind of a primordial feminist.

208

Gentian

It had been raining hard all night; when the morning dawned clear, everything looked vivid and unnatural. The wet leaves on the trees and hedges seemed to emit a real green light of their own; the tree trunks were black and dark, and the spots of moss on them stood out distinctly.

A tall old woman was coming quickly up the street. She had on a stiffly starched calico gown, which sprang and rattled as she walked. She kept smoothing it anxiously. "Gittin every mite of the stiff'nin out," she murmured to herself.

She stopped at a long cottage house, whose unpainted walls, with white window-facings and wide sweep of shingled roof, looked dark and startling through being sodden with rain.

There was a low stone wall by way of fence, with a gap in it for a gate.

She had just passed through this gap when the house door opened, and a woman put out her head.

"Is that you, Hannah?" she said.

"Yes, it's me." She laid a hard emphasis on the last word; then she sighed heavily.

"Hadn't you better hold your dress up comin through that wet grass, Hannah? You'll git it all bedraggled."

"I know it. I'm a-gittin every mite of the stiffnin out on't. I worked half the forenoon ironin on't yesterday, too. Well, I thought I'd got to git over here and fetch a few of these fried cakes. I thought maybe Alfred would relish 'em for his breakfast; and he'd got to have 'em while they was hot; they ain't good for nothin cold; and I didn't have a soul to send—never do. How is Alfred this mornin, Lucy?"

"'Bout the same, I guess."

"Ain't had the doctor yit?"

"No." She had a little, patient, pleasant smile on her face, looking up at her questioner.

The women were sisters. Hannah was Hannah Orton, unmarried. Lucy was Mrs. Tollet. Alfred was her sick husband. Hannah's long, sallow face was deeply wrinkled. Her wide mouth twisted emphatically as she talked.

"Well, I know one thing. If he was my husband he'd *have* a doctor."

Mrs. Tollet's voice was old, but there was a childish tone in it, a sweet uncertain pipe.

"No, you couldn't make him, Hannah; you couldn't, more 'n me. Alfred was alluz just so. He ain't never thought nothin of doctors, nor doctors' stuff."

"Well, I'd make him take somethin. In my opinion he needs somethin bitter." She screwed her mouth as if the bitter morsel were on her own tongue.

"Lor'! he wouldn't take it, you know, Hannah."

"He'd have to. Gentian would be good for him."

"He wouldn't touch it."

"I'd make him, if I put it in his tea unbeknownst to him."

"Oh, I wouldn't dare to."

"Land, I guess, I'd dare to. If folks don't know enough to take what's good for 'em, they'd oughta be made to, by hook or crook. I don't believe in deceivin generally, but I don't believe the Lord would have let folks have the faculty for deceivin in 'em if it wa'n't to be used for good sometimes. It's my opinion Alfred won't last long if he don't have somethin pretty soon to strengthen him up and give him a start. Well, ain't no use talkin. I've got to git home and put this dress in the wash tub agin, I s'pose. I never see such a sight—just look at that! You'd better give Alfred those cakes before they git cold."

"I shouldn't wonder if he relished 'em. You was real good to think of it, Hannah."

"Well, I'm a-goin. Every mite of the stiff'nin's out. Sometimes it seems as if there weren't no end to the work. I didn't know how to git out this mornin, anyway."

When Mrs. Tollet entered the house, she found her husband in a wooden rocking chair with a calico cushion, by the kitchen window. He was a short, large-framed old man, but he was very thin. There were great hollows in his yellow cheeks.

"What you got there, Lucy?"

"Some griddle cakes Hannah brought."

"Griddle cakes!"

"They're real nice-lookin ones. Don't you think you'd relish one or two, Alfred?"

"If you and Hannah want griddle cakes, you can have griddle cakes."

"Then you don't want to have one, with some maple molasses on it? They've kept hot; she had 'em covered up."

"Take 'em away!"

She set them meekly on the pantry shelf. Then she came back and stood before her husband, gentle deprecation in her soft old face and in the whole poise of her little slender body.

"What *will* you have for breakfast, Alfred?"

"I don't know. Well, you might as well fry a little slice of bacon and git a cup of tea."

"Ain't you most afeared of—bacon, Alfred?"

"No, I ain't. If anybody's sick, they can tell what they want themselves 'bout as well's anybody can tell 'em. They don't have any hankerin a'ter anythin unless it's good for 'em. When they need anythin, natur gives 'em a longin a'ter it. I wish you'd hurry up and cook that bacon, Lucy. I'm awful faint at my stomach."

She cooked the bacon and made the tea with no more words. Indeed, it was seldom that she used as many as she used now. Alfred Tollet, ever since she had married him had been the sole autocrat of all her little Russias; her very thoughts had followed after him, like sheep.

After breakfast she went about putting her house in order for the day. When that was done, and she was ready to sit down with her sewing, she found that her husband had fallen asleep in his chair. She stood over him a minute, looking at his pale old face with the sincerest love and reverence. Then she sat down by the window and sewed, but not long. She got her bonnet and shawl stealthily, and stole out of the house. She sped quickly down the village street. She was light-footed for an old woman. She slackened her pace when she reached the village store, and crept hesitatingly into the great lumbering rank-smelling room, with its dark, newly sprinkled floor. She bought a bar of soap; then she stood irresolute.

"Anything else this mornin, Mis' Tollet?" The proprietor himself, a narrow-shouldered irritable man, was waiting on her. His tone was impatient. Mrs. Tollet was too absorbed to notice it. She stood hesitating.

"Is there anything else you want?"

"Well—I don't know; but—perhaps I'd better have—ten cents' worth of gentian." Her very lips were white; she had an expression of frightened, guilty resolution. If she had asked for strychnine, with a view to her own bodily destruction, she would not have had a different look.

The man mistook it, and his conscience smote him. He thought his manner had frightened her, but she had never noticed it.

"Goin to give your husband some bitters?" he asked, affably, as he handed her the package.

She started and blushed. "No—I—thought some would be good for me."

"Well, gentian is a first-rate bitter. Good mornin, Mis' Tollet."

She was trembling all over when she rached the house door. There is a subtle, early raised wind which blows spirits about like leaves, and she had come into it with her little paper of gentian. She had hidden the parcel in her pocket before she entered the kitchen. Her husband was awake. He turned his wondering, half-resentful eyes towards her without moving his head.

"Where have you been, Lucy?"

"I—just went down to the store a minute, Alfred, while you was asleep."

"What for?"

"A bar of soap."

Alfred Tollet had always been a very healthy man until this spring. Some people thought his illness was alarming now, more from its un-wontedness and consequent effect on his mind, than from anything serious in its nature. However that may have been, he had complained of great depression and languor all the spring, and had not attempted to do any work.

It was the beginning of May now.

"If Alfred can only git up May hill," Mrs. Tollet's sister had said to her, "he'll git along all right through the summer. It's a dreadful tryin time."

So up May hill, under the white apple and plum boughs, over the dandelions and the young grass, Alfred Tollet climbed, pushed and led faithfully by his loving old wife. At last he stood triumphantly on the summit of that fair hill, with its sweet, wearisome ascent. When the first of June came, people said, "Alfred Tollet's a good deal better."

He began to plant a little and bestir himself.

"Alfred's out workin in the garden," Mrs. Tollet told her sister one afternoon. She had strolled over to her house, with her knitting, after dinner.

"You don't say so! Well, I thought when I see him Sunday that he was lookin better. He's got through May, and I guess he'll pull through. I did feel kinda worried 'bout him over one spell—Why, Lucy, what's the matter?"

"Nothin. Why?"

"You looked at me dreadful kind of queer and distressed, I thought."

"I guess you must have imagined it, Hannah. There ain't nothin the matter." She tried to look unconcernedly at her sister, but her lips were trembling.

"Well, I don't know 'bout it. You look kinda queer now. I guess you walked too fast comin over here. You alluz did race."

"Maybe I did."

"For the land's sake, just see that dust you tracked in! I've got to git the dust pan and brush now, and sweep it up."

"I'll do it."

"No, set still. I'd rather see to it myself."

As the summer went on, Alfred Tollet continued to improve. He was as hearty as ever by September. But his wife seemed to lose as he gained. She grew thin, and her small face had a solemn, anxious look. She went out very little. She did not go to church at all, and she had been a devout church-goer. Occasionally she went over to her sister's, that was all. Hannah watched her shrewdly. She was a woman who arrived at conclusions slowly, but she never turned aside from the road to them.

"Look-a here, Lucy," she said one day. "I know what's the matter with you; there's somethin on your mind, and I think you'd better out with it."

The words seemed propelled like bullets by her vehemence. Lucy shrank down and away from them, her pitiful eyes turned up toward her sister.

"Oh, Hannah, you scare me; I don't know what you mean."

"Yes, you do. Do you s'pose I'm blind? You're worrying yourself to death, and I want to know the reason why. Is it anything 'bout Alfred?"

"Yes—don't, Hannah."

"Well, I'll go over and give him a piece of my mind. I'll see—"

"Oh, Hannah, don't! It ain't him. It's me—it's me."

"What on earth have you done?"

Mrs. Tollet began to sob.

"For the land sake, stop cryin and tell me."

"Oh, I give him—gentian."

"Lucy Ann Tollet, are you crazy? What if you did give him gentian. I don't see nothin to take on about."

"I—deceived him, and it's been most killin me to think on't ever since."

"What do you mean?"

"I put it in his tea, the way you said."

"And he never knew it?"

"He kinda complained 'bout its tastin bitter, and I told him 'twas his mouth. He asked me if it didn't taste bitter to me, and I said, 'No.' I don't know what's to become of me. Then I had to be careful 'bout puttin too much on't in his tea, that I was afraid he wouldn't get enough. So I put little sprinklins in the bread and pies and everythin I cooked. And when he'd say nothin tasted right nowadays, and somehow everything was kinda bitterish, I'd tell him it must be his mouth."

"Look here, Lucy, you didn't eat everythin with gentian in it yourself?"

"Course I did."

"For the land sake!"

"I s'pose the stuff must have done him good; he's picked up ever since he begun takin it. But I can't git over my deceivin of him so. I've 'bout made up my mind to tell him."

"Well, all I've got to say is you're a big fool if you do. I declare, Lucy Ann Tollet, I never saw such a woman. The idee of your worryin over such a thing as that when it's done Alfred good, too! Perhaps you'd rather he'd died?"

"Sometimes I think I had most rather."

"Well!"

In the course of a few days Mrs. Tollet did tell her husband. He received her disclosure in precisely the way she had known that he would. Her nerves received just the shock which they were braced to meet.

They had come home from meeting on a Sunday night. Mrs. Tollet stood before him; she had not even taken off her shawl and little black bonnet.

"Alfred," said she, "I've got somethin to tell you. It's been on my mind a long time. I meant it all for the best, but I've been doin somethin wrong. I've been deceivin of you. I give you gentian last spring when you was so poorly. I put little sprinklins on't into everything you ate. And I didn't tell the truth when I said 'twas your mouth and it didn't taste bitter to me."

The old man half closed his eyes, and looked at her intently; his mouth widened out rigidly. "You put a little gentian into everything I ate unbeknownst to me, did you?" said he. "Hm!"

"Oh, Alfred, don't look at me so! I meant it all for the best, but I was afeard you wouldn't git well without you had it, Alfred. I was dreadful worried about you; you didn't know nothin about it, but I was. I laid awake nights a-worryin and prayin. I know I did wrong; it wa'n't right to deceive you, but it was along of my worryin and my thinkin so much of you, Alfred. I was afeard you'd die and leave me all alone; and —it most killed me to think on't."

Mr. Tollet pulled off his boots, then pattered heavily about the house, locking the doors and making preparations for retiring. He would not speak another word to his wife about the matter, though she kept on with her piteous little protestations.

Next morning, while she was getting breakfast, he went down to the store. The meal, a nice one—she had taken unusual pains with it—was on the table when he returned; but he never glanced at it. His hands were full of bundles, which he opened with painstaking deliberation. His wife watched apprehensively. There was a new teapot, a pound of tea, some bread and cheese, also a salt mackerel.

Mrs. Tollet's eyes shone round and big; her lips were white. Her husband put a pinch of tea in the new teapot, and filled it with boiling water from the kettle.

"What are you a-doin, Alfred?" she asked, feebly.

"I'm just goin to make sure I have some tea, and somethin to eat without any gentian in it."

"Oh, Alfred, I made these corn cakes on purpose, and they are real light. They ain't got no gentian in 'em, Alfred."

He sliced his bread and cheese clumsily, and sat down to eat them in stubborn silence.

Mrs. Tollet, motionless at her end of the table, stared at him with an appalled look. She never thought of eating anything herself.

After breakfast, when her husband started out to work, he pointed at the mackerel. "Don't you touch that," said he.

"But, Alfred—"

"I ain't got nothin more to say. Don't you touch it."

Never a morning had passed before but Lucy Tolbert had set her house in order; today she remained there at the kitchen table till noon, and did not put away the breakfast dishes.

Alfred came home, kindled up the fire, cooked and ate his salt mackerel imperturbably; and she did not move or speak till he was about to go away again. Then she said, in a voice which seemed to speak of itself, "Alfred!"

He did not turn his head.

"Alfred, you must answer me. I'm in earnest. Don't you never want me to cook anything for you again?"

"No, I'm afeard of gittin things that's bitter."

"I won't never put any gentian in anything again. Alfred, won't you let me get supper?"

"No, I won't. I don't want to talk no more about it. In futur I'm a-goin to cook my vittles myself, and that's all there is about it."

"Alfred, if you don't want me to do nothin for you, maybe—you'll think I ain't earnin my own vittles, maybe—you'd rather I go over to Hannah's—"

She sobbed aloud when she said that. He looked startled, and eyed her sharply for a minute. The other performer in the little melodrama which this thwarted, arbitrary old man had arranged was adopting a role which he had not anticipated, but he was still going to abide by his own.

"Maybe 'twould be just as well," said he. Then he went out the door.

Hannah Orton was in her kitchen sewing when her sister entered.

"For the land sake, Lucy, what is the matter?"

"I've left him—I've left Alfred! Oh! oh!"

Lucy Tollet gasped for breath; she sank into a chair, and leaned her head against the wall. Hannah got some water.

"Don't, Lucy—there, there! Drink this, poor lamb!"

She did not quite faint. She could speak in a few minutes. "He bought him a new teapot this mornin, Hannah, and some bread and cheese and salt mackerel. He's goin to do his own cookin; he don't want me to do nothin more for him; he's afeard I'll put gentian in it. I've left him! I've come to stay with you!"

"You told him, then?"

"I had to; I couldn't go on no longer. He wouldn't let me touch that mackerel, and it oughta have been soaked. It was salt enough to kill him."

"Serve him right if it did."

"Hannah Orton, I ain't a-goin to have a thing said agin Alfred."

"Well, if you want to stand up for Alfred Tollet, you can. You alluz would stand up for him agin your own folks. If you want to keep on carin for such a miserable, set, unfeelin—"

"Don't you say another word, Hannah—not another one; I won't hear it."

"I ain't a-goin to say nothin; there ain't any need of your bein so fierce. Now don't cry so, Lucy. We shall git along real nice here together. You'll get used to it a'ter a little while, and you'll see you are a good deal better off without him; you've been nothin but just a slave ever since you was married. Don't you s'pose I've seen it? I've pitied you so, I didn't know what to do. I've seen the time when I'd like to ha' shook Alfred."

"Don't, Hannah."

"I ain't a-goin to say nothin more. You just stop cryin, and try and be calm, or you'll be sick. Have you had any dinner?"

"I don't want none."

"You've got to eat somethin, Lucy Ann Tollet. There ain't no sense in your givin up so. I've got a nice little piece of lamb, and some peas and string beans left over, and I'm a-goin to get 'em. You've got to eat 'em, and then you'll feel better. Look-a here, I want to know if Alfred drove you out of the house 'cause you give him gentian. I ain't got it through my head yet."

"I asked him if he'd rather have me go, and he said maybe 'twould be just as well. I thought I shouldn't have no right to stay if I couldn't get his meals for him."

"Right to stay! Lucy Ann Tollet, if it wa'n't for the grace of the Lord, I believe you'd be a simpleton. I don't understand no such goodness. I alluz thought it would run into foolishness some time, and I believe it has with you. Well, don't worry no more about it; set up and eat your dinner. Just smooth out that mat under your feet a little; you've got it all balled up."

No bitter herb could have added anything to the bitterness of that first dinner which poor Lucy Tollet ate after she had left her own house. Time and custom lessened, but not much, the bitterness of the subsequent ones. Hannah had sewed for her living all her narrow, single life; Lucy shared her work now. They had to live frugally; still they had enough. Hannah owned the little house in which she lived.

Lucy Tollet lived with her through the fall and winter. Her leaving her husband started a great whirlpool of excitement in this little village.

Hannah's custom doubled; people came ostensibly for work, but really for information. They quizzed her about her sister, but Hannah could be taciturn. She did her work and divulged nothing, except occasionally when she was surprised. Then she would let fall a few little hints, which were not at Lucy's expense.

They never saw Mrs. Tollet; she always ran when she heard anyone coming. She never went out to church nor on the street. She grew to have a morbid dread of meeting her husband or seeing him. She would never sit at the window, lest he might go past. Hannah could not understand this; neither could Lucy herself.

Hannah thought she was suffering less, and was becoming weaned from her affection, because she did so. But in reality she was suffering more, and her faithful love for her imperious old husband was strengthening.

All the autumn and winter she stayed and worked quietly; in the spring she grew restless, though not perceptibly. She had never bewailed herself much after the first; she dreaded her sister's attacks on Alfred. Silence as to her own grief was her best way of defending him.

Towards spring she often let her work fall in her lap, and thought. Then she would glance timidly at Hannah, as if she knew what her thoughts were; but Hannah was no mind reader. Hannah, when she set out for meeting one evening in May, had no conception whatever of the plan which was all matured in her sister's mind.

Lucy watched her out of sight; then she got herself ready quickly. She smoothed her hair, put on her bonnet and shawl, and started up the road towards her old home. There was no moon, but it was clear and starry. The blooming trees stood beside the road like sweet, white spring angels. There was a whippoorwill calling somewhere over across the fields. Lucy Tollet saw neither stars nor blooming trees; she did not hear the whippoorwill. That hard, whimsical old man in the little weather-beaten house ahead towered up like a grand giant between the white trees and this one living old woman; his voice in her ears drowned out all the sweet notes of the spring birds.

When she came in sight of the house there was a light in the kitchen window. She crept up to it softly and looked in. Alfred was standing there with his hat on. He was looking straight at the window, and he saw her the minute her little pale face came up above the sill.

He opened the door quickly and came out. "Lucy, is that you?"

"Oh, Alfred, let me come home! I'll never deceive you agin!"

"You just go straight back to Hannah's this minute!"

She caught hold of his coat. "Oh, Alfred, don't—don't drive me away agin! It'll kill me this time; it will! it will!"

"You go right back."

She sank right down at his feet then, and clung to them. "Alfred, I won't go; I won't! I won't! You sha'n't drive me away agin. Oh, Alfred, don't drive me away from home! I've lived here with you for fifty year a'most. Let me come in and cook for you, and do for you agin. Oh, Alfred, Alfred!"

"See here, Lucy—git up; stop takin on so. I want to tell you somethin. You just go back to Hannah's and don't you worry. You set down and wait a minute. There!"

Lucy looked at him. "What do you mean, Alfred?"

"Never you mind; you just go right along."

Lucy Tollet sped back along the road to Hannah's, hardly knowing what she was about. It is doubtful if she realized anything but a blind obedience to her husband's will, and a hope of something roused by a new tone in his voice. She sat down on the doorstep and waited, she did not know for what. In a few minutes she heard the creak of heavy boots, and her husband came in sight. He walked straight up to her.

"I've come to ask you to come home, Lucy. I'm a-feelin kinda poorly this spring, and—I want you to stew me up a little gentian. That you give me afore done me a sight of good."

"Oh, Alfred!"

"That's what I'd got laid out to do when I see you at the window, Lucy, and I was a-goin to do it."

Charles W. Chesnutt

(1858-1932)

*C*harles W. Chesnutt, though born in Cleveland, Ohio, spent
*his formative years and early manhood in North Carolina, the setting
for his best narratives. When he was twenty-five, he returned to Cleveland to become, first, a court reporter and, later, one of the first American Negroes to succeed as a fiction writer. He began to sell stories in
1887 and in 1899 won wide readership with two collections of short
tales,* The Conjure Woman *and* The Wife of His Youth, *subtitled and*
Other Stories of the Color Line. *These books, rather than the three
novels that followed them, contained his best writing.*

*Chesnutt's first book introduced a noteworthy narrator, venerable
Uncle Julius, whose dialect stories instruct newly established Northern
employers—and incidentally readers—concerning black superstitions
and racial relationships. In "The Conjurer's Revenge," first published in
the* Overland Monthly *in 1889, the framework's stuffy diction sharply
contrasts with the raconteur's vernacular speech, recorded here by a
black author intimately acquainted with it. The wry ending shows that
Uncle Julius, for all his innocent appearance, is a shrewd operator.*

The Conjurer's Revenge

Sunday was sometimes a rather dull day at our place. In the morning, when the weather was pleasant, my wife and I would drive to town, a distance of about five miles, to attend the church of our choice. The afternoons we spent at home, for the most part, occupying ourselves with the newspapers and magazines, and the contents of a fairly good library. We had a piano in the house, on which my wife played with skill and feeling. I possessed a passable baritone voice, and could accompany myself indifferently well when my wife was not by to assist me. When these resources failed us, we were apt to find it a little dull.

One Sunday afternoon in early spring—the balmy spring of North Carolina, when the air is in that ideal balance between heat and cold where one wishes it would always remain—my wife and I were seated on the front piazza, she wearily but conscientiously plowing through a missionary report, while I followed the impossible career of the blonde heroine of a rudimentary novel. I had thrown the book aside in disgust, when I saw Julius coming through the yard, under the spreading elms, which were already in full leaf. He wore his Sunday clothes, and advanced with a dignity of movement quite different from his week-day slouch.

"Have a seat, Julius," I said, pointing to an empty rocking chair.

"No, thanky, boss. I'll just set here on the top step."

"Oh, no, Uncle Julius," exclaimed Annie. "Take this chair. You will find it much more comfortable."

The old man grinned in appreciation of her solicitude, and seated himself somewhat awkwardly.

"Julius," I remarked, "I am thinking of setting out scuppernong vines on that sand hill where the three persimmon trees are; and while I'm working there, I think I'll plant watermelons between the vines, and get a little something to pay for my first year's work. The new railroad will be finished by the middle of summer, and I can ship the melons North and get a good price for them."

"If you are gwine to have any more plowin to do," replied Julius, "I 'spect you'll have to buy another creetur, 'cause hit's as much as them hosses can do to tend to the work they got now."

"Yes, I had thought of that. I think I'll get a mule; a mule can do more work, and doesn't require as much attention as a horse."

"I wouldn't 'vise you to buy no mule," remarked Julius, with a jerk of his head.

"Why not?"

"Well, you may 'low hit's all foolish'ness, but if I was in your place I wouldn't buy no mule."

"But that isn't a reason; what objections have you to a mule?"

"Fact is," continued the old man in a serious tone, "I don't like to drive a mule. I's alluz afeared I might be imposin on some human creetur. Ev'y time I cuts a mule with a hickory, 'pears to me most likely I's cuttin some of my own relations, or somebody else what can't he'p theyse'ves."

"What put such an absurd idea into your head?" I asked.

My question was followed by a short silence, during which Julius seemed engaged in a mental struggle.

"I dunno as hit's worth while to tell you this," he said, at length. "I don't hardly 'spect for you to b'lieve it. Does you 'member that club-footed man what hilt the hoss for you the other day when you was gittin out'n the rockaway down to Marse Archie McMillan's store?"

"Yes, I believe I do remember seeing a club-footed man there."

"Did you ever see a club-footed nigger before or since?"

"No, I can't remember that I ever saw a club-footed colored man," I replied after a moment's reflection.

"You and Mis' Annie wouldn't want to b'lieve me, if I was to 'low that that man was once a mule?"

"No," I replied, "I don't think it very likely that you could make us believe it."

"Why, Uncle Julius!" said Annie severely, "what ridiculous nonsense!"

This reception of the old man's statement reduced him to silence, and it required some diplomacy on my part to induce him to vouchsafe an explanation. The prospect of a long, dull afternoon was not alluring, and I was glad to have the monotony of Sabbath quiet relieved by a plantation legend.

"When I was a young man," began Julius, when I had finally prevailed upon him to tell us the story, "that club-footed nigger—his name is Primus—used to belong to old Marse Jim McGee, over on the Lumberton plank road. I used to go over there to see a woman what lived on the plantation; that's how I come to know all about it. This here Primus was the liveliest hand on the place, alluz a-dancin, and drinkin, and runnin round, and singin and pickin the banjo; 'ceptin once in a while, when he 'lowed he wa'n't treated right about somep'm another, he'd git so sulky and stubborn that the white folks couldn't hardly do nothin with him.

"It was 'gin the rules for any of the hands to go way from the plantation at night. But Primus didn't mind the rules, and went when he felt like it. And the white folks pretend like they didn't know it, for Primus was dangerous when he got in them stubborn spells, and they'd rather not fool with him.

"One night in the spring of the year, Primus slipped off from the plantation, and went down on the Wilmington Road to a dance gun by some of the free niggers down there. They was a fiddler, and a banjo, and a jug gwine round on the outside, and Primus sung and dance till long about two o'clock in the mornin, when he start for home. As he come along back, he tuck a nigh-cut 'cross the cotton fields and long by the edge of the Min'al Spring Swamp, so as to git shet of the patrols what rid up and down the big road for to keep the darkies from runnin round nights. Primus was saunterin long, studyin 'bout the good time he'd had with the gals, when, as he was gwine by a fence corner, what should he hear but somep'm grunt. He stopped a minute to listen, and he heard somep'm grunt again. Then he went over to the fence where he heard the fuss, and there laying in the fence corner, on a pile of pine straw, he seed a fine fat shoat.

"Primus look hard at the shoat, and then started home. But somehow or nother he couldn't git away from that shoat; when he tuck one step for'ards with one foot, the other foot 'peared to take two steps back'ards, and so he kept naturally gittin closer and closer to the shoat. It was the beatinest thing! The shoat just 'peared to charm Primus, and first thing you know, Primus found hisse'f way up the road with the shoat on his back.

"If Primus had've knowed whose shoat that was, he'd a-managed to git past it somehow or nother. As it happen, the shoat b'long to a conjure man what lived down in the free-nigger settlement. 'Course the conjure man didn't have to work his roots but a little while 'fore he found out who tuck his shoat, and then the trouble begun. One mornin, a day or so later, and before he got the shoat eat up, Primus didn't go to work when the horn blow, and when the overseer went to look for him, they war no trace of Primus to be discovered nowhere. When he didn't come back in a day or so more, ev'ybody on the plantation 'lowed he had runned away. His master a'vertise him in the papers and offered a big reward for him. The nigger-catchers fotch out they dogs, and track him down to the edge of the swamp, and then the scent gun out. And that was the last anybody seed of Primus for a long, long time.

"Two or th'ee weeks a'ter Primus disappear, his master went to town one Sad'day. Marse Jim was standin in front of Sandy Campbell's barroom, up by the old wagon yard, when a poor white man from down

on the Wilmington Road come up to him and ax him, kinda careless
like, if he didn't want to buy a mule.

" 'I dunno,' says Marse Jim. 'It 'pends on the mule and on the price.
Where is the mule?'

" 'Just round here, back of old Tom McAllister's store,' says the poor
white man.

" 'I reckon I'll have a look at the mule,' says Marse Jim, 'and if he
suits me, I dunno but what I mought buy him.'

"So the poor white man tuck Marse Jim round back of the store, and
there stood a monst'ous fine mule. When the mule see Marse Jim, he
gun a whinny, just like he knowed him before. Marse Jim look at the
mule, and the mule 'peared to be sound and strong. Marse Jim 'lowed
they 'peared to be somep'm familious 'bout the mule's face, specially
his eyes; but he hadn't lost ne'er mule, and didn't have no recomem-
brance of havin seed the mule before. He ax the poor buckra where he
got the mule, and the poor buckra say his bru'r raise the mule down on
Rockfish Creek. Marse Jim was a little 'spicious of seein a poor white
man with such a fine creetur, but he finally 'greed to give the man fifty
dollars for the mule—'bout half what a good mule was worth them days.

"He tied the mule behind the buggy when he went home, and put
him to plowin cotton the next day. The mule done mighty well for
th'ee or four days, and then the niggers 'mence to notice some queer
things about him. They was a meadow on the plantation where they
used to put the horses and mules to pastur. Hit was fence off from the
corn field on one side, but on the other side'n the pastur was a tobacco
patch, what wa'n't fence off, 'cause the beastisses don't none on 'em
eat tobacco. They don't know what's good! Tobacco is like religion:
the good Lord made it for people, and they ain't no other creetur what
can 'preciate it. The darkies notice that the first thing the new mule
done, when he was turnt into the pastur, was to make for the tobacco
patch. Course they didn't think nothin on it, but next mornin, when
they went to catch him, they 'scovered that he had eat up two whole
rows of tobacco plants. A'ter that they had to put a halter on him, and
tie him to a stake, or e'se they wouldn't 've been ne'er leaf of tobacco
left in the patch.

"Another day one of the hands, named Dolphus, hitch the mule up,
and drive up here to this here vineyard—that was when old Marse Dugal
own this place. Marse Dugal had kilt a yearlin, and the neighbor white
folks all sont over for to git some fresh beef, and Marse Jim had sont
Dolphus for some too. They was a wine-press in the yard where Dolphus
left the mule a-standin, and right in front of the press they was a tub of
grape juice just pressed out, and a little on one side a barrel about half
full of wine what had been standin two or th'ee days and had begun to
git sorta sharp to the taste. They was a couple of boards on top of this

here barrel, with a rock laid on 'em to hold 'em down. As I was a-sayin, Dolphus left the mule standin in the yard, and went into the smoke-house for to git the beef. By and by, when he come out, he seed the mule a stagg'rin 'bout the yard; and 'fore Dolphus could git there to find out what was the matter, the mule fell right over on his side, and laid there just like he was dead.

"All the niggers 'bout the house run out there for to see what was the matter. Some say the mule had the colic; some say one thing and some another, till by and by one of the hands seed the top was off'n the barrel, and run and looked in.

"'Fore the Lord!' he say, 'that mule drunk! he been drinkin the wine.' And sure enough, the mule had passed by the tub of fresh grape-juice and push the cover off'n the barrel, and drunk two or th'ee gallon of the wine what had been standin long enough for to begin to git sharp.

"The darkies all made a great 'miration 'bout the mule gittin drunk. They never hadn't seed nothin like it in they born days. They poured water over the mule, and tried to sober him up. But it wa'n't no use, and Dolphus had to take the beef home on his back and leave the mule there, till he slept off his spree.

"I don't 'member whether I told you or no, but when Primus disappear from the plantation, he left a wife behind him, a monst'ous good-lookin yellow gal, name Sally. When Primus had been gone a month or so, Sally 'mence for to git lonesome; and tuck up with another young man name Dan, what b'long on the same plantation. One day this here Dan tuck the new mule out in the cotton field for to plow, and when they was gwine long the turn row, who should he meet but this here Sally? Dan look round and he didn't see the overseer nowhere; so he stop a minute for to run on with Sally.

"'Howdy, honey,' says he. 'How you feelin this mornin?'

"'First rate,' 'spond Sally.

"They was lookin at one another, and they didn't ne'er one on 'em pay no 'tention to the mule, who had turnt his head round and was lookin at Sally as hard as he could, and stretchin his neck and raisin his years, and whinnyin kinda soft to hisse'f.

"'Yas, honey,' 'lows Dan, 'and you gwine to feel first rate long as you sticks to me. For I's a better man than that low-down runaway nig-ger Primus that you been wastin your time with.'

"Dan had let go the plow handle and had put his arm round Sally, and was just gwine to kiss her, when somep'm cotch him by the scruff of the neck and flung him way over in the cotton patch. When he pick hisse'f up, Sally had gone kitin down the turn row, and the mule was standin there lookin as ca'm and peaceful as a Sunday mornin.

"First Dan had 'lowed it was the overseer what had cotch him wastin his time. But they wa'n't no overseer in sight, so he 'cluded it must've been the mule. So he pitch into the mule and lammed him hard as he could. The mule tuck it all, and 'peared to be as humble as a mule could be, but when they was makin the turn at the end of the row, one of the plow lines got under the mule's hind leg. Dan retch down to git the line out, sorta careless like, when the mule haul off and kick him clean over the fence into a brier patch on the other side.

"Dan was mighty sore from his wounds and scratches, and was laid up for two or th'ee days. One night the new mule got out'n the pastur, and went down to the quarters. Dan was layin there on his pallet, when he heard somep'm bangin away at the side of his cabin. He raise one shoulder and look round, when what should he see but the new mule's head stickin in the window, with his lips drawed back over his toofs, grinnin and snappin at Dan just like he want to eat him up. Then the mule went round to the door, and kick away like he want to break the door down, till by and by somebody come along and driv him back to the pastur. When Sally come in a little later from the big house, where she'd been waitin on the white folks, she found poor Dan nigh about dead, he was so scared. She 'lowed Dan had had the nightmare. But when they look at the door they seed the marks of the mule's hoofs, so they couldn't be no mistake about what had happen.

"Course the niggers they told they master 'bout the mule's gwines-on. First he didn't pay no 'tention to it, but a'ter a while he told 'em if they didn't stop they foolishness, he gwine tie some on 'em up. So a'ter that they didn't say nothin more to they master, but they kept on noticin the mule's queer ways just the same.

"Long 'bout the middle of the summer they was a big camp meetin broke out down on the Wilmington Road, and nigh 'bout all the poor white folks and free niggers in the settlement got 'ligion, and lo and behold! mongst 'em was the conjure man what own the shoat what charmed Primus.

"This conjure man was a Guinea nigger, and before he was sot free had used to b'long to a gent'eman down in Sampson County. The conjure man say his daddy was a king, or a governor, or some sorta what-you-may-call-'em way over yander in Afficky, where the niggers come from, before he was stoled away and sold to the speculators. The conjure man had he'ped his master out'n some trouble or 'nother with his goofer, and his master had sot him free, and bought him a tract of land down on the Wilmington Road. He pretend to be a cow doctor, but everybody knowed what he really was.

"The conjure man hadn't more than come through good, before he was tuck sick with a cold what he cotch kneeling on the ground so long by the mourners' bench. He kept gittin worser and worser, till one day he sent word up to Marse Jim McGee's plantation, and ax Pete, the nigger what tuck care of the mules, for to come down there that night and fetch that mule what his master had bought from the poor white man durin o' the summer.

"Pete didn't know what the conjure man was drivin at, but he didn't dast to stay 'way. And so that night, when he'd done eat his bacon and his hoe cake and drunk his 'lasses and water, he put a bridle on the mule, and rid him down to the conjure man's cabin. When he got to the door. He felt mighty dubious 'bout gwine in, but he was bleedst to do it, he knowed he couldn't he'p hisse'f.

" 'Pull the string,' says a weak voice. And when Pete lift the latch and went in, the conjure man was layin on the bed, lookin pale and weak, like he didn't have much longer for to live.

" 'Is you fotch the mule?' says he.

"Pete say yas, and the conjure man kept on.

" 'Br' Pete,' says he, 'I's been a monst'ous sinner man, and I's done a power of wickedness endurin of my days, but the good Lord is wash my sins away, and I feels now that I's bound for the kingdom. And I feels, too, that I ain't gwine to git up from this bed no more in this world, and I wants to undo some o' the harm I done. And that's the reason, Br' Pete, I sont for you to fetch that mule down here. You 'member that shoat I was up to your plantation inquirin about last June?"

" 'Yas,' says Br' Pete, 'I 'member your axin 'bout a shoat you had lost.'

" 'I dunno whether you ever larnt it or not,' says the conjure man, 'but I done knowed your master's Primus had tuck the shoat, and I was bound to git even with him. So one night I cotch him down by the swamp on his way to a candy pullin, and I th'owed a goofer mixtry on him, and turnt him to a mule, and got a poor white man to sell the mule, and we 'vided the money. But I don't want to die till I turn Br' Primus back again.'

"Then the conjure man ax Pete to take down one or two gourds off'n a shelf in the corner, and one or two bottles with some kind of mixtry in 'em, and set 'em on a stool by the bed. And then he ax him to fetch the mule in.

"When the mule come in the door, he gin a snort, and started for the bed, just like he was gwine to jump on it.

" 'Hold on there, Br' Primus!' the conjure man hollered. 'I's monst'ous weak, and if you 'mence on me, you won't never have no chance for to git turn back no more.'

"The mule seed the sense of that, and stood still. Then the conjure man tuck the gourds and bottles, and 'mence to work the roots and yarbs, and the mule 'mence to turn back into a man—first his years, then the rest of his head, then his shoulders and arms. All the time the conjure man kept on workin roots; and Pete and Primus could see he was gittin weaker and weaker all the time.

" 'Br' Pete,' says he, by and by, 'gimme a drink o' them bitters out'n that green bottle on the shelf yander. I's gwine fast, and it'll gimme strenk for to finish this work.'

"Br' Pete look up on the mantelpiece, and he seed a bottle in the corner. It was so dark in the cabin he couldn't tell whether it was a green bottle or no. But he hilt the bottle to the conjure man's mouth, and he tuck a big mouthful. He hadn't more than swallowed it 'fore he 'mence to holler:

" 'You gimme the wrong bottle, Br' Pete; this here bottle's got pizen in it, and I's done for this time, sure. Hold me up, for the Lord's sake, till I git through turnin Br' Primus back.'

"So Pete hilt him up, and he kept on workin the roots, till he got the goofer all tuck off'n Br' Primus 'ceptin one foot. He hadn't got this foot more than half turnt back before his strenk gun out entirely, and he drop the roots and fell back on the bed.

" 'I can't do no more for you, Br' Primus,' says he, 'but I hopes you will forgive me for what harm I done you. I knows the good Lord done forgive me, and I hope to meet you both in glory. I sees the good angels waitin for me up yander, with a long white robe and a starry crown, and I'm on my way to jine 'em.' And so the conjure man died, and Pete and Primus went back to the plantation.

"The darkies made a great 'miration when Primus come back. Marse Jim let on like he didn't believe the tale the two niggers told; he says Primus had runned away, and stay till he got tired of the swamps, and then come back on him to be fed. He tried to 'count for the shape of Primus's foot by sayin Primus got his foot smash, or snake-bit, or somep'm, whiles he was 'way, and then stayed out in the woods where he couldn't git it cured straight, 'stid o' comin long home where a doctor could a-tended to it. But the niggers all notice they master didn't tie Primus up, nor take on much 'cause the mule was gone. So they 'lowed they master must've had his 'spicions 'bout that conjure man."

My wife had listened to Julius's recital with only a mild interest. When the old man had finished it she remarked—

"That story does not appeal to me, Uncle Julius, and is not up to your usual mark. It isn't pathetic, it has no moral that I can discover, and I can't see why you should tell it. In fact, it seems to me like nonsense."

The old man looked puzzled as well as pained. He had not pleased the lady, and he did not seem to understand why.

"I'm sorry ma'm," he said reproachfully, "if you don't like that tale. I can't make out what you means by some of them words you use, but I'm tellin nothin but the truth. Course I didn't see the conjure man turn him back, for I wasn't there. But I been hearin the tale for twenty-five years, and I ain't got no 'casion for to 'spute it. They's so many things a body knows is lies, that they ain't no use gwine round findin fault with tales that mought just as well be so as not. F'instance, they's a young nigger gwine to school in town, and he come out here the other day and 'lowed that the sun stood still and the yea'th turnt round every day on a kind o' axletree. I told that young nigger if he didn't take hisse'f 'way with them lies, I'd take a buggy trace to him; for I sees the yea'th standin still all the time, and I sees the sun gwine round it, and if a man can't b'lieve what he sees, I can't see no use in livin—mought's well die and be where we can't see nothin. And another thing what proves the tale 'bout this old Primus is the way he goes on if anybody ax him how he come by that club foot. I axed him one day, mighty polite and civil, and he call me a old fool, and got so mad he ain't spoke to me since. But this is a queer world, any way you can fix it," concluded the old man with a weary sigh.

"If you makes up your mind not to buy that mule, sir," he added as he rose to go, "I knows a man what's got a good hoss he wants to sell— leastways, that's what I heared. I'm gwine to prayer meetin tonight, and I'm gwine right by the man's house, and if you'd like to look at the hoss, I'll ax him to fetch him round."

"Oh yes," I said, "you can ask him to stop in, if he is passing. There will be no harm in looking at the horse, though I rather think I shall buy a mule."

Early next morning the man brought the horse up to the vineyard. At that time I was not a very good judge of horse flesh. The horse appeared sound and gentle, and, as the owner assured me, he had no bad habits. The man wanted a huge price for the horse, but finally agreed to accept a much smaller sum, upon payment of which I became possessed of a very fine-looking animal. But alas for the deceitfulness of appearances! I soon ascertained that the horse was blind in one eye, and that the sight of the other was very defective, and not a month elapsed before my purchase developed most of the diseases that horse flesh is heir to, and a more worthless, broken-winded, spavined quadruped never disgraced the noble name of horse. After worrying through two or three months of life, he expired one night in a fit of the colic. I replaced him with a mule, and Julius henceforth had to take his chances of driving some metamorphosed unfortunate.

Circumstances that afterwards came to my knowledge created in my mind a strong impression that Julius may have played a more than unconscious part in this transaction. Among other significant facts was his appearance, the Sunday following the purchase of the horse, in a new suit of store clothes, which I had seen displayed in the window of Mr. Solomon Cohen's store, on my last visit to town, and had remarked on account of their striking originality of cut and pattern. As I had not recently paid Julius any money, and as he had no property to mortgage,

I was driven to conjecture to account for his possession of the means to buy the clothes. Of course I would not charge him with duplicity unless I could prove it, at least to a moral certainty, but for a long time afterwards I took his advice only in small doses and with great discrimination.

James Whitcomb Riley

(1849-1916)

*A*lthough *James Whitcomb Riley was chiefly famous in his heyday as a writer of poems in dialect, he invaded this collection by writing a prose piece for lecture audiences that was perhaps his funniest creation.*

Born and reared in Greenfield, Indiana, and educated in the village school, Riley foiled his lawyer father's attempt to steer him into the legal profession by going out on the road, first as a sign painter and later as a patent-medicine-show performer, and eventually, working on newspapers. He started as a Hoosier dialect poet when working for the Indianapolis Journal, *writing under various pen names for that paper and others. When his poems became popular beyond Indiana, he collected a dozen in* The Old Swimmin'-Hole and 'Leven More Poems *(1883) and ascribed the book to "Benj. F. Johnson of Boone," an uneducated farmer who boasted that he wrote "from the hart out." But the true author made sure that he got credit by placing his name in brackets after Johnson's. In this collection and more than forty others, Riley wrote, as he put it, verse about "the kind of people I knew and especially . . . verse that I could read just as if it were being spoken for the first time." Persuaded that "all true dialect-writers are also endowed with native histrionic capabilities," he constantly "took naturally to anything theatrical" and was remarkably successful on platforms throughout the United States.*

In "How to Tell a Story," Mark Twain used the piece that follows to illustrate the difference between a comic story, a short joke with a snapper that anybody can tell, and a humorous story, "a work of art— high and delicate art"—that "only an artist can tell." Twain gives as an example a comic story taking "only a minute and a half to tell," one that "isn't worth the telling." By contrast:

Put into the humorous-story form it takes ten minutes, and is about the funniest thing I have ever listened to—as James Whitcomb Riley tells it.

He tells it in the character of a dull-witted old farmer who has just heard it for the first time, thinks it is unspeakably funny, and is trying to repeat it. . . . But he can't remember it; so he gets all mixed up and wanders helplessly round and round, putting in tedious details that don't belong in the tale and only retard it; taking them out conscientiously and putting in others that are just as useless; . . . and so on, and so on, and so on, . . . at the end of ten minutes the audience have laughed until they are exhausted, and the tears are running down their faces.

The simplicity and innocence and sincerity and unconsciousness of the old farmer are perfectly simulated, and the result is a performance which is thoroughly charming and delicious. This is art — and fine and beautiful, and only a master can compass it; but a machine could tell the other story.

As Twain says, in the form of a joke, the skeletal narrative had been popular all over the world for centuries. Indexers of folktale types cite numerous appearances of this one in many countries. John Wardroper, a passionate collector of chestnuts, in Jest upon Jest (1970), cites reincarnations in 1765, 1780, and 1811 joke books. The staying power of the jest was indicated in 1929 when Erich Maria Remarque included a version in his tremendously popular war novel, All Quiet on the Western Front. The antiquity of the story, of course, makes the vast delight of Riley's old farmer on hearing it amusing. Otherwise, the joke itself is relatively unimportant. What is most important is the comic character of the teller and his excruciatingly inept way of unfolding his narrative.

The Old Soldier's Story
(As Told before the New England Society in New York City)

Since we have had no stories tonight, I will venture, Mr. President, to tell a story that I have heretofore heard at nearly all the banquets I have ever attended. It is a story simply, and you must bear with it kindly. It is a story as told by a friend of us all, who is immoderately fond of a funny story, and who, unfortunately, attempts to tell a funny story himself—one that he has been particularly delighted with. Well, he is not a storyteller, and especially he is not a funny storyteller. His funny stories, indeed, are oftentimes touchingly pathetic. But to such a story as he tells, being a good-natured man and kindly disposed, we have to listen, because we do not want to wound his feelings by telling him that we have heard that story a great number of times, and that we have heard it ably told by a great number of the people from the time that we were children. But, as I say, we can not hurt his feelings. We can not stop him; we can not kill him; and so the story generally proceeds. He selects a very old story always, and generally tells it in about this fashion:—

I heerd an awful funny thing the other day—ha! ha! I don't know whether I can git it off or not, but anyhow I'll tell it to you. Well!—let's see now how the fool thing goes. Oh, yes!—Why there was a fellow one time—it was during the army and this fellow that I started in to tell you about was in the war and—ha! ha!—there was a big fight a-goin on. And this fellow was in the fight, and it was a big battle and bullets a-flyin every which way, and bombshells a-bustin, and cannonballs a-flyin round promiscuous, and this fellow right in the midst of it, you know, and all excited and het up and chargin away.

And the first thing you know along come a cannonball and shot his head off—ha! ha! ha! Hold on here a minute!—No, sir; I'm a-gittin ahead of my story. No, no, it didn't shoot his *head* off—I'm gittin the cart before the horse there. Shot his *leg* off; that was the way. Shot his leg off; and down the poor fellow dropped, and, of course, in that condition was perfectly helpless, you know, but yit with presence of mind to know that he was in a dangerous condition if somep'm wasn't done for him right away. So he seen a comrade a-chargin by that he knowed, and he hollers to him and called him by name—I disremember now what the fellow's name was. . . .

Well, that's got nothing to do with the story, anyway. He hollers to him, he did, and says, "Hello, there," he says to him. "Here, I want you to come here and give me a lift. I got my leg shot off, and I want you to pack me back to the rear of the battle—where the doctors always is, you know, during a fight"—and he says, "I want you to pack me back there where I can get meddy-cinal attention, or I'm a dead man, for I got my leg shot off," he says. "And I want you to pack me back there so's the surgeons can take care of me."

Well—the fellow, as luck would have it, recognized him and run to him and throwed down his own musket, so's he could pick him up. And he stooped down and picked him up and kinda halfway shouldered him and halfway helt him between his arms like, and then he turned and started back with him—ha! ha! ha!

Now mind, the fight was still a-goin on—and right at the hot of the fight, and the fellow, all excited, you know, like he was, and the soldier that had his leg shot off gettin kinda fainty like, and his head kinda stuck back over the fellow's shoulder that was carryin him. And he hadn't got more'n a couple o' rods with him when another cannonball come along and tuck his head off, sure enough!—and the curiousest thing about it was—ha! ha!—that the fellow was a-packin him didn't know that he had been hit agin at all, and back he went—still carryin the deceased back—ha! ha! ha!—to where the doctors could take care of him—as he thought.

Well, his cap'n happened to see him, and he thought it was a rather curious proceedins—a soldier carryin' a dead body out of the fight, don't you see? And so he hollers at him, and he says to the soldier, the cap'n did, he says, "Hullo, here! where you goin with that thing?" the cap'n said to the soldier who was a-carryin the fellow that had his leg shot off. Well, his head, too, by that time.

So he says, "Where you goin with that thing?" the cap'n said to the soldier who was a-carryin away the fellow that had his leg shot off.

Well, the soldier he stopped—kinda haltin, you know, like a private soldier will when his presidin officer says to him. "Why," he says, "Cap, it's a comrade o' mine and the poor fellow has got his leg shot off, and I'm a-packin him back to where the doctors is. And there was nobody to help him, and the fellow woulda died in his tracks— or track, ruther—if it hadn't a-been for me, and I'm a-packin him back where the surgeons can take care of him, where he can get medical attendance—or his wife's a widow!" he says, "'cause he's got his leg shot off!"

Then Cap says, "You blame fool you, he's got his *head* shot off!"

So then the fellow slacked his grip on the body and let it slide down on the ground, and looked at it a minute, all puzzled you know, and says, "Why he told me it was his leg!" Ha! ha! ha!

Alfred Henry Lewis
(Dan Quin)

(ca. 1858-1914)

*T*he *life and the career of Alfred Henry Lewis up to the time he became a very successful writer of local color stories with Far-Western settings and characters hardly seemed to predict his achievements. Born in Cleveland, Ohio, where he practiced law until 1881, he visited the Southwest briefly, then became a Kansas City journalist, and, eventually, a Washington, D.C., correspondent and editor. His Western travels, however, had been as a wandering cowboy, and his experiences furnished him with materials for his fictions. These were contributed to magazines from the late 1890s until his death and were collected in six books:* Wolfville *(1897),* Sandburrs *(1900),* Wolfville Days *(1902),* Wolfville Nights *(1908),* Wolfville Folks *(1908), and* Faro Nell and Her Friends *(1913).*

His stories, set in Arizona's cattle and mining country, are reminiscences and yarns told in dialect by the Old Cattleman and are more often than not humorous ones. The frameworks of the stories are unusually skimpy for the period, indicating merely that the raconteur is an old-timer and that the writer is a tenderfoot whose chief chores are getting him to talk, listening, and recording the monologues. In a preface to Wolfville, *from which the story that follows is drawn, Lewis says that he has decided to leave to Frederic Remington, the illustrator, the job of picturing the town, its leading inhabitants, and the Old Cattleman. "The style," he says, "will be crude, abrupt, and meagre, but I trust it will prove as satisfactory to the reader as it has to me." Actually, the quoted prose is packed with locutions and phrasings that are much like those of post-Civil War Phunny Phellows. In the story about the jocose Jaybird, the Old Cattleman treats two serious happenings—a stampede and a killing—with much more levity than his real counterpart probably would have.*

Jaybird Bob's Joke

Old Cattleman

A. H. Lewis, *Wolfville* (N.Y., 1892, frontispiece).

"Whatever makes this here Jaybird Bob believe he's a humorist?" said the Old Cattleman one afternoon as we slowly returned from a walk. "Whatever it is misleads him to so deem himself is surely too many for me. Doc Peets tells him himse'f one day he's plumb wrong.

"'You-all's naturally a somber, morose party,' says Doc Peets this time, 'and nothing jocose or jocund about you. Your disposition, Jaybird, don't no more run to jokes than a prairie dog's.'

"'Which I would admire to know why not,' says Jaybird Bob.

"'Well,' goes on Doc Peets, 'you thinks too slow—too much like a cow in a swamp. Your mind moves sluggish thataway, and sorta sinks to the hocks each step. If you was born to be funny, your intellects would be limber and frivolous.'

"'Bein all this is personal to me,' says Jaybird Bob, 'I takes leave to regard you as wrong. My jokes is good, high-grade jokes, and when you-all talks of me being morose, it's a mere case of bluff.' And so

Jaybird goes on a-holdin of himse'f funny, until we-alls has him to bury.

"No; Jaybird ain't his sure-'nough name; it's just a handle to his 'dentity, so we-alls picks it up handy and easy. Jaybird's real name is Graingerford—Poindexter Graingerford. But the same is cumbersome and unwieldy a whole lot; so when he first trails into Wolfville we-alls considers among ourse'fs and settles it's a short cut to call him 'Jaybird Bob,' thataway. And we does.

"It's on the spring roundup, this-here Jaybird first develops that he regards himse'f witty. It's in the mornin as we-alls has saddled up and lines out to comb the range roundabout for cattle. There's a tenderfoot along whose name is Todd, and as he's canterin off, Jaybird comes a-curvin up on his bronco and reaches over and tails this shorthorn's pony.

"What's tailin a pony? It's ridin up from the rear and takin a half hitch on your saddle with the tail of another gent's pony, and then spurrin by, and swappin ends with the whole outfit—gent, hoss and all.

"It's really too tumultuous for a joke, and maybe breaks the pony's neck, maybe the rider's. But whether he saves his neck or no, the party whose pony is thus tailed alluz emerges therefrom disheveled and wrought up and hotter than a wolf. So no one plays this here joke much, not till he's ready to get shot at.

"As I says, this Jaybird watches Todd as he rides off. Bein new on the range thataway, Todd don't ride easy. A cow saddle ain't built like these-here Eastern hulls, nohow. The stirrup is two inches further back for one thing, and it's compiled a heap different other ways. Bein unused to cow saddles, and for that matter cow ponies, this Todd lops over forrard and beats with his elbow like he's a curlew or somethin flyin, and I reckons it's such proceedins makes Jaybird allow he's goin to be funny and tail Todd's pony.

"As I explains, he capers along after Todd and reaches over and gets a handful of the pony's tail. And then, wrappin it round his saddle-horn, he goes by on the jump and spreads Todd and his bronco promiscuous about the scene. This here Todd goes along the grass on all fours like a jack-rabbit.

"Which Todd, I reckons, is the hostilest gent in southeast Arizona. Before even he offers to get up, he lugs out his six-shooter and makes some mighty sincere gestures thataway to shoot Jaybird. But he's slow with his weapon, bein spraddled out on the grass, and it gives Dave Tutt and Enright a chance to jump in between and stop the deal.

"We-alls picks Todd up, and rounds up his pony—which scrambles to its feet and is now a-cavortin round like its mind is overturned—and explains to him that this-here is a joke. But he's surly and relentless about it, and it don't take no hawk to see he don't forgive Jaybird a little bit.

"'Tailin a gent's pony,' says Todd, 'is no doubt thrillin amusement for folks lookin on, but there's nothin of a redeemin nature in it from the standpoint of the party whose pony's upheaved thataway. Not to be misunderstood at this here crisis,' goes on this Todd, 'I wants to announce that from now forrard, life will have but one purpose with me, which'll be to down the next gent whoever tails a pony of mine. The present incident goes as a witticism; but you can gamble the next won't be so regarded.'

"That sorta ends the talk, and all of us but the cook and the hoss-hustlers being in the saddle by now, we disperses ourse'fs through the scenery to work the cattle and proceed with the roundup we-alls is on. We notes, though, that tailin Todd's pony don't go agin with safety.

"It's when we-alls rides away that Doc Peets—who's out with the roundup, though he ain't got no cattle-brand himse'f—tells Jaybird he's not a humorist, like I already repeats.

"But, as I suggests, this Jaybird Bob can't believe it none. He's mighty sure about his jokes bein excellent good jokes, and while it's plain Todd ain't got no confidence in him and distrusts him complete since he tips over his bronco that mornin, it looks like Jaybird can't let him alone. And them misdeeds of Jaybird's keeps goin on, until by the merest mistake—for it's an accident if ever one happens in the cow country—this here tenderfoot shoots up Jaybird and kills him for good.

"It looks to us like it's a special Providence to warn folks not to go projectin about, engaged in what you might call physical jests none. Still, this-here removal of Jaybird don't take place till mighty near the close of the roundup. And intervenin he's pirootin round, stackin the cards and settin up hands on the poor shorthorn continuous.

"One of Jaybird's jokes—'one of his best,' Jaybird calls it—results in stampedin the herd of cattle we-alls is bringin along at the time—bein all cows and their calves—to a brandin pen. Which there's two thousand, big and little, in the bunch. And Jaybird's humor puts 'em to flight like so many blackbirds. And it takes two days hard ridin for the whole out-fit to bring 'em together agin.

"Among other weaknesses this Todd imports from the States is, he's afraid of snakes. Rattlesnakes is his abhorrence, and if each is a disem-bodied spirit he can't want 'em further off. He's alluz alarmed that maybe, somehow, a rattlesnake will come pokin in under his blankets nights, and camp with him while he's asleep. And this here wretched Jaybird fosters them delusions.

"'About them serpents,' I overhears Jaybird say to him one evenin while we-alls is settin round; —all but Moore and Tutt, who's ridin herd; ' 'bout them serpents; a gent can't be too particular. It looks like they has but one hope, which is to crawl into a gent's blankets and sleep some with him. Which, if he moves or turns over, they simply emits a buzz and grabs him. I knows of forty folks who's bit thataway by snakes, and ne'er a one lives to explain the game.'

" 'Be rattlesnakes thick in Arizona?' I hears Todd say to this Jaybird.

" 'Be they thick?' answers Jaybird. 'Well, I sure wishes I had whiskey for all the rattlesnakes that is hereabouts. I don't want to go overstatin' the census to a gent who is out playin for information and who's learnin fast, but I s'pose now that there ain't none less than a billion snakes in southeast Arizona alone. If I could saw off the little passel of cattle I has on this range, you can gamble I'd pull my freight tomorrow. It's all right for such old Cimmarons as Enright, and such parties as that saw-bones Peets, to go bluffin about there bein no rattlesnakes to speak of, and that they couldn't p'izen you to death nohow; but you bet I ain't seen forty of my dearest friends cash in of snake bites, and not learn nothin. And almost every time it's a rattlesnake as comes slidin into bed with 'em while they's locked in dreams and who gets hot and goes to chewin of 'em because they wants to turn out before the snake does. Rattlesnakes thataway wants to sleep till it's fourth drink time and the sun's way up yonder. And when a gent goes to rollin out of his blankets say sunup, it makes 'em monstrous angry to be disturbed; and the first he knows of where they be and how they look on early risin, their teeth's in him up to the guard, and before night there's one less gent to cook for, and an extra saddle rides along in the grub-wagon when they next moves camp.'

"Of course all this is a heap impressive to Todd; and while Enright and Peets both tells him Jaybird's havin fun with him, you can see he's mortal afraid every night when he spreads his blankets, and he makes a circle about where he sleeps, with a horsehair lariat he's got from a Mexican, and who tells him it'll tickle the snakes' necks when they goes to crawl across it, and make 'em keep away.

"The way this here Jaybird manages to stampede the bunch that time is thisaway. Jaybird comes ridin in from the cattle about three hours before sunup, to turn out Tutt, who is due to take his place on herd. Jaybird's got a rawhide rope that he's dragged about in the grass, which makes it damp and cold. As Jaybird rides up to camp he sees this Todd rolled in his blankets, snorin to beat four of a kind.

"Naturally Jaybird's out to be joyous in a second. He rides up close to this he'pless shorthorn as he lays asleep, and tosses a loop of his wet rawhide across his countenance where it's turned up in the moonlight. As it settles down cold and startlin on Todd's skin, Jaybird yells:

" 'Snake, Todd! There's a rattlesnake on you bigger 'n a dog.'

"Jaybird says later as how this Todd behaves tremendous. He b'iles up into the atmosphere with a howl like a wolf; and grabbin a blanket in each hand, he starts out over the plains in a state of frenzy. Which the worst is he charges headlong toward the herd; and what with them shrieks he volunteers, and the blankets flappin and wavin, there ain't a cow in the bunch who stays in her right mind a moment. Which she springs to her feet, and, takin her offspring along, goes surgin up into the hills for good. You couldn't head or stop 'em then. It's the completest case of the stampede I ever turns out to behold.

"No; this here Todd never gathers the rights of the eepisode. He's that peevish and violent by nature no one tells him it's Jaybird; and unless, in the light of knowin more, he has since figgered out the truth, he allows to this day a rattlesnake as big as a roll of blankets tries to recline on his face that time.

"To keep peace in camp and not let him go to pawin round for real trouble with the festive Jaybird, Enright stands in to cap the game himse'f, and picks it up in confab with this Todd the next day as how he sees the rattlesnake, and that it's mighty near bein a whopper.

"'It's sure,' says Enright, when he and Todd is conversin thereon, 'the most giant serpent I ever sees without the aid of liquor. And when he goes stealin off into the gloom, bein amazed and rattled by your cries, he leaves, so far as I'm concerned, a trail of relief behind. You-all can gamble, I wasn't interruptin of no such snake, nor makin of no pretexts for his detainment.'

"'What for was his rattles like?' says Todd; and he gets pale at the mere sound of Enright's talk.

"'As to them rattles,' says Enright, like he's mighty thoughtful tryin to recall 'em to mind, 'as to this reptile's rattles, it's that dark that while I sees 'em I couldn't but jest. So far as I notes anythin they looks like a belt full of cartridges, sorta corrugated and numerous.'

"Now this here which I relates, while no doubt burnin experiences to Todd, is after all harmless enough. And to people not careful about the basis of their glee it might do some to laugh at. But it all closes up on a play with nothin gay nor merry in it; leastwise not for Jaybird Bob.

"This here finish joke of Jaybird's transpires one evenin as the cook's startin in to rustle some chuck. The grub-wagon's been stopped in the mouth of Peeled Pine Canyon. Every gent's in camp but this here tenderfoot Todd. Enright, who's actin as roundup boss for the outfit—for everybody's cattle's bein worked together thataway like we alluz does—has sent Todd peerin round for cattle, way off in the valley into which the Peeled Pine Canyon opens. This here shorthorn's due to be back any time now, 'cause it's only a question of how far up the valley does he go. He don't run no show to be lost, for nothin less aerial than goats could climb out of the canyon he's in, and therefore he's bound to find camp.

"Of course, knowin every gent's station in the day's ridin, we-alls is plenty aware that this tenderfoot Todd is some'eres above us in the valley. None of the rest of us is turnin our minds to him, probably, except Jaybird Bob. It all of a bump like a buckin pony strikes Jaybird that he's missin an unusual chance to be buoyant.

"'What for a play would it be,' says Jaybird, rousin up from where he lays watchin the cook slice salt hoss for the fryin pan. 'What for a game it would be, I says, for a passel of us to lay out up the draw and bushwhack this-here untaught person Todd as he comes ridin down to camp? We-alls could hop out at him, a-whoopin and shoutin, and bein wrapped up in blankets, he allows it's sure Indians and goes plumb locoed.'

"'You-all will keep harrowin away at this Todd party, Jaybird,' says Enright, 'until you arises from the game loser. Now I don't reckon none I'd play Apache if I'm you. There's too much effort in bein an Apache thataway. I'd lay here and think up some joke which don't demand so much industry, and ain't calc'lated to scare an innocent gent to death.'

"But Jaybird wouldn't listen. He falls into admiration of his scheme, and at last Tutt and Jack Moore allows they'll go along and play they's aborigines with Jaybird, and note how the tenderfoot stands the racket.

"As long as this here Jaybird's bound to make the play,' says Jack Moore to Enright, talkin one side, 'it's a heap better to have the conservative element represented in the deal. So I puts it up, it's a good sage move for me and Tutt to stand in. We-alls will come handy to pull Jaybird and the shorthorn apart if they gets their horns locked in the course of them gaieties.'

"Enright takes the same view; so Jaybird and Moore and Tutt wanders off up the canyon a mile, and lays in wait surreptitious to head off Todd. Jack tells me the story when him and Tutt come ridin back with the corpse.

"'This is how we does,' says Jack. 'Me and Tutt and deceased—which last is Jaybird all right enough—is ensconced behind a p'int of rocks. Jaybird's got his blanket wrapped round him so he looks like a savage. It ain't long when we-alls hears the tenderfoot comin down the canyon; it's likely he's half-mile away. He's runnin onto us at a road gait, and when he's about two hundred yards off Jaybird turns out a yell to make you shiver, shakes a load or two out'n his gun, goes surgin out from round the p'int of rocks, and charges straight at this unthinkin tenderfoot. It is due to truth to say, me and Tutt follows this Jaybird's suit, only not so violent as to whoops.

"'Does it scare up the tenderfoot? Well, it surely alarms him a heap. He takes Jaybird for an Indian and makes no question; which the same is nowise strange; I'd took him for a savage myse'f, only I knows it's Jaybird. So, as I remarks, it horrifies the tenderfoot on end, and at the first sight of Jaybird he whirls his pony and lights out up that valley like antelope.

"'Naturally we-alls follows: Jaybird leadin, a-whoopin, and a-shootin, and throwin no end of spirit into it. It's a success, this piece of wit is, up to this juncture, and Jaybird puts a heap of zest into it.

"'The weak spot in all this here humor grows out of the idees this tenderfoot's been gainin, and the improvements he's been makin while stragglin about in our society. I unhesitatingly states that if this-here joke is pulled off by Jaybird when Todd first enters our midst, it might have been the victory of his life. But Jaybird defers it too long. The tenderfoot has acquired a few Western ways, enough to spoil the fun and send poor Jaybird a-curvin to his home on high.

"'This is what that shorthorn does that teaches me he's learnin. While he's humpin off up the canyon, and me and Jaybird and Tutt is stampedin along in pursuit, the fugitive throws loose his six-shooter, and without even turnin his head or lookin at us, he unhooks the entire bundle of lead our way.

"'Which the worst feature of it is, this backhanded, blind shootin is a winner. The very first shot smites Jaybird plumb through the hat, and he goes off his pony without even mentionin about it to either Tutt or me.

"'That's all there is to the report. Dave and me pulls up our broncos, abandons the joke, lays Jaybird across his saddle like a sack of corn, and returns to state the case.'

"'Whatever did you-alls do with this frightened stranger?' asks Enright.

"'Which we never does nothin,' says Jack. 'The last I beholds he's flyin up the valley, hittin nothin but the high places. And assumin his project is to get away, he's succeedin admirable. As he vanishes, I should judge from his motion he's reloadin his gun. And from the luck he has with Jaybird, Tutt and me is led to believe there's no real object in followin him no further. I don't press my society on no gent, surely not on some locoed tenderfoot thataway who's pulled his gun and is done blazin away erratic, without purpose or aim.

"'Don't you and Tutt know here he is at?' demands Enright.

"'Which we surely don't,' says Tutt. 'If his hoss holds and he don't swerve none from the direction he's p'intin out in when he fades from view, he's got to be over in the San Simon country by tomorrow mornin when we eats our grub, and that's half way to the Borax Desert. If you yearns for my impressions,' concludes Jack, 'drawn from a-seein of him depart, I'm free to say I don't reckon you-alls is goin to meet this-here tenderfoot none soon.'

"And that's about the size of it. Jack calls the turn. Jaybird's last joke alarms this tenderfoot Todd plum out'n Arizona, and there ain't none of us ever sees hair, horn, nor hoof-mark of him no more. And he takes with him, this Todd does, the boss pony in our bunch."

Edward Noyes Westcott

(1846-1898)

*E*dward Noyes Westcott *was a one-book man. His novel,* David Harum, A Story of American Life, *written after he retired from business and finished on his deathbed, was published posthumously the year he died. Westcott was born and educated through high school in Syracuse, in central New York, the setting for his book. He drew upon his experiences as a banker in his hometown, experiences which had acquainted him well with the life and the characters of the neighboring countryside.* David Harum, *purportedly drawn from life, is a New York State version of probably the most popular of all nineteenth-century American humorous types—a scantily educated countryman whose keen mind and practical experience enable him to understand human nature and say perceptive things about his associates as he tells stories about them. Although Westcott's novel has an overall plot of sorts, its appeal derives in large part from a number of stories that David and his sister tell.*

The novel's appeal was widespread. The book sold half a million copies during its first twenty months in print. (The per capita equivalent in 1980 would have been about three times as great.) By 1965 David Harum *actually had sold one and a quarter million copies, had been translated into a number of languages, and had done well as a play and even better as a motion picture, with Will Rogers typecast in the leading role.*

The title "The Horse Trader" has been given by the editors to a portion of the novel's first chapter and all of the second, which form a unit. The first two chapters of the book were the last ones written, "prefixed to the story as it then stood in order to introduce David and Aunt Polly to the reader at the very beginning." Since it began, American humor had used deals in horses as a favorite subject matter.

The Horse Trader

David Harum

David Harum (New York: D. Appleton & Company, Publishers, 1900, p. 224).

"I guess I'll take a look at the *Tribune*," said David, unfolding that paper.

Mrs. Bixbee went on with her needlework, with an occasional side glance at her brother, who was immersed in the gospel of his politics. Twice or thrice she opened her lips as if to address him, but apparently some restraining thought interposed. Finally the impulse to utter her mind culminated. "Dave," she said, "d'you know what Deacon Perkins is sayin about you?"

David opened his paper so as to hide his face, and the corners of his mouth twitched as he asked in return, "Well, what's the deacon sayin now?"

"He's sayin," she replied, in a voice mixed of indignation and apprehension, "that you sold him a balky horse, and he's goin to have the law on ye."

David's shoulders shook behind the sheltering page, and his mouth expanded in a grin.

"Well," he replied after a moment, lowering the paper and looking gravely at his companion over his glasses, "next to the deacon's religious experience, them of lawin and hoss tradin air his strongest p'ints, and he works the whole on 'em to once sometimes."

The evasiveness of this generality was not lost on Mrs. Bixbee, and she pressed the point with "Did ye? and will he?"

"Yes, and no, and maybe and maybe not," was the categorical reply.

"Well," she answered with a snap, "maybe you call that an answer. I s'pose if you don't want to let on you won't, but I do believe you've been playing some trick on the deacon, and won't own up. I do wish," she added, "that if you had to get rid of a balky horse onto somebody, you'd have picked out somebody else."

"When you got a balker to dispose of," said David gravely, "you can't always pick and choose. First come, first served." Then he went on more seriously: "Now I'll tell ye. Quite a while ago—in fact, not long after I come to enjoy the privilege of the deacon's acquaintance—we had a deal. I wa'n't just on my guard, knowin him to be a deacon and all that, and he lied to me so splendid that I was took in, clean over my head. He done me so brown I was burnt in places, and you could smell smoke around me for some time."

"Was it a horse?" asked Mrs. Bixbee gratuitously.

"Well," David replied, "maybe it *had* been some time, but at that particular time the only thing to determine that fact was that it wa'n't nothin else."

"Well, I declare!" exclaimed Mrs. Bixbee, wondering not more at the deacon's turpitude than at the lapse in David's acuteness, of which she had an immense opinion, but commenting only on the former. "I'm 'mazed at the deacon."

"Yes'm," said David with a grin, "I'm quite a liar myself when it comes down to the hoss business, but the deacon can give me both bowers every hand. He done it so slick that I had to laugh when I come to think it over—and I had witnesses to the whole confab, too, that he didn't know of, and I could've showed him up in great shape if I'd had a mind to."

"Why didn't ye?" said Aunt Polly, whose feelings about the deacon were undergoing a revulsion.

"Well, to tell ye the truth, I was so completely skunked that I hadn't a word to say. I got rid of the thing for what it was worth for hide and tallow, and 'stid of squealin round the way you say he's doin, like a stuck pig, I kept my tongue between my teeth and laid to git even some time."

"You ought to've had the law on him," declared Mrs. Bixbee, now fully converted. "The old scamp!"

"Well," was the reply, "I gen'ally prefer to settle out of court, and in this particular case, where I might a been willin t' admit that I'd been did up, I didn't feel much like swearin to it. I reckoned the time'd come when maybe I'd git the laugh on the deacon, and it did, and we're pretty well settled now in full."

"You mean this last performance?" asked Mrs. Bixbee. "I wish you'd quit beatin about the bush and tell me the whole story."

"Well, it's like this, then, if you *will* have it. I was over to Whiteboro a while ago on a little matter of worldly business, and I seen a couple of fellows halter-exercisin a hoss in the tavern yard. I stood round a spell watchin 'em, and when he come to a standstill I went and looked him over, and I liked his looks, first rate.

" 'For sale?' I says.

" 'Well,' says the chap that was leadin him, 'I never see the hoss that wa'n't, if the price was right.'

" 'Yourn?' I says.

" 'Mine and hisn,' he says, noddin his head at the other fellow.

" 'What ye askin for him?' I says.

" 'One fifty,' he says.

"I looked him all over again, pretty careful, and once or twice I kinda shook my head 's if I didn't quite like what I seen, and when I got through I sorta half turned away without sayin anythin, 's if I'd seen enough.

" 'They ain't a scratch nor a pimple on him,' says the fellow, kinda resentin my looks. 'He's sound and kind, and 'll stand without hitchin, and a lady can drive him 's well as a man.'

" 'I ain't got anythin ag'in him,' I says, 'and probably that's true, every word on 't. But one fifty's a considerable price for a hoss these days. I hain't no pressin use for another hoss, and, in fact,' I says, 'I've got one or two for sale myself.'

" 'He's worth two hundred just as he stands,' the fellow says. 'He hain't had no trainin, and he can draw two men in a road wagon better 'n fifty.'

"Well, the more I looked at him the better I liked him, but I only says, 'Just so, just so; he may be worth the money, but just as I'm fixed now, he ain't worth it to *me*, and I hain't got that much money with me if he was,' I says.

"The other fellow hadn't said nothin up to that time, and he broke in now. 'I s'pose you'd take him for a gift, wouldn't ye?' he says, kinda sneerin.

" 'Well, yes,' I says, 'I dunno but I would if you'd throw in a pound of tea and a halter.'

"He kinda laughed, and says, 'Well, this ain't no gift enterprise, and I guess we ain't goin to trade. But I'd like to know,' he says, 'just as a matter of curiosity, what you'd say he *was* worth to ye.'

" 'Well,' I says, 'I come over this mornin to see a fellow that owed me a trifle o' money. Exceptin of some loose change, what he paid me is all I got with me,' I says, takin out my wallet. 'That wad's got a hundred and twenty-five into it, and if you'd sooner have your hoss and halter than the wad,' I says, 'why I'll bid ye good day.'

" 'You're offerin one twenty-five for the hoss and halter?' he says.

" 'That's what I'm doin,' I says.

" 'You've made a trade,' he says, puttin out his hand for the money and handin the halter to me."

"And didn't ye suspicion nothin when he took ye up like that?" asked Mrs. Bixbee.

"I did smell woolen some," said David, "but I had the *hoss* and they had the *money*, and as fur as I could see, the critter was all right. Howsomever, I says to 'em; 'This here's all right, fur as it's gone, but you've talked pretty strong 'bout this hoss. I don't know who you fellows be, but I can find out,' I says.

"Then the first fellow that done the talkin 'bout the hoss put in and says, 'They hain't been one word said to you about this hoss that wa'n't gospel truth—not one word.' And when I come to think on 't afterward," said David with a half-laugh, "it maybe wa'n't *gospel* truth, but it was good enough *jury* truth. I guess this ain't over and above interestin to ye, is it?" he asked after a pause, looking doubtfully at his sister.

"Yes, 'tis," she asserted. "I'm lookin forward to where the deacon comes in. But you just tell it your own way."

"I'll git there all in good time," said David, "but some o' the p'int o' the story 'll be lost if I don't tell ye what come first."

"I allow to stand it 's long 's you can," she said encouragingly, "seein what work I had gettin ye started. Did ye find out anythin 'bout them fellows?"

"I asked the barn man if he knowed who they was, and he said he never seen 'em till the yestidy before, and didn't know 'em from Adam. They come along with a couple of hosses, one drivin and t' other leadin—the one I bought. I asked him if they knowed who I was, and he said one on 'em asked him, and he told him. The fellow said to him, seein me drive up: 'That's a pretty likely lookin hoss. Who's drivin him?' And he says to the fellow: 'That's David Harum, from over to Homeville. He's a great fellow for hosses,' he says."

"Dave," said Mrs. Bixbee, "them chaps just laid for ye, didn't they?"

"I reckon they did," he admitted, "and they was as slick a pair as was ever drawed to," which expression was lost upon his sister. David rubbed the fringe of yellowish-gray hair which encircled his bald pate for a moment.

"Well," he resumed, "after the talk with the barn man, I smelt woolen stronger 'n ever. But I didn't say nothin, and had the mare hitched and started back. Old Jinny drives with one hand, and I could watch the new one all right, and as we come along I begun to think I wa'n't stuck after all. I never see a hoss travel evener and nicer, and when we come to a good level place I sent the old mare along the best she knew, and the new one never broke his gait, and kept right up 'ithout 'parently half tryin; and Jinny don't take most folks' dust, either. I swan! 'Fore I got home I reckoned I'd just as good as made seventy-five, anyway!"

"Then they wa'n't nothin the matter with him, after all," commented Mrs. Bixbee in rather a disappointed tone.

"The meanest thing top of the earth was the matter with him," declared David. "But I didn't find it out till the next afternoon, and then I found it out good. I hitched him to the open buggy and went round by the East Road, 'cause that ain't so much traveled. He went along all right till we got a mile or so out of the village, and then I slowed him down to a walk. Well, sir, scat my —! he hadn't walked more 'n a rod 'fore he come to a dead standstill. I clucked and gidapped and finally took the gad to him a little. But he only just kinda humped up a little and stood like he'd took root."

"Well, now!" exclaimed Mrs. Bixbee.

"Yes'm," said David. "I was stuck in every sense of the word."

"What d'ye do?"

"Well, I tried all the tricks I knowed—and I could lead him—but when I was in the buggy he wouldn't stir till he got good and ready, and then he'd start of his own accord and go on a spell, and—"

"Did he keep it up?" Mrs. Bixbee interrupted.

"Well, I should say he did. I finally got home with the critter, but I thought one time I'd either have to lead him or spend the night on the East Road. He balked five separate times, varyin in length, and it was dark when we struck the barn."

"I should have thought you'd a wanted to kill him," said Mrs. Bixbee, "and the fellows that sold him to ye, too."

"They *was* times," David replied, with a nod of his head, "when if he'd a fell down dead, I wouldn't have figgered on puttin a band on my hat, but it don't never pay to git mad with a hoss; and as for the fellow I bought him of, when I remembered how he told me he's stand without hitchin, I swan! I had to laugh. I did for a fact. 'Stand without hitchin!' He, he, he!"

"I guess you wouldn't think it was so awful funny if you hadn't gone and stuck that horse onto Deacon Perkins—and I don't see how you done it."

"Maybe that is part of the joke," David allowed, "and I'll tell ye the rest on't. The next day I hitched the new one to the democrat wagon and put in a lot of straps and rope, and started off for the East Road again. He went first rate till we come to about the place where we had the first trouble, and sure enough, he balked again. I leaned over and hit him a smart cut on the off shoulder, but he only humped a little and never lifted a foot. I hit him another lick, with the self-same result. Then I got down and I strapped that animal so 't he couldn't move nothin but his head and tail, and got back into the buggy. Well, by and by, it may a-been ten minutes or it may a-been more or less—it's slow settin behind a balkin hoss—he was ready to go on his own account, but he couldn't budge. He kinda looked round, much as to say, 'What on earth's the matter?' and then he tried another move and then another, but no go. Then I got down and took the hobbles off, and then climbed back into the buggy and says 'cluck!' to him, and off he stepped as chipper as could be, and we went joggin along all right, maybe two mile, and when I slowed up, up he come again. I gin him another clip in the same place on the shoulder, and I got down and tied him up again, and the same thing happened as before, on'y it didn't take him quite so long to make up his mind about startin, and we went some further without a hitch. But I had to go through with the performance the third time before he got it into his head that if he didn't go when *I* wanted he couldn't go when *he* wanted, and that didn't suit him; and when he felt the whip on his shoulder it meant business."

"Was that the end of his balkin?" asked Mrs. Bixbee.

"I had to give him one more go-round," said David, "and after that I didn't have no more trouble with him. He showed symptoms at times, but a touch of the whip on the shoulder always fetched him. I always carried them straps, though, till the last two or three times."

"Well, what's the deacon kickin about then?" asked Aunt Polly. "You're just saying you broke him of balkin."

"Well," said David slowly, "some hosses will balk with some folks and not with others. You can't most generally tell."

"Didn't the deacon have a chance to try him?"

"He had all the chance he asked for," replied David. "Fact is, he done most of the sellin, as well as the buyin, himself."

"How's that?"

"Well," said David, "it come about like this: After I'd got the hoss where I could handle him I begun to think I'd had some interestin and valuable experience, and it wa'n't scarcely fair to keep it all to myself. I didn't want no patent on 't, and I was willin to let some other fellow git a piece. So one mornin, week before last—let's see: week ago Tuesday it was, and a mighty nice mornin it was, too—one o' them days that kinda liberal up your mind—I allowed to hitch up and drive past the deacon's and back, and maybe git somethin to strengthen my faith, et cetery, in case I run acrost him. Well, 's I come along I seen the deacon putterin round, and I waved my hand to him and went by a-kitin. I went up the road a ways and killed a little time, and when I come back there was the deacon as I expected. He was leanin over the fence, and as I jogged up he hailed me, and I pulled up.

" 'Mornin, Mr. Harum,' he says.

" 'Mornin, deacon,' I says. 'How are ye? and how's Mis' Perkins these days?'

" 'I'm fair,' he says; 'fair to middlin. But Mis' Perkins is ailin some—as *usual*,' he says."

"They do say," put in Mrs. Bixbee, "that Mis' Perkins don't have much of a time herself."

"Guess she has all the time they is," answered David.

"Well," he went on, "we passed the time o' day and talked a spell about the weather and all that, and finally I straightened up the lines as if I was goin on, and then I says, 'Oh, by the way,' I says. 'I just thought on 't. I heard Dominie White was lookin for a hoss that'd suit him.'

" 'I ain't heard,' he says. But I see in a minute he had—and it really was a fact—and I says, 'I've got a roan colt, risin five, that I took on a debt a spell ago, that I'll sell reasonable, that's as likely and nice every way a young hoss as ever I owned. I don't need him,' I says, 'and didn't want to take him, but it was that or nothin at the time, and glad to git it, and I'll sell him at a bargain. Now what I want to say to you, deacon, is this: that hoss would suit the dominie to a T, in my opinion, but the dominie won't come to me. Now if *you* was to say to him—bein in his church and all that,' I says, 'that you could git him the right kind of a hoss, he'd believe you, and you and me'd be doin a little stroke of business and a favor to the dominie into the bargain. The dominie's well off,' I says, 'and can afford to drive a good hoss.' ' "

"What did the deacon say?" asked Aunt Polly, as David stopped for breath.

"I didn't expect him to jump down my throat," he answered. "But I seen him prick up his ears, and all the time I was talkin I noticed him lookin my hoss over, head and foot. 'Now I 'member,' he says, 'hearin somethin 'bout Mr. White's lookin for a hoss, though when you first spoke on 't it had slipped my mind. Of course,' he says, 'they ain't any real reason why Mr. White shouldn't deal with you direct, and yit maybe I *could* do more with him 'n you could. But,' he says, 'I wa'n't cal'latin to go t' the village this mornin, and I sent my hired man off with my drivin hoss. Maybe I'll drop round in a day or two,' he says, 'and look at the roan.'

" 'You mightn't catch me,' I says, 'and I want to show him myself; and more 'n that,' I says, 'Doug Robinson's after the dominie. I'll tell ye,' I says, 'you just git in 'ith me and go down and look at him, and I'll send ye back or drive ye back, and if you've got anythin special on hand you needn't be gone three quarters of an hour,' I says."

"He come, did he?" inquired Mrs. Bixbee.

"He done *so*," said David sententiously, "just as I knowed he would, after he'd hemmed and hawed about so much, and he rode a mile and a half livelier 'n he done in a good while, I reckon. He had to pull that old broadbrim of hisn down to his ears, and don't you forgit it. He, he, he, he! The road was just *full* o' hosses. Well, we drove in the yard, and I told the hired man to unhitch the bay hoss and fetch out the roan, and while he was bein unhitched the deacon stood round and never took his eyes offn him, and I knowed I wouldn't sell the deacon no roan hoss *that* day, even if I wanted to. But when he come out, I begun to crack him up, and I talked hoss for all I was worth. The deacon looked him over in a don't-care kind of a way, and didn't 'parently give much heed to what I was sayin. Finally I says, 'Well, what do you think of him?' 'Well,' he says, 'he seems to be a likely enough critter, but I don't believe he'd suit Mr. White—'fraid not,' he says. 'What you askin for him?' he says. 'One-fifty,' I says, 'and he's a cheap hoss at the money'; but" added the speaker with a laugh, "I knowed I might's well 've said a thousand. The deacon wa'n't buyin no roan colts that mornin."

"What did he say?" asked Mrs. Bixbee.

"'Well,' he says, 'well, I guess you ought to git that much for him; but I'm 'fraid he ain't what Mr. White wants.' And then, 'That's quite a hoss we come down with,' he says. 'Had him long?' 'Just long enough to git 'quainted with him,' I says. 'Don't you want the roan for your own use?' I says. 'Maybe we could shade the price a little.' 'No,' he says, 'I guess not. I don't need another hoss just now.' And then, after a minute, he says, 'Say, maybe the bay horse we drove'd come nearer the mark for White if he's all right. Just as soon I'd look at him?' he says. 'Well, I hain't no objections, but I guess he's more of a hoss than the dominie 'd care for, but I'll go and fetch him out,' I says. So I brought him out and the deacon looked him over. I see it was a case of love at first sight, as the story books say. 'Looks all right,' he says. 'I'll tell ye,' I says, 'what the fellow I bought him of told me.' 'What's that?' says the deacon. 'He said to me,' I says, ' "That hoss ain't got a scratch nor a pimple on him. He's sound and kind and 'll stand without hitchin, and a lady could drive him as well's a man." '

"'That's what he said to me,' I says, 'and it's every word on't true. You've seen whether or not he can travel,' I says, 'and so far's I've seen, he ain't 'fraid o' nothin.' 'D'ye want to sell him?' the deacon says. 'Well,' I says, 'I ain't offerin him for sale. You'll go a good ways, 'fore you'll strike such another; but, of course, he ain't the only hoss in the world, and I never had anythin in the hoss line I wouldn't sell at *some* price.' 'Well,' he says, 'what d'ye ask for him?' 'Well,' I says, 'if my own brother was to ask me that question, I'd say to him two hundred dollars, cash down, and I wouldn't hold the offer open an hour,' I says."

"My!" ejaculated Aunt Polly. "Did he take you up?"

"'That's more'n I give for a hoss in a good while,' he says, shakin his head, 'and more'n I can afford, I'm 'fraid.' 'All right,' I says, 'I can afford to keep him'; but I knew I had the deacon same as the woodchuck had Skip. 'Hitch up the roan,' I says to Mike. 'The deacon wants to be took up to his house.'

'Is that your last word?' he says. 'That's what it is,' I says. 'Two hundred, cash down.'"

"Didn't you dast to trust the deacon?" asked Mrs. Bixbee.

"Polly," said David, "they's a number of holes in a ten-foot ladder."

Mrs. Bixbee seemed to understand this rather ambiguous rejoinder.

"He must a-squirmed some," she remarked.

David laughed.

"The deacon ain't much used to payin the other fellow's price," he said, "and it was like pullin teeth; but he wanted that hoss more 'n a cow wants a calf, and after a little more squimmidgin he hauled out his wallet and forked over. Mike come out with the roan, and off the deacon went, leadin the bay hoss."

"I don't see," said Mrs. Bixbee, looking up at her brother, "that after all they was anythin you said to the deacon that he could catch holt on."

"They wa'n't nothin," he replied. "The only thing he can complain about's what I *didn't* say to him."

"Hain't he said anythin to ye?" Mrs. Bixbee inquired.

"He, he, he, he! He hain't but once, and they wa'n't but little of it then."

"How?"

"Well, the day but one after the deacon sold himself Mr. Stickin Plaster I had an errand three-four mile or so up past his place, and when I was comin back along 'bout four or half past, it come on to rain like all possessed. I had my old umbrel—though it didn't hinder me from gettin more or less wet—and I sent the old mare along for all she knew. As I come to within a mile from the deacon's house, I seen somebody on the road, and when I come up closer I see it was the deacon himself, in trouble, and I kinda slowed up to see what was goin on. There he was, settin all humped up, with his old broad-brim hat slopin down his back, a-sheddin water like a roof. Then I seen him lean over and larrup the hoss with the ends of the line for all he was worth. It appeared he hadn't no whip, and it wouldn't done him no good if he'd had. Well, sir, rain or no rain, I just pulled up to watch him. He'd just larrup a spell, and then he'd set back; and then he'd lean over and try it again, harder 'n ever. Scat my —! I thought I'd die a-laughin. I couldn't hardly cluck to the mare when I got ready to move on. I drove alongside and pulled up. 'Hullo, deacon,' I says, 'what's the matter?' He looked up at me, and I won't say he was the maddest man I ever see, but he was long ways the maddest-*lookin* man, and he shook his fist at me just like one of the unregenerate. 'Consarn ye, Dave Harum!' he says, 'I'll have the law on ye for this.' 'What for?' I says, 'I didn't make it come on to rain, did I?' I says. 'You know mighty well what for,' he says. 'You sold me this *damned beast*,' he says, 'and he's balked with me *nine times* this afternoon, and I'll fix ye for 't,' he says. 'Well, Deacon,' I says, 'I'm 'fraid the squire's office 'll be shut up before you *git* there, but I'll take any word you'd like to send. You know I told you,' I says, 'that he'd stand still 'ithout hitchin.' And at that he only just kinda choked and spluttered. He was so mad he couldn't say nothin, and on I drove, and when I got forty rod or so I looked back, and there was the deacon a-comin along the road with as much of his shoulders as he could git under his hat and *leadin* his new hoss. He, he, he, he! Oh, my stars and garters! Say, Polly, it paid me for bein born into this vale o' tears. It did, I declare for 't!"

Aunt Polly wiped her eyes on her apron.

"But, Dave," she said, "did the deacon really say *that word*?"

"Well," he replied, "if 'twa'n't that it was the prettiest imitation on 't that ever I heard."

"David," she continued, "don't you think it pretty mean to badger the deacon so 't he swore and than laugh 'bout it? And I s'pose you've told the story all over."

"Mis' Bixbee," said David emphatically, "if I'd paid good money to see a funny show, I'd be a blamed fool if I didn't laugh, wouldn't I? That spectacle of the deacon cost me considerable, but it was more 'n worth it. But," he added, "I guess the way the thing stands now I ain't so much out, on the whole."

Mrs. Bixbee looked at him inquiringly.

"Of course, you know Dick Larrabee?" he asked.

She nodded.

"Well, three-four days after the shower, and the story 'd got around some—as *you* say, the deacon is considerable of a talker—I got holt of Dick—I've done him some favors, and he naturally expects more—and I says to him: 'Dick,' I says, 'I hear 't Deacon Perkins has got a hoss that don't suit him—hain't got knee action enough at times,' I says, 'and maybe he'll sell him reasonable.' 'I've heerd somethin about it,' says Dick, laughin. 'One o' them kind o' hosses you don't like to git catched out in the rain with,' he says. 'Just so,' I says. 'Now,' I says, 'I've got a notion 't I'd like to own that hoss at a price, and that maybe *I* could git him home even if it did rain. Here's a hundred and ten,' I says, 'and I want you to see how fur it'll go to buyin him. If you git me the hoss you needn't bring none on 't back. Want to try?' 'All right,' he says, and took the money. 'But,' he says, 'won't the deacon suspicion that it comes from you?' 'Well,' I says, 'my portrait ain't on none o' the bills, and I reckon *you* won't tell him so, out and out,' and off he went. Yistidy he come in, and I says, 'Well, done anythin?' 'The hoss is in your barn.' 'Good for you!' I says. 'Did you make anythin?' 'I'm satisfied,' he says. 'I made a ten-dollar note.' And that's the net results on 't," concluded David, "that I've got the hoss and he cost me just thirty-five dollars."

Mark Twain

Samuel Langhorne Clemens (Mark Twain)

(1835-1910)

*L*ike other American humorists, Samuel Clemens did work of *several sorts before he hit his stride as Mark Twain. Born and brought up in Hannibal, Missouri, he learned printing there and then traveled eastward as far as New York City as a tramp printer. Back home, he set type in St. Louis and Keokuk and then was a Mississippi River cub and steamboat pilot until 1861. Following his very brief wartime service, he went to the Far West, did some pocket mining, and then turned news-paper reporter in Nevada and then worked as a reporter in San Francisco. After that, he wrote travel letters from the Sandwich Islands, New York City, Europe, and the Holy Land. A book of revised and expanded letters,* The Innocents Abroad *(1869), and another about his life in the West,* Roughing It *(1871), established him as a very popular humorist. After his marriage, he settled in Hartford, Connecticut, and there wrote his most ad-mired books:* The Adventures of Tom Sawyer *(1876),* Life on the Missis-sippi *(1883),* Adventures of Huckleberry Finn *(1884), and* A Connecticut Yankee in King Arthur's Court *(1889). He continued to write until his death, notably producing* Pudd'nhead Wilson *(1894),* The Man That Cor-rupted Hadleyburg *(1900),* Captain Stormfield's Visit to Heaven *(1909), and an autobiography that was published after his death, in 1924.*

Mark Twain had ties with every group of nineteenth-century American humorists. As a youth, Sam Clemens read the antebellum writers; as a young printer, he put their stories into type; over the years, as Mark Twain, he often echoed them; and, when he helped edit an anthology, Mark Twain's Library of Humor, *he saw to it that it did well by them and by the Funny Fellows. He started as a newspaper comic writer, gave comic lectures during many years, and used techniques typical of the school. He greatly admired local colorists, made a lecture tour jointly with one of them (George Washington Cable), and in his best books was a local color writer himself.*

Even in Twain's semifactual travel books, memorable passages were local color interludes. "Jim Baker's Blue-Jay Yarn" was part of the second chapter and all of the third of a book about travels in Europe, A Tramp Abroad *(1880). Wandering in the Neckar Woods, long associated with fairy tales about talking beasts, and mocked by some derisive ravens, the author recalls a California mining camp hermit and the story he had told about a frustrated blue-jay. The characterization of Jim Baker in both the framework of the story and his monologue, as well as the yarn-spinning skill he displays, make it what many critics feel is Twain's best short narrative. Bernard DeVoto says of it:*

The story exhibits a good many aspects of Mark Twain's humor. It is a narrative interlude . . . a passage in which the argument of the book halts while Mark Twain is overhearing the talk of men who are leisurely and entertained. Its material comes from the Negro's bestiary, interstitial with his boyhood in Hannibal; and in this way the humor rises from fantasy, from the imaginative mythmaking of the slaves on the frontier. But also, Jim Baker, the narrator, exists; he is a creation from the world of reality. He lives, and no fantasy has gone into his creation, but only the sharp perception of an individual. His patient, exploratory mind actually works before our eyes and no one can doubt him. His speech has been caught so cunningly that its rhythms produce complete conviction. Fantasy is thus an instrument of realism and the humor of Mark Twain merges into the fiction that is his highest reach.

Like much great humor, "Jim Baker's Blue-Jay Yarn" has touches of pathos that give it warm humanity.

Mark Twain's second piece in the present collection, "Frescoes from the Past," is a chapter transferred from Adventures of Huckleberry Finn *before it was published to* Life on the Mississippi. *It embodies some of Huck's wonderful storytelling to recount a confrontation that was a favorite of frontier humorists — the ritualistic exchange of imaginative boasts before a fight and then the fight itself. The vauntings of Kentuckians and boatmen had been heard and reported in the Hannibal of Sam Clemens's boyhood. The Hannibal* Journal *printed a poem that included a boast that rang like the brags of Twain's raftsmen.*

I'll flog the Young Earthquake
 The earth I will physic;
 Volcanoes I'll strangle,
 Or choke with the phthisic.

And a hundred tales contained comic boasts; Clemens may well have set type for some. Years after leaving Hannibal, the author remembered the shouts of an exboatman he had heard in the town's streets. His raftsmen's vauntings outdo earlier boasts in their imaginative extravagance. And the ending of the story, though it followed a popular postwar pattern, was funnier than the brutal descriptions of fights in most prewar versions. The chapter is enriched by the style not only of the boasters but also of Huck — one of the great vernacular vehicles America has produced.

Jim Baker's Blue-Jay Yarn

Jim Baker

Mark Twain's Library of Humor (p. 417).

One never tires of poking about in the dense woods that clothe all these lofty Neckar hills to their tops. The great deeps of a boundless forest gave a beguiling and impressive charm in any country; but German legends and fairy tales have given these an added charm. They have peopled all that region with gnomes, and dwarfs, and all sorts of mysterious and uncanny creatures. At the time I am writing of, I had been reading so much of this literature that sometimes I was not sure but I was beginning to believe in the gnomes and fairies as realities.

One afternoon I got lost in the woods about a mile from the hotel, and presently fell into a train of dreamy thought about animals which talk, and kobolds, and enchanted folk, and the rest of the pleasant legendary stuff; and so, by stimulating my fancy, I finally got to imagining I glimpsed small flitting shapes here and there down the columned aisles of the forest. It was a place which was peculiarly meet for the occasion. It was a pine wood, with so thick and soft a carpet of brown needles that one's footfall made no more sound than if he were treading on wool; the tree-trunks were as round and straight and smooth as pillars, and stood close together; they were bare of branches to a point about twenty-five feet above ground, and from there upward so thick with boughs that not a ray of sunlight could pierce through. The world was bright with sunshine outside, but a deep and mellow twilight reigned in there, and also a silence so profound that I seemed to hear my own breathings.

When I had stood ten minutes, thinking and imagining, and getting my spirit in tune with the place, and in the right mood to enjoy the supernatural, a raven suddenly uttered a hoarse croak over my head. It made me start; and then I was angry because I started. I looked up, and the creature was sitting on a limb right over me, looking down at me. I felt something of the same sense of humiliation and injury which one feels when he finds that a human stranger has been clandestinely inspecting him in his privacy and mentally commenting upon him. I eyed the raven, and the raven eyed me. Nothing was said during some seconds. Then the bird stepped a little way along his limb to get a better point of observation, lifted his wings, stuck his head far down below his shoulders toward me, and croaked again—a croak with a distinctly insulting expression about it. If he had spoken in English he could not have said any more plainly than he did say in raven, "Well, what do *you* want here?" I felt as foolish as if I had been caught in some mean act by a responsible being, and reproved for it. However, I made no reply; I would not bandy words with a raven. The adversary waited a while, with his shoulders still lifted, his head thrust down between them, and his keen bright eye fixed on me; then he threw out two or three more insults, which I could not understand, further than that I knew a portion of them consisted of language not used in church.

I still made no reply. Now the adversary raised his head and called. There was an answering croak from a little distance in the wood,—evidently a croak of inquiry. The adversary explained with enthusiasm, and the other raven dropped everything and came. The two sat side by side on the limb and discussed me as freely and offensively as two great naturalists might discuss a new kind of bug. The thing became more and more embarrassing. They called in another friend. This was too much. I saw that they had the advantage of me, and so I concluded to get out of the scrape by walking out of it. They enjoyed my defeat as much as any low white people could have done. They craned their necks and laughed at me (for a raven *can* laugh, just like a man), they squalled insulting remarks after me as long as they could see me. They were nothing but ravens—I knew that,—what they thought about me could be a matter of no consequence,—and yet when even a raven shouts after you, "What a hat!" "O, pull down your vest!" and that sort of thing, it hurts you and humiliates you, and there is no getting around it with fine reasoning and pretty arguments.

Animals talk to each other, of course. There can be no question about that; but I suppose there are very few people who can understand them. I never knew but one man who could. I knew he could, however, because he told me so himself. He was a middle-aged, simple-hearted miner, who had lived in a lonely corner of California, among the woods and mountains, a good many years, and had studied the ways of his only neighbors, the beasts and the birds, until he believed he could accurately translate any remark which they made. This was Jim Baker. According to Jim Baker, some animals have only a limited education, and use only very simple words, and scarcely ever a comparison or a flowery figure; whereas, certain other animals have a large vocabulary, a fine command of language and a ready and fluent delivery; consequently these latter talk a great deal; they like it; they are conscious of their talent, and they enjoy "showing off." Baker said, that after long and careful observation, he had come to the conclusion that the blue-jays were the best talkers he had found among birds and beasts. Said he:

"There's more *to* a blue-jay than any other creature. He has got more moods and more different kinds of feelings than other creatures; and, mind you, whatever a blue-jay feels, he can put into language. And no mere commonplace language, either, but rattling, out-and-out book-talk—and bristling with metaphor, too—just bristling! And as for command of language—why, *you* never see a blue-jay stuck for a word. No man ever did. They just boil out of him! And another thing: I've noticed a good deal, and there's no bird, or cow, or anything that uses as good grammar as a blue-jay. You may say a cat uses good grammar. Well, a cat does—but you let a cat get excited, once; you let a cat get to pulling fur with another cat on a shed, nights, and you'll hear grammar that will give you the lockjaw. Ignorant people think it's the *noise* which fighting cats make that is so aggravating, but it ain't so; it's the sickening grammar they use. Now I've never heard a jay use bad grammar but very seldom; and when they do, they are as ashamed as a human; they shut right down and leave.

"You may call a jay a bird. Well, so he is, in a measure—because he's got feathers on him, and don't belong to no church, perhaps; but otherwise he is just as much a human as you be. And I'll tell you for why. A jay's gifts, and instincts, and feelings, and interests, cover the whole ground. A jay hasn't got any more principle than a Congressman. A jay will lie, a jay will steal, a jay will deceive, a jay will betray; and four times out of five, a jay will go back on his solemnest promise. The sacredness of an obligation is a thing which you can't cram into no blue-jay's head. Now, on top of all this, there's another thing: a jay can outswear any gentleman in the mines. You think a cat can swear. Well, a cat can; but you give a blue-jay a subject that calls for his reserve powers, and where is your cat? Don't talk to *me*—I know too much about this thing.

And there's yet another thing; in the one little particular of scolding—just good, clean, out-and-out scolding—a blue jay can lay over anything, human or divine. Yes, sir, a jay is everything that a man is. A jay can cry, a jay can laugh, a jay can feel shame, a jay can reason and plan and discuss, a jay likes gossip and scandal, a jay has got a sense of humor, a jay knows when he is an ass just as well as you do—maybe better. If a jay ain't human, he better take in his sign, that's all. Now I'm going to tell you a perfectly true fact about some blue-jays.

"When I first begun to understand jay language correctly, there was a little incident that happened here. Seven years ago, the last man in this region but me moved away. There stands his house—been empty ever since; a log house, with a plank roof—just one big room, and no more; no ceiling—nothing between the rafters and the floor. Well, one Sunday morning I was sitting out here in front of my cabin with my cat, taking the sun, and looking at the blue hills, and listening to the leaves rustling so lonely in the trees, and thinking of the home away yonder in the States, that I hadn't heard from in thirteen years, when a blue-jay lit on that house, with an acorn in his mouth, and says, 'Hello, I reckon I've struck something!' When he spoke, the acorn dropped out of his mouth and rolled down the roof, of course, but he didn't care; his mind was all on the thing he had struck. It was a knot-hole in the roof. He cocked his head to one side, shut one eye and put the other one to the hole, like a possum looking down a jug; then he glanced up with his bright eyes, gave a wink or two with his wings—which signifies gratification, you understand—and says, 'It looks like a hole, it's located like a hole—blamed if I don't believe it *is* a hole!'

"Then he cocked his head down and took another look; he glances up perfectly joyful this time; winks his wings and his tail both, and says, 'Oh, no, this ain't no fat thing, I reckon! If I ain't in luck!—why it's a perfectly elegant hole!' So he flew down and got that acorn, and fetched it up and dropped it in, and was just tilting his head back with the heavenliest smile on his face, when all of a sudden he was paralyzed into a listening attitude, and that smile faded gradually out of his countenance like breath off'n a razor, and the queerest look of surprise took its place. Then he says, 'Why I didn't hear it fall!' He cocked his eye at the hole again, and took a long look; raised up and shook his head; stepped around to the other side of the hole and took another look from that side; shook his head again. He studied a while, then he just went into the *de*tails—walking round and round the hole, and spied into it from every point of the compass. No use. Now he took a thinking attitude on the comb of the roof, and scratched the back of his head with his right foot for a minute, and finally says, 'Well, it's too many for *me*, that's certain; must be a mighty long hole; however, I ain't got no time to fool around here, I got to 'tend to business; I reckon it's all right—chance it, anyway!'

"So he flew off and fetched another acorn and dropped it in, and tried to flirt his eye to the hole quick enough to see what become of it, but he was too late. He held his eye there as much as a minute; then he raised up and sighed, and says, 'Consound it, I don't seem to understand this thing, no way; however, I'll tackle her again.' He fetched another acorn and done his level best to see what become of it, but he couldn't. He says, 'Well, *I* never stuck no such a hole as this before; I'm of the opinion it's a totally new kind of hole.' Then he begun to get mad. He held in for a spell, walking up and down the comb of the roof, and shaking his head and muttering to himself; but his feelings got the upper hand of him presently, and he broke loose and cussed himself black in the face. I never see a bird take on so about a little thing. When he got through he walks to the hole and looks in again for half a minute; then he says, 'Well, you're a long hole, and a deep hole, and a mighty singular hole altogether—but I've started to fill you, and I'm d—d if I *don't* fill you, if it takes a hundred years!'

"And with that, away he went. You never see a bird work so since you was born. He laid into his work like a nigger, and the way he hove acorns into that hole for about two hours and a half was one of the most exciting and astonishing spectacles I ever struck. He never stopped to take a look any more—he just hove 'em in, and went for more. Well, at last he could hardly flop his wings, he was so tuckered out. He comes a-drooping down, once more, sweating like an ice-pitcher, drops his acorn in and says, '*Now* I guess I've got the bulge on you by this time!' So he bent down for a look. If you'll believe me, when his head come up again he was just pale with rage. He says, 'I've shoveled acorns enough in there to keep the family thirty years, and if I can see a sign of *one* of 'em, I wish I may land in a museum with a belly full of sawdust in two minutes!'

"He just had strength enough to crawl up on to the comb and lean his back agin the chimbly, and then he collected his impressions and begun to free his mind. I see in a second that what I had mistook for profanity in the mines was only just the rudiments, as you may say.

"Another jay was going by, and heard him doing his devotions, and stops to inquire what was up. The sufferer told him the whole circumstances, and says, 'Now yonder's the hole, and if you don't believe me, go and look for yourself.' So this fellow went and looked, and comes back and says, 'How many did you say you put in there?' 'Not any less than two tons,' says the sufferer. The other jay went and looked again. He couldn't seem to make it out, so he raised a yell, and three more jays come. They all examined the hole, they all made the sufferer tell it over again, then they all discussed it, and got off as many leather-headed opinions about it as an average crowd of humans could have done.

"They called in more jays; then more and more, till pretty soon this whole region 'peared to have a blue flush about it. There must have been five thousand of them; and such another jawing and disputing and ripping and cussing, you never heard. Every jay in the whole lot put his eye to the hole, and delivered a more chuckled-headed opinion about the mystery than the jay that went there before him. They examined the house all over, too. The door was standing half-open, and at last one old jay happened to go and light on it and look in, Of course, that knocked the mystery galley-west in a second. There lay the acorns, scattered all over the floor. He flopped his wings and raised a whoop. 'Come here!' he says, 'Come here, everybody; hang'd if this fool hasn't been trying to fill up a house with acorns!' They all came a-swooping down like a blue cloud, and as each fellow lit on the door and took a glance, the whole absurdity of the contract that the first jay had tackled hit him home and he fell over backwards suffocating with laughter, and the next jay took his place and done the same.

"Well, sir, they roosted around here on the house-top and the trees for an hour, and guffawed over that thing like human beings. It ain't no use to tell me a blue-jay hasn't got a sense of humor, because I know better. And memory too. They brought jays here from all over the United States to look down that hole, every summer for three years. Other birds too. And they could all see the point, except an owl that came from Nova Scotia to visit the Yo Semite, and he took this thing in on his way back. He said he couldn't see anything funny in it. But then, he was a good deal disappointed about Yo Semite, too."

Frescoes from the Past

Huckleberry Finn
Adventures of Huckleberry Finn
(New York: Charles Webster Publishing Co., 1885, p. 61).

By way of illustrating keelboat talk and manners, and that now-departed and hardly-remembered raft-life, I will throw in, in this place, a chapter from a book which I have been working at, by fits and starts, during the past five or six years, and may possibly finish in the course of five or six more. The book is a story which details some passages in the life of an ignorant village boy, Huck Finn, son of the town drunkard of my time out west, there. He has run away from his persecuting father, and from a persecuting good widow who wishes to make a nice, truth-telling, respectable boy of him; and with him a slave of the widow's has also escaped. They have found a fragment of a lumber-raft (it is high water and dead summer time), and are float-ing down the river by night and hiding in the willows by day,—bound for Cairo whence the negro will seek freedom in the heart of the free

States. But in a fog, they pass Cairo without knowing it. By and by they begin to suspect the truth, and Huck Finn is persuaded to end the dismal suspense by swimming down to a huge raft which they have seen in the distance ahead of them, creeping aboard under cover of the darkness, and gathering the needed information by eavesdropping: —

But you know a young person can't wait very well when he is impatient to find a thing out. We talked it over, and by and by Jim said it was such a black night, now, that it wouldn't be no risk to swim down to the big raft and crawl aboard and listen, — they would talk about Cairo, because they would be calculating to go ashore to buy whiskey or fresh meat or something. Jim had a wonderful level head, for a nigger: he could most always start a good plan when you wanted one.

I stood up and shook my rags off and jumped into the river, and struck out for the raft's light. By and by, when I got down nearly to her, I eased up and went slow and cautious. But everything was all right — nobody at the sweeps. So I swum down along the raft till I was most abreast the camp fire in the middle, then I crawled aboard and inched along and got in among some bundles of shingles on the weather side of the fire. There was thirteen men there — they was the watch on deck of course. And a mighty rough-looking lot, too. They had a jug, and tin cups, and they kept the jug moving. One man was singing — roaring, you may say; and it wasn't a nice song — for a parlor anyway. He roared through his nose, and strung out the last word of every line very long. When he was done they all fetched a kind of Injun war-whoop, and then another was sung. It begun: —

> "There was a woman in our towdn,
>   In our towdn did dwed'l (dwell,)
> She loved her husband dear-i-lee,
>   But another man twyste as wed'l.
> Singing too, riloo, riloo, riloo,
>   Ri-too, riloo, rilay---e,
> She loved her husband dear-i-lee,
>   But another man twyste as wed'l."

And so on — fourteen verses. It was kind of poor, and when he was going to start on the next verse one of them said it was the tune the old cow died on; and another one said: "Oh, give us a rest." And another one told him to take a walk. They made fun of him till he got mad and jumped up and begun to cuss the crowd, and said he could lam any thief in the lot.

They was all about to make a break for him, but the biggest man there jumped up and says: —

"Set whar you are, gentlemen. Leave him to me, he's my meat."

Then he jumped up in the air three times, and cracked his heels together every time. He flung off a buckskin coat that was all hung with fringes, and says, "You lay thar tell the chawin-up's done;" and flung his hat down, which was all over ribbons, and says, "You lay thar tell his sufferin's is over."

Then he jumped up in the air and cracked his heels together again, and shouted out:—

"Whoo-oop! I'm the old original iron-jawed, brass-mounted, copper-bellied corpse-maker from the wilds of Arkansaw!—Look at me! I'm the man they call Sudden Death and General Desolation! Sired by a hurricane, dam'd by an earthquake, half-brother to the cholera, nearly related to the small-pox on the mother's side! Look at me! I take nineteen alligators and a bar'l of whiskey for breakfast when I'm in robust health, and a bushel of rattlesnakes and a dead body when I'm ailing! I split the everlasting rocks with my glance, and I squench the thunder when I speak! Blood's my natural drink, and the wails of the dying is music to my ear! Cast your eye on me, gentlemen!—and lay low and hold your breath, for I'm bout to turn myself loose!"

All the time he was getting this off, he was shaking his head and looking fierce, and kind of swelling around in a little circle, tucking up his wrist-bands, and now and then straightening up and beating his breast with his fist, saying, "Look at me, gentlemen!" When he got through, he jumped up and cracked his heels together three times, and let off a roaring "whoo-oop! I'm the bloodiest son of a wildcat that lives!"

Then the man that had started the row tilted his old slouch hat down over his right eye; then he bent stooping forward, with his back sagged and his south end sticking out far, and his fists a-shoving out and drawing in in front of him, and so went around in a little circle about three times, swelling himself up and breathing hard. Then he straightened, and jumped up and cracked his heels together three times before he lit again (that made them cheer), and he began to shoot like this:

"Whoo-oop! bow your neck and spread, for the kingdom of sorrow's a-coming! Hold me down to the earth, for I feel my powers a-working! whoo-oop! I'm a child of sin, *don't* let me get a start! Smoked glass, here, for all! Don't attempt to look at me with the naked eye, gentlemen! When I'm playful I use the meridians of longitude and parallels of latitude for a seine, and drag the Atlantic Ocean for whales! I scratch my head with the lightning and purr myself to sleep with the thunder! When I'm cold, I bile the Gulf of Mexico and bathe in it; when I'm hot I fan myself with an equinoctial storm; when I'm thirsty I reach up and suck a cloud dry like a sponge; when I range the earth hungry, famine follows in my tracks! Whoo-oop! Bow your neck and spread! I put my hand on the sun's face and make it night in the earth; I bite a piece out of the moon and hurry the seasons; I shake myself and crumble the mountains! Contemplate me through leather—*don't* use the naked eye! I'm the man with a petrified heart and biler-iron bowels! The massacre of isolated communities is the pastime of my idle moments, the destruction of nationalities the serious business of my life! The boundless vastness of the great American desert is my enclosed property, and I bury my dead on my own premises!" He jumped up and cracked his heels together three times before he lit (they cheered him again), and as he come down he shouted out: "Whoo-oop! bow your neck and spread, for the pet child of calamity's a-coming!"

Then the other one went to swelling around and blowing again—the first one—the one they called Bob; next, the Child of Calamity chipped in again, bigger than ever; then they both got at it at the same time, swelling round and round each other and punching their fists most into each other's faces, and whooping and jawing like Injuns; then Bob called the Child names, and the Child called him names back again; next, Bob called him a heap rougher names, and the Child come back at him with the very worst kind of language; next, Bob knocked the Child's hat off, and the Child picked it up and kicked Bob's ribbony hat about six foot; Bob went and got it and said never mind, this warn't going to be the last of this thing, because he was a man that never forgot and never forgive, and so the Child better look out, for there was a time a-coming, just as sure as he was a living man, that he would have to answer to him with the best blood in his body. The Child said no man was willinger than he for that time to come, and he would give Bob fair warning, *now*, never to cross his path again, for he could never rest till he had waded in his blood, for such was his nature, though he was sparing him now on account of his family, if he had one.

Both of them was edging away in different directions, growling and shaking their heads and going on about what they was going to do; but a little black-whiskered chap skipped up and says:—

"Come back here, you couple of chicken-livered cowards, and I'll thrash the two of ye!"

And he done it, too. He snatched them, he jerked them this way and that, he booted them around, he knocked them sprawling faster than they could get up. Why, it warn't two minutes till they begged like dogs—and how the other lot did yell and laugh and clap their hands all the way through, and shout "Sail in, Corpse-Maker!" "Hi! at him again, Child of Calamity!" "Bully for you, little Davy!" Well, it was a perfect pow-wow for a while. Bob and the Child had red noses and black eyes when they got through. Little Davy made them own up that they was sneaks and cowards and not fit to eat with a dog or drink with a nigger; then Bob and the Child shook hands with each other, very solemn, and said they had always respected each other and was willing to let bygones be bygones. So then they washed their faces in the river; and just then there was a loud order to stand by for a crossing, and some of them went forward to man the sweeps there, and the rest went aft to handle the after-sweeps.

I laid still and waited for fifteen minutes, and had a smoke out of a pipe that one of them left in reach; then the crossing was finished, and they stumped back and had a drink around and went to talking and singing again. Next they got out an old fiddle, and one played, and another patted juba, and the rest turned themselves loose on a regular old-fashioned keel-boat breakdown. They couldn't keep that up very long without getting winded, so by and by they settled around the jug again.

They sung "jolly, jolly raftsman's the life for me," with a rousing chorus, and then they got to talking about differences betwixt hogs, and their different kind of habits; and next about women and their different ways; and next about what ought to be done with the Injuns; and next about what a king had to do, and how much he got; and next about how to make cats fight; and next about what to do when a man has fits; and next about differences betwixt clear-water rivers and muddy-water ones. The man they called Ed said the muddy Mississippi water was wholesomer to drink than the clear water of the Ohio; he said if you let a pint of this yaller Mississippi water settle, you would have about a half to three-quarters of an inch of mud in the bottom, according to the stage of the river, and then it warn't no better than Ohio water—what you wanted to do was to keep it stirred up—and when the river was low, keep mud on hand to put in and thicken the water up the way it ought to be.

The Child of Calamity said that was so; he said there was nutritiousness in the mud, and a man that drunk Mississippi water could grow corn in his stomach if he wanted to. He says:—

"You look at the graveyards; that tells the tale. Trees won't grow worth shucks in a Cincinnati graveyard, but in a Sent Louis graveyard they grow upwards of eight hundred foot high. It's all on account of the water the people drunk before they laid up. A Cincinnati corpse don't richen a soil any."

And they talked about how Ohio water didn't like to mix with Mississippi water. Ed said if you take the Mississippi on a rise when the Ohio is low, you'll find a wide band of clear water all the way down the east side of the Mississippi for a hundred mile or more, and the minute you get out a quarter of a mile from shore and pass the line, it is all thick and yaller the rest of the way across. Then they talked about how to keep tobacco from getting mouldy, and from that they went into ghosts and told about a lot that other folks had seen; but Ed says:—

"Why don't you tell something that you've seen yourselves? Now let me have a say. Five years ago I was on a raft as big as this, and right along here it was a bright moonshiny night, and I was on watch and boss of the stabboard oar forrard, and one of my pards was a man named Dick Allbright, and he come along to where I was sitting, forrard—gaping and stretching, he was—and stooped down on the edge of the raft and washed his face in the river, and come and set down by me and got out his pipe, and had just got it filled, when he looks up and says,—

" 'Why looky-here,' he says, 'ain't that Buck Miller's place, over yander in the bend?'

" 'Yes,' says I, 'it is—why?' He laid his pipe down and leaned his head on his hand, and says,—

" 'I thought we'd be furder down.' I says,—

" 'I thought it too, when I went off watch'—we was standing six hours on and six off—'but the boys told me,' I says, 'that the raft didn't seem to hardly move, for the last hour,'—says I, 'though she's a slipping along all right, now,' says I. He give a kind of groan, and says,—

" 'I've seed a raft act so before, along here,' he says, ' 'pears to me the current has most quit above the head of this bend durin' the last two years,' he says.

"Well, he raised up two or three times, and looked away off and around on the water. That started me at it, too. A body is always doing what he sees somebody else doing, though there mayn't be no sense in it. Pretty soon I see a black something floating on the water away off to stabboard and quartering behind us. I see he was looking at it, too. I says,—

" 'What's that?' He says, sort of pettish,—

" ' 'Tain't nothing but an old empty bar'l.'

" 'An empty bar'l!' says I, 'why,' says I, 'a spy-glass is a fool to *your* eyes. How can you tell it's an empty bar'l?' He says,—

" 'I don't know; I reckon it ain't a bar'l, but I thought it might be,' says he.

" 'Yes,' I says, 'so it might be, and it might be anything else, too; a body can't tell nothing about it, such a distance as that,' I says.

"We hadn't nothing else to do, so we kept on watching it. By and by I says,—

" 'Why, looky-here, Dick Allbright, that thing's a-gaining on us, I believe.'

"He never said nothing. The thing gained and gained, and I judged it must be a dog that was about tired out. Well, we swung down into the crossing, and the thing floated across the bright streak of the moonshine, and, by George, it *was* a bar'l. Says I,—

" 'Dick Allbright, what made you think that thing was a bar'l, when it was half a mile off,' says I. Says he,—

" 'I don't know.' Says I,—

" 'You tell me, Dick Allbright.' Says he—

" 'Well, I knowed it was a bar'l; I've seen it before; lots has seen it; they says it's a hanted bar'l.'

"I called the rest of the watch, and they come and stood there, and I told them what Dick said. It floated right along abreast, now, and didn't gain any more. It was about twenty foot off. Some was for having it aboard, but the rest didn't want to. Dick Allbright said rafts that had fooled with it had got bad luck by it. The captain of the watch said he didn't believe in it. He said he reckoned the bar'l gained on us because it was in a little better current than what we was. He said it would leave by and by.

"So then we went to talking about other things, and we had a song, and then a breakdown; and after that the captain of the watch called for another song; but it was clouding up, now, and the bar'l stuck right thar in the same place, and the song didn't seem to have much warm-up to it, somehow, and so they didn't finish it, and there warn't any cheers, but it sort of dropped flat, and nobody said anything for a minute. Then everybody tried to talk at once, and one chap got off a joke, but it warn't no use, they didn't laugh, and even the chap that made the joke didn't laugh at it, which ain't usual. We all just settled down glum, and watched the bar'l, and was oneasy and oncomfortable. Well, sir, it shut down black and still, and then the wind begin to moan around, and next the lightning begin to play and the thunder to grumble. And pretty soon there was a regular storm, and in the middle of it a man that was running aft stumbled and fell and sprained his ankle so that he had to lay up. This made the boys shake their heads. And every time the lightning come, there was that bar'l with the blue lights winking around it. We was always on the look-out for it. But by and by, towards dawn, she was gone. When the day come we couldn't see her anywhere, and we warn't sorry, neither.

"But next night about half-past nine, when there was songs and high jinks goin on, here she comes again, and took her old roost on the stabboard side. There warn't no more high jinks. Everybody got solemn; nobody talked; you couldn't get anybody to do anything but set around moody and look at the bar'l. It begun to cloud up again. When the watch changed, the off watch stayed up, 'stead of turning in. The storm ripped and roared around all night, and in the middle of it another man tripped and sprained his ankle, and had to knock off. The bar'l left towards day, and nobody see it go.

"Everybody was sober and down in the mouth all day. I don't mean the kind of sober that comes of leaving liquor alone,—not that. They was quiet, but they all drunk more than usual,—not together, but each man sidled off and took it private, by himself.

"After dark the off watch didn't turn in; nobody sung, nobody talked; the boys didn't scatter around, neither; they sort of huddled together, forrard; and for two hours they set there, perfectly still, looking steady in the one direction, and heaving a sigh once in a while. And then, here come the bar'l again. She took up her old place. She staid there all night; nobody turned in. The storm come on again, after midnight. It got awful dark; the rain poured down; hail, too; the thunder boomed and roared and bellowed; the wind blowed a hurricane; and the lightning spread over everything in big sheets of glare, and showed the whole raft as plain as day; and the river lashed up white as milk as far as you could see for miles, and there was that bar'l jiggering along, same as ever. The captain ordered the watch to man the after-sweeps for a crossing, and nobody would go,—no more sprained ankles for them, they said. They wouldn't even *walk* aft. Well then, just then the sky split wide open, with a crash, and the lightning killed two men of the after watch, and crippled two more. Crippled them how, say you? Why, *sprained their ankles!*

"The bar'l left in the dark betwixt lightnings, toward dawn. Well, not a body eat a bite at breakfast that morning. After that the men loafed around, in twos and threes, and talked low together. But none of them herded with Dick Allbright. They all give him the cold shake. If he come around where any of the men was, they split up and sidled away. They wouldn't man the sweeps with him. The captain had all the skiffs hauled up on the raft, alongside of his wigwam, and wouldn't let the dead men be took ashore to be planted; he didn't believe a man that got ashore would come back; and he was right.

"After night come, you could see pretty plain that there was going to be trouble if that bar'l come again; there was such a muttering going on. A good many wanted to kill Dick Allbright, because he'd seen the bar'l on other trips, and that had an ugly look. Some wanted to put him ashore. Some said, let's all go ashore in a pile, if the bar'l comes again.

"This kind of whispers was still going on, the men being bunched together forrard watching for the bar'l, when, lo and behold you! here she comes again. Down she comes, slow and steady, and settles into her old tracks. You could a heard a pin drop. Then up comes the captain, and says,—

"Boys, don't be a pack of children and fools; I don't want this bar'l to be dogging us all the way to Orleans, and *you* don't; well, then, how's the best way to stop it? Burn it up,—that's the way. I'm going to fetch it aboard,' he says. And before anybody could say a word, in he went.

"He swum to it, and as he come pushing it to the raft, the men spread to one side. But the old man got it aboard and busted in the head, and there was a baby in it! Yes sir; a stark-naked baby. It was Dick Allbright's baby; he owned up and said so.

"'Yes,' he says, a-leaning over, 'yes, it is my own lamented darling, my poor lost Charles William Allbright deceased,' says he,—for he could curl his tongue around the bulliest words in the language when he was a mind to, and lay them before you without a jint started, anywheres. Yes, he said he used to live up at the head of this bend, and *one night he choked his child,* which was crying, not intending to kill it, — which was prob'ly a lie, — and then he was scared, and buried it in a bar'l, before his wife got home, and off he went, and struck the northern trail and went to rafting; and this was the third year that the bar'l had chased him. He said the bad luck always begun light, and lasted till four men was killed, and then the bar'l didn't come any more after that. He said if the men would stand it one more night, — and was a-going on like that, — but the men had got enough. They started to get out a boat to take him ashore and lynch him, but he grabbed the little child all of a sudden and jumped overboard with it hugged up to his breast and shedding tears, and we never see him again in this life, poor old suffering soul, nor Charles William neither."

"*Who* was shedding tears?" says Bob; "was it Allbright or the baby?"

"Why, Allbright, of course; didn't I tell you the baby was dead? Been dead three years — how could it cry?"

"Well, never mind how it could cry — how could it *keep* all that time?" says Davy. "You answer me that."

"I don't know how it done it," says Ed. "It done it, though — that's all I know about it."

"Say — what did they do with the bar'l?" says the Child of Calamity.

"Why, they hove it overboard, and it sunk like a chunk of lead."

"Edward, did the child look like it was choked?" says one.

"Did it have its hair parted?" says another.

"What was the brand on that bar'l, Eddy?" says a fellow they called Bill.

"Have you got the papers for them statistics, Edmund?" says Jimmy.

"Say, Edwin, was you one of the men that was killed by the lightning?" says Davy.

"Him? O, no, he was both of 'em," says Bob. Then they all haw-hawed.

"Say, Edward, don't you reckon you'd better take a pill? You look bad — don't you feel pale?" says the Child of Calamity.

"O, come, now, Eddy," says Jimmy, "show up; you must a kept part of that bar'l to prove the thing by. Show us the bunghole — *do* — and we'll all believe you."

"Say, boys," says Bill, "less divide it up. That's thirteen of us. I can swaller a thirteenth of the yarn, if you can worry down the rest."

Ed got up mad and said they could all go to some place which he ripped out pretty savage, and then walked off aft cussing to himself, and they yelling and jeering at him, and roaring and laughing so you could hear them a mile.

"Boys, we'll split a watermelon on that," says the Child of Calamity;

and he came rummaging around in the dark amongst the shingle bundles where I was, and put his hand on me. I was warm and soft and naked; so he says "Ouch!" and jumped back.

"Fetch a lantern or a chunk of fire here, boys—there's a snake here as big as a cow!"

So they run there with a lantern, and crowded up and looked in on me.

"Come out of that, you beggar!" says one.

"Who are you?" says another.

"What are you after here? Speak up prompt, or overboard you go."

"Snake him out, boys. Snatch him out by the heels."

I began to beg, and crept out amongst them trembling. They looked me over, wondering, and the Child of Calamity says:—

"A cussed thief! Lend a hand and less heave overboard!"

"No," says Big Bob, "less get out the paint-pot and paint him a sky-blue all over from head to heel, and *then* heave him over."

"Good! that's it. Go for the paint, Jimmy."

When the paint come, and Bob took the brush and was just going to begin, the others laughing and rubbing their hands, I begun to cry, and that sort of worked on Davy, and he says:—

"'Vast there! He's nothing but a cub. I'll paint the man that teches him!"

So I looked around on them, and some of them grumbled and growled, and Bob put down the paint, and the others didn't take it up.

"Come here to the fire, and less see what you're up to here," says Davy. "Now set down there and give an account of yourself. How long have you been aboard here?"

"Not over a quarter of a minute, sir," says I.

"How did you get dry so quick?"

"I don't know, sir. I'm always that way, mostly."

"Oh, you are, are you? What's your name?"

I warn't going to tell my name. I didn't know what to say, so I just says:

"Charles William Allbright, sir."

Then they roared—the whole crowd; and I was mighty glad I said that, because maybe the laughing would get them in a better humor.

When they got done laughing, Davy says:—

"It won't hardly do, Charles William. You couldn't have growed this much in five year, and you was a baby when you come out of the bar'l, you know, and dead at that. Come, now, tell a straight story, and nobody'll hurt you, if you ain't up to anything wrong. What *is* your name?"

"Aleck Hopkins, sir. Aleck James Hopkins."

"Well, Aleck, where did you come from here?"

"From a trading-scow. She lays up the bend yonder. I was born on

her. Pap has traded up and down here all his life; and he told me to swim
off here, because when you went by he said he would like to get some
of you to speak to a Mr. Jonas Turner, in Cairo, and tell him—"

"Oh, come!"

"Yes, sir, it's as true as the world; Pap he says—"

"Oh, your grandmother!"

They all laughed, and I tried again to talk, but they broke in on me
and stopped me.

"Now, looky-here," says Davy; "you're scared, and so you talk wild.
Honest, now, do you live in a scow, or is it a lie?

"Yes, sir, in a trading scow. She lays up at the head of the bend. But
I warn't born in her. It's our first trip."

"Now you're talking! What did you come aboard here, for? To steal?"

"No, sir, I didn't.—It was only to get a ride on the raft. All boys does
that."

"Well, I know that. But what did you hide for?"

"Sometimes they drive the boys off."

"So they do. They might steal. Looky-here; if we let you off this
time, will you keep out of these kind of scrapes hereafter?"

" 'Deed I will, boss. You try me."

"All right, then. You ain't but little ways from shore. Overboard
with you, and don't you make a fool of yourself another time this way.
—Blast it, boy, some raftsmen would rawhide you till you were black
and blue!"

I didn't wait to kiss good-bye, but went overboard and broke for
shore. When Jim come along by and by, the big raft was away out of
sight around the point. I swum out and got aboard, and was mighty
glad to see home again.

The boy did not get the information he was after, but his adventure
has furnished the glimpse of the departed raftsman and keelboatman
which I desire to offer in this place.

Linguistic Note

Linguistic Note

For centuries, writers of comic literature have utilized dialect differences as part of their armament. Aristophanes, writing for Athenians, satirized the behavior of Spartans and Thebans through his representation of their speech. Catullus deflated the pretensions of the parvenu Arrius by noting his pronunciation of *h*- where it did not belong. Chaucer's Reeve made fun of the Cambridge students (and of his fellow pilgrim the Miller) by using forms of northern English not yet acceptable in London. Shakespeare paid his respects to the Irish, Scots, and Welsh in the army of Henry V. And, from colonial times, American authors in various regions have portrayed, generally with some sympathy, the speech of groups familiar to them but less afflicted with formal schooling.

These writers were not systematic dialectologists. They were not working from detailed analyses of the pronunciation, grammar, and vocabulary of the groups they were portraying—what present-day linguists call contrastive sketches. They simply chose a few features by which the language of their characters was identifiable to them and to the audience for whom they were writing. These writers were successful, at least in their appeal to the reading public of their day, if we may judge by the reception their works received and by the number of times these works were reprinted.

Walter Blair has offered his explanation of the decline of public interest in dialect literature. Possibly the widening of general education has made the descendants of Down East Yankees and Mississippi roarers a little sensitive about the language once used (and sometimes still used) in their communities. Possibly this spread of general education, accompanied by the turning away of the schools from such time-honored if pedestrian chores as reading and writing and ciphering, has made us less concerned with departures from conventional orthographic and grammatical niceties. If there has been as yet no chairman of an English department who signs his name with an *X*, as was remarked in the opening scene of the musical comedy *Louisiana Purchase*, there are enough examples of illiterate quarterbacks in their senior years in high school to make Sut Lovingood and Simon Suggs seem like a pair of intellectuals. And the fractionating of society by the automobile and the one-class suburb has meant that we no longer have the casual contacts our parents had with the uneducated. When we no longer hear speech approximating that of Uncle Remus or David Harum as a matter of course, we find it difficult to understand the conventions by which writers such as J. C. Harris and Edward Westcott represented that speech. Furthermore, as we examine closely the conventions used by various writers, we find several problems—and not mere inconsistencies—in our appreciation of them.

First, many representation of dialect features are simply bad spellings of words that are pronounced more or less the same everywhere and are rarely misspelled in practice; for example, *wuz* for *was,* *wimmen* for *women.* Among the literary comedians of the 1860s and later (for example, Artemus Ward, Petroleum V. Nasby, Bill Arp, and Josh Billings), such spellings ran riot.

A second problem is that very often a feature that is probably shared by all characters in a work is indicated as peculiar to a limited group. In *Adventures of Huckleberry Finn*, the narrator consistently uses the *-ing* participle, but the black runaway Jim uses *-in.* Yet, in antebellum Hannibal, a white boy of Huck's background (and indeed white adult males several cuts above him) would normally use *-in.* Whether the author or the editor was responsible, there is only one *-in* participle in "The Big Bear of Arkansas," though it would have been normal usage on the frontier.

On the other hand, some of the most typical regional pronunciations are not represented because the resources of the English alphabet are inadequate. Even William Gilmore Simms, who tried hard—perhaps, some say, too hard—to represent accurately the dialects of his native South Carolina, provided no suggestion of the distinctive low-country pronunciation of /e/ and /o/, as in *date* and *boat.* No novelist portraying the speech of the Deep South has attempted to represent the diphthong [əɪ] in *bird.* (For older proletarian speech in New York City, where *coil* and *curl* were homonymous, some recent authors have used such reverse spellings as *earl boiner.*) No representation of Canadian, eastern Virginian, or low-country South Carolinian speech hints at the centered beginnings of /ai/ and /au/, as in *ice* and *house.* Nor is there any way to represent tempo, timbre, or intonation, often more striking cues to dialect than articulation of vowels and consonants.

Finally, the best representations of a dialect may be misinterpreted if the reader does not have, or even know, the filter—the author's own speech—through which the dialect is interpreted. The "broad *a*'" pronunciation of *laugh* is naturally represented as *larf* by eastern New Englanders who do not pronounce the /-r/ in barn, but Midwesterners would pronounce the /-r/ as they read it. Midwesterners almost always pronounce the casual honorific *brer* "brother" (as used in the stories of Joel Chandler Harris and Charles Waddell Chesnutt) not only with final /-r/ but rhyming with *bear*; many of them also hear Upland Southern *right* as homonymous with *rat*, providing opportunity for embarrassment when a Southerner asks a Midwestern hostess for a piece of *ice*.

These observations are paralleled in the experience of elementary teachers. As children struggle to learn to read, too much emphasis on the proper phonetic rendering of what is read may interfere with comprehension. To many people—not all of them uneducated—the *th-* in *them* is merely another way of representing the sound /d-/, just as to others *horse* and *hoarse, cot* and *caught, barn* and *born,* and *wile* and *while* are homophonous. However different the regional varieties of pronunciation may be, a willing pupil guided by a patient teacher can master the conventions of written English; conversely, anything written will normally be read in terms of the reader's own speech. To me, *chair* and *cheer* are homonyms, but I never confuse them in writing.

In order to make the dialect humor of the nineteenth century accessible to twentieth-century readers, I have tried to normalize the spellings as far as possible without distorting the flavor of the original. Each exception must justify itself by suggesting the flavor of the dialect rather than by attempting to replicate it. For example, such spellings as *hoss, git, 'oman (woman),* and *obleedge (oblige)* are kept, since they offer little trouble.

Where authors differ in the way they represent a given sound or word, I have tried to adopt a convention that will create the least trouble for readers. *After* is represented variously by our authors as *arter, atter,* and *a'ter.* I have adopted the last, which permits a reader to make stressed vowels of various qualities. When I am inconsistent, it is again in the interest of comprehension: *yearth* (or *yea'th*) for *earth* offers no problems, but *yearly* and *yearn* for *early* and *earn* can be misunderstood. Occasionally, with the same intent, I substitute a convention of my own for that of the author: *Br' Rabbit* seems a good representation of Harris's casual honorific. As a corollary, I have resisted the temptation to "improve" the dialect by making it more consistent, even when I have a pretty good idea of what the author might have said. For example, other spellings by Finley Peter Dunne suggest that Mr. Dooley, like many other Americans (not all of Hibernian extraction), pronounced *again* "against" to rhyme with *sin,* but I have left the spelling *again* as Dunne wrote it. Where there are inconsistencies—Josh Billings vacillates between *-in* and *-ing* for the participial ending—I feel that any of our authors has the right of self-contradiction that Walt Whitman asserted for himself.

In dealing with grammar and vocabulary I have trod very gingerly. However exotic the dialect, the grammatical signals are usually clear: the use of *ain't*, the use of multiple negation (*ain't nobody never makes no pound cake no more*), and the omission of the verb *to be* (*we going tomorrow*) present little difficulty. When authors alternate *see* and *seed* as the past tense, they are only reflecting American usage. Several of the older and less-educated speakers interviewed for the linguistic atlases have actually offered *see, seed, seen,* and *saw* in the course of an interview. And converting the action of Chesnutt's conjurer from *working his roots* to *performing his incantations* would be incongruous. Some terms may be obscure. The context may tell readers that a *doggery* or a *grocery* was a place where liquor was dispensed, licitly or otherwise; but, when Dunne follows *the flying machine* with *the Croker Machine*, even present-day New Yorkers would rarely catch in the last an allusion to Tammany Hall (itself fading into the mists of history). For the benefit of the curious, a list of similar words and personalities follows.

The number of changes I have made varies with the author. I have dealt most drastically with the literary comedians. Conversely, the two selections from Mark Twain I have left untouched: the blue-jay story offers no problems of interpretation, and, though the dialect is more elaborately represented in the visit to the raft, the preface to *Adventures of Huckleberry Finn* suggests a careful attempt on the part of the author to represent consistently a kind of speech with which he was intimately familiar.

Wherever possible, my interpretations have drawn on the regional linguistic atlases, which, under the leadership of Hans Kurath, have given us, over the past half-century, a wealth of detail on American regional vernaculars. Walter Blair and I have profited both from my own experience as field-worker and editor and from discussions with other dialectologists who have been interested in these problems and some of whom have made interesting analyses of the accuracy with which authors have represented local speech: Sumner Ives (Joel Chandler Harris), William Evans (George Washington Cable), Charles William Foster (Charles Chesnutt), James Austin (Bill Arp), James W. Downer (James Russell Lowell), and especially my student and friend the late Walter Avis (Thomas Chandler Haliburton).

Most important, though, is the fact that every selection is included not as a specimen of dialectal paleontology but because it is funny in its own right. The humor is of various sorts: the mordant satire in Birdoffredum Sawin's letter, the impudent roguery of Simon Suggs, the saccharine sentimentality of "Gentian" and "The Minister's House-keeper," and the folk wisdom of David Harum. Most of these selections I had never read before, but sheer delight in the humor made me almost oblivious to the infernal labor of editing. I hope that in their edited form they will bring delight to a generation of Americans who in their deep concern with moral values have become almost afraid to laugh at themselves.

Raven I. McDavid, Jr.
Chicago
October 20, 1980

Forgotten Words and Personalities

Forgotten Words and Personalities

Australian ballot The usual ballot in twentieth-century American elections but, when introduced during the late nineteenth century, hailed as a cure for voting fraud since it was officially printed, was often serially numbered, and was of uniform quality and color ("On Reform Candidates")

bald face Raw whiskey ("A Tight Race Considerin")

banquette Sidewalk, usually one raised above street level which is still known in the New Orleans area ("Posson Jone'")

bell-wether A tame sheep fitted with a bell to help herdsmen find the herd ("The Minister's Housekeeper")

big Cleveland Grover Cleveland (1837-1908), president of the United States (1885-1889, 1893-1897), physically a symbol of the solid conservative wing of the Democratic Party ("On Reform Candidates")

b'ilin Boiling, for the whole b'ilin, meaning the whole crowd

Bluenose A Nova Scotian ("The Clockmaker")

bridewell The unofficial name for the Chicago House of Correction (as often used for its counterparts in English cities); along with Cook County Hospital, successor to the old pesthouse, still a favorite target for the futile crusades of frenetic liberal reformers ("On Reform Candidates")

bunko steerer In confidence games and other swindles, the "roper" who locates and enlists the cooperation of willing victims ("On Reform Candidates")

cake walk A popular American dance often involving contests with prizes for the most eccentric steps ("On Reform Candidates")

camfire Camphor ("The Harp of a Thousand Strings")

Campbell Minstrels A popular minstrel company of the mid-nineteenth century ("Interview with President Lincoln")

carminative balsam, Jaynes's A proprietary medicine reputed to relieve colic, grippe, and flatulence ("Why He Should Not Be Drafted")

carry the pall Serve as pall bearer at a funeral ("On Reform Candidates")

Charter Haitch (1828-1893) Carter Harrison who was serving his fifth term as "reform mayor" of Chicago when assassinated ("On Reform Candidates")

chickens A gambling game using dice ("The Big Bear of Arkansas")

chippen-bird A tree sparrow ("The Big Bear of Arkansas")

come through To experience the extreme emotions of religious conversion ("The Conjurer's Revenge")

Cowan, Edgar (1805-1888) Senator from Pennsylvania (1861-1867) ("The Reward of Virtue")

Coxey, "General" Jacob Sechler (1854-1951) Massilon, Ohio, industrialist who led a march of the unemployed to Washington, D.C., in 1893, which demanded public works bonds for projects similar to those adopted by the Public Works Administration in 1933 ("On the Victorian Era")

cried Announced in public, as the banns for an impending marriage ("The Courtin")

Croker Machine From Richard Croker (1841-1922), for seventeen years the leader of Tammany Hall, the once all-powerful Democratic organization in Manhattan ("On the Victorian Era")

Croton water Water from the Croton Reservoir in Westchester County, New York, used for the New York City water supply since 1842; often reputed to be a powerful laxative by confusion with Croton oil, of unrelated etymology ("A Tight Race Considerin")

democrat wagon A light, two-seated wagon ("The Horse Trader")

Dick horse A stallion ("Simon Suggs Attends a Camp Meeting")

didapper A Carolina grebe, or a small bird resembling one, that dives for its food ("A Tight Race Considerin")

doggery A saloon

Doolittle, James R. (1815-1897) Republican senator from Wisconsin (1857-1869) ("The Reward of Virtue")

east of State Street and south of Jackson Boulevard the "levee," in the late nineteenth century, a concentration of brothels and saloons and of hard-core Chicago machine politics ("On Reform Candidates")

Eyre, Governor Edward John Eyre who, as governor of Jamaica, suppressed an insurrection in 1865 in what opponents claimed was a grossly brutal fashion; a trial conducted by a court of inquiry resulted in his exoneration ("The Tower of London")

fastin spit Hunger(?) ("On Charity")

Fenian A member of an organization of Irish-American activists formed in 1856 and flourishing until the twentieth century, antecedent of the present-day Irish Republican Army ("On the Victorian Era")

fish-skin Money (*Biglow Papers*)

flujuns Euphemism for Hell ("How Sally Hooter Got Snakebit")

gossoon Garçon, waiter ("On Reform Candidates")

Grinnell, Josiah B. (1821-1891) Republican congressman from Iowa (1863-1867) ("The Reward of Virtue")

grocery A saloon

Hamlin, Hannibal L. (1809-1891) Democratic senator from Maine (1848-1857) who became a Republican in 1856 and was vice president under Lincoln (1861-1865) ("Bill Arp to Abe Linkhorn")

Hard-Shell Baptist Primitive, old-school, conservative Baptist opposed to foreign missions ("The Harp of a Thousand Strings")

lewed Cheated ("Simon Suggs Attends a Camp Meeting")

made tie A tie already knotted that can be slipped on without tying, a symbol of lower-middle-class insecurity ("On Reform Candidates")

mastodon A highly esteemed variety of cotton ("A Tight Race Considerin")

Memphis and New Orleans unpleasantnesses 1866 fights between local whites and the blacks supported by the army of occupation ("The Reward of Virtue")

Nye, Bill Edger W. Nye (1850-1896), an American humorist ("On the Victorian Era")

Onion League Club Union League Club of Chicago, which, like its counterparts in other northern cities, was a wealthy citadel of ostentatious patriotism, virtue, and Republicanism ("On Reform Candidates")

Orangey A Protestant Irishman or Irish-American, especially one from Ulster, named from adherence to the cause of William of Orange in 1688 ("On the Victorian Era")

perch A measure of stone equal to 25 cubic feet ("Live Yankees")

pic Picayune, a small coin of little value ("A Tight Race Considerin")

quitte Syrup at the point of crystallizing ("Posson Jone'")

Randall, Alexander W. (1819-1872) U.S. postmaster general (1865-1869) after whom Camp Randall, and the stadium on its site in Madison, Wisconsin, were named ("The Reward of Virtue")

red eye Whiskey of very poor quality ("How Sally Hooter Got Snakebit")

Rhode Island greening A type of apple ("Live Yankees")

rockaway Type of pleasure carriage, originally with a standing canopy and removable side curtains ("The Conjurer's Revenge")

Rousseau, Lowell H. (1818-1869) Congressman from Kentucky (1865-1867) who attacked Iowa's Congressman Josiah B. Grinnell in June 1866 when Grinnell failed to apologize adequately for making offensive remarks; reprimanded, Rousseau resigned but was immediately reelected ("The Reward of Virtue")

salt hoss Corned beef ("Jaybird Bob's Joke")

Scanlan, Michael ("Tim") (1836-1917) Minor Irish-American poet from Chicago ("Mr. Dooley to Mr. Hennessy on the Victorian Era")

Sea Island A highly prized variety of long staple cotton grown chiefly along the coast of South Carolina and Georgia ("A Tight Race Considerin")

Seward, William H. (1801-1872) Governor of New York (1839-1843), senator from New York (1849-1861), and U.S. secretary of state (1861-1869) ("The Reward of Virtue")

shite-poke A type of heron that defecates when startled ("The Big Bear of Arkansas")

shoat An adolescent porker weaned but not yet ready for market ("The Conjurer's Revenge")

smell woolen To suspect fraud, that is, to suspect that someone is pulling the wool over one's eyes ("The Horse Trader")

soft sawder Soft soap, sweet talk, flattery ("The Clockmaker")

Stevens, Thaddeus (1792-1868) Congressman from Pennsylvania elected several times (first in 1848), extremist in advocating punishment of the South, who led the drive for the impeachment of President Andrew Johnson ("The Reward of Virtue")

Sumner, Charles (1811-1874) Senator from Massachusetts (1851-1874), extremist in attacking the South and advocating its punishment ("The Reward of Virtue")

tew around Bustle, fuss, mess ("The Minister's Housekeeper")

Trumbull, Jonathan (1813-1896) Radical Republican senator from Illinois (1855-1873) who was hostile toward President Andrew Johnson ("The Reward of Virtue")

Wade, Benjamin (1800-1878) Radical Republican senator from Ohio (1851-1869) ("The Reward of Virtue")

wake To conduct a wake for (a wake with only small beer would epitomize the poverty of the family) ("On Charity")

Wilcox, Ella Wheeler (1850-1919) American sentimental poet who was popular but whose work was of low quality ("On the Victorian Era")

Yankeeing Cheating ("The Standing Candidate")

Selected Bibliography

Selected Bibliography

General Studies

American Dialect Humor

Bier, Jesse. *The Rise and Fall of American Humor* (New York, 1968).

Blair, Walter. *Horse Sense in American Humor* (Chicago, 1942; New York, 1962).

Blair, Walter, ed. *Native American Humor* (New York, 1937; San Francisco, 1960), pp. 3-196.

Blair, Walter, and Hamlin Hill. *America's Humor: From Poor Richard to Doonesbury* (New York, 1978).

Brooks, G. L. "Dialect in Literature," in *English Dialects* (London, 1963), pp. 184-209.

Ives, Sumner A. "A Theory of Literary Dialect," *Tulane Studies in English*, 2 (1950), 137-81.

Rourke, Constance. *American Humor: A Study of the National Character* (New York, 1931, 1965).

Rubin, L. D., and Others. *The Comic Imagination in American Literature* (New Brunswick, 1973).

Thorp, Willard. *American Humorists* (Minneapolis, 1964).

Rustic Yankees

Dorson, Richard M. *Jonathan Draws the Long Bow* (Cambridge, Massachusetts, 1946).

Royot, Daniel. *L'Humour Américain des Puritains aux Yankees* (Lyon, 1980).

Frontier Storytellers

Boatright, Mody C. *Folk Laughter on the American Frontier* (New York, 1949).

Cohen, Hennig, and William B. Dillingham, eds. *Humor of the Old Southwest* (Boston, 1964), pp. ix-xxiv.

Inge, M. Thomas, and Others. *The Frontier Humorists: Critical Views* (Hamden, Connecticut, 1975).

Meine, Franklin J., ed., *Tall Tales of the Southwest* (New York, 1930), pp. xv-xxxii.

Yates, Norris W. *William T. Porter and the Spirit of the Times: A Study of the Big Bear School of Humor* (Baton Rouge, Louisiana, 1957).

Funny Fellows

Clemens, Will M. *Famous Funny Fellows* (New York, 1882).

Lukens, Henry Clay. "American Literary Comedians," *Harper's*, 80 (1890), 783-97.

Pattee, F. L. *American Literature since 1870* (New York, 1915), pp. 25-44.

Local Colorists

Pattee, F. L. *American Literature since 1870* (New York, 1915), pp. 63-98, 220-70, 294-320.

Rhode, Robert D. *Setting in the American Short Story of Local Color* (The Hague, 1975).
Simpson, Claude M., ed. *The Local Colorists* (New York, 1960).
Warfel, Harry R., and G. Harrison Orians, eds. *American Local Color Stories* (New York, 1941).

Studies of Individual Authors

Browne, Charles Farrar

Austin, James C. *Artemus Ward* (New York, 1964).
Seitz, Don C. *Artemus Ward* (New York, 1919).

Cable, George Washington

Butcher, Philip. *George W. Cable* (New York, 1962).
Evans, William. "French Literary Dialect in *The Grandissimes*," *American Speech*, 46 (1971), 210-22.
Evans, William, "Dialect and Diglossia in G. W. Cable's 'Belles Damoiselles Plantation,' " *Journal of the Linguistic Association of the Southwest*, X (1981).
Turner, Arlin. *George W. Cable, A Biography* (Durham, North Carolina, 1956).

Chesnutt, Charles W.

Andrews, C. L. "Charles W. Chesnutt's Conjure Stories," *Southern Literary Journal*, 7 (1975), 78-99.
Chesnutt, Helen M. *Charles Waddell Chesnutt, Pioneer of the Color Line* (Baton Rouge, Louisiana, 1952).
Foster, Charles W. *The Phonology of the Conjure Tales of Charles W. Chesnutt* (Publications of the American Dialect Society, 55, 1971).

Clemens, Samuel Langhorne

Blair, Walter. *Mark Twain & "Huck Finn"* (Berkeley, California, 1960, 1973).
Carkeet, David. "The Dialects in *Huckleberry Finn*," *American Literature*, 51 (1979), 315-32.
Gibson, William. *The Art of Mark Twain* (New York, 1976).
Paine, A. B. *Mark Twain: A Biography*, 3 vols. (New York, 1912).
Pederson, Lee A. "Mark Twain's Missouri Dialects," *American Speech*, 42 (1967), 261-78.
Pederson, Lee A. "Negro Speech in *Huckleberry Finn*," *Mark Twain Journal*, 13 (1965), 1-4.
Rulon, C. M. "Geographical Delimitation of the Dialect Areas in *Huckleberry Finn*," *Mark Twain Journal*, 14 (1966), 9-12.
Smith, Henry Nash. *Mark Twain: The Development of a Writer* (Cambridge, Massachusetts, 1962).

Crockett Almanack Anonymous Authors

Dorson, Richard M., ed. *Davy Crockett, American Comic Legend* (New York, 1939).
Rourke, Constance. *Davy Crockett* (New York, 1934).
Seelye, John. "A Well-Wrought Crockett," in *Toward a New American Literary History: Essays in Honor of Arlin Turner*, L. J. Budd, E. H. Cady, and C. L. Anderson, eds. (Durham, North Carolina, 1980), pp. 91-110.

Dunne, Finley Peter

Dunne, Philip, ed. *Mr. Dooley Remembers* (New York, 1963).
Ellis, Elmer. *Mr. Dooley's America: A Life of Finley Peter Dunne* (New York, 1941).

Freeman, Mary E. Wilkins

Brand, A. G. "Misanthropy as Propaganda," *New England Quarterly*, 50 (1977), 83-100.

Foster, Edward. *Mary E. Wilkins Freeman* (New York, 1956).
Westbrook, P. D. *Mary Wilkins Freeman* (New York, 1967).

Haliburton, Thomas Chandler

Avis, Walter S. "A Note on the Speech of Sam Slick," *The Sam Slick Anthology*, R. E. Watters, ed. (Toronto, 1939), pp. xix-xxviii.
Chittick, V. L. O. *Thomas Chandler Haliburton* (New York, 1924).

Harris, George Washington

Current-Garcia, Eugene. "Sut Lovingood's Rare Ripe Southern Garden," *Studies in Short Fiction,* 9 (1972), 117-29.
Day, Donald. "The Life of George Washington Harris," *Tennessee Historical Quarterly,* 6 (1947), 3-38.
Rickels, Milton. *George Washington Harris* (New York, 1965).

Harris, Joel Chandler

Bickley, R. Bruce. *Joel Chandler Harris* (New York, 1978).
Cousins, P. M. *Joel Chandler Harris: A Biography* (Baton Rouge, Louisiana, 1968).
Ives, Sumner A. "Dialect Differentiation in the Stories of Joel Chandler Harris," *American Literature,* 27 (1955), 85-96.
Ives, Sumner A. *The Phonology of the Uncle Remus Stories* (Publications of the American Dialect Society, 22, 1954).

Hooper, Johnson Jones

Hoole, W. Stanley. *Alias Simon Suggs* (University, Alabama, 1952).

Lewis, Henry Clay

Anderson, John Q. *Louisiana Swamp Doctor: Life and Writings of Henry Clay Lewis* (Baton Rouge, Louisiana, 1962).

Locke, David Ross

Austin, James C. *Petroleum V. Nasby (David Ross Locke)* (New York, 1965).
Harrison, John M. *The Man Who Made Nasby* (Chapel Hill, North Carolina, 1969).

Lowell, James Russell

Blair, Walter. "James Russell Lowell," in *American Writers,* Supplement I, Part 2 (New York, 1979), pp. 404-26.
Downer, James W. "Features of New England Speech in James Russell Lowell's *Biglow Papers,*" unpublished doctoral dissertation, University of Michigan, 1958.
Duberman, Martin. *James Russell Lowell* (Boston, 1966).
Howard, Leon. *Victorian Knight-Errant* (Berkeley, California, 1952).

Paulding, James Kirke

Herold, Amos L. *James Kirke Paulding, Versatile American* (New York, 1926).
Paulding, William T. *Literary Life of James Kirke Paulding* (New York, 1867).

Riley, James Whitcomb

Crowder, Richard. *Those Innocent Years* (Indianapolis, 1957).
Dickey, Marcus. *The Maturity of James Whitcomb Riley* (Indianapolis, 1922).
Revell, Donald G. *James Whitcomb Riley* (New York, 1970).

Robb, John S.

Spotts, Carle Brooks. "The Development of Fiction on the Missouri Frontier," *Missouri Historical Review,* 29 (1935), 100-38.

Shaw, Henry Wheeler

Day, Donald. *Uncle Sam's Uncle Josh* (Boston, 1953).
Kesterton, D. B. *Josh Billings (H. W. Shaw)* (New York, 1973).

Smith, Charles H.

Austin, James C., and Wayne Pike. "The Language of Bill Arp," *American Speech,* 48 (1973), 84-97.
Christie, Annie May. "Civil War Humor: Bill Arp," *Civil War History,* 2 (1956), 103-19.

Smith, F. Hopkinson

Moyne, Ernest J. "Mark Twain and the Baroness Alexandra Gripenberg," *American Literature,* 45 (1973), 370-78.

Smith, Seba

Rickels, Patricia, and Milton Rickels. *Seba Smith* (Boston, 1977).
Wyman, Mary Alice. *Two American Pioneers: Seba Smith and Elizabeth Oakes Smith* (New York, 1927).

Stowe, Harriet Beecher

Foster, Charles H. *The Rungless Ladder: Harriet Beecher Stowe and New England Puritanism* (Durham, North Carolina, 1954).

Taliaferro, Harden E.

Boggs, Ralph S. "North Carolina Folktales Current in the 1820's," *Journal of American Folklore,* 47 (1934), 269-88.
Walser, Richard. "Biblio-biography of Skitt Taliaferro," *North Carolina Historical Review,* 55 (1978), 375-95.
Williams, Cratis D. "Mountain Customs, Social Life, and Folk Yarns in *Fisher's River Scenes and Characters,*" *North Carolina Folklore,* 16 (1968), 143-52.

Thompson, William Tappan

Ellison, George R. "William Tappan Thompson and the *Southern Miscellany,*" *Mississippi Quarterly,* 23 (1970), 155-68.
Miller, H. Prentice. "The Background and Significance of *Major Jones's Courtship,*" *Georgia Historical Quarterly,* 30 (1946), 267-96.

Thorpe, Thomas Bangs

Blair, Walter. "T. B. Thorpe and His Masterpiece," in *The Frontier Humorists* (Hamden, Connecticut, 1975), pp. 105-17.
Current-Garcia, Eugene. "Thomas Bangs Thorpe and the Literature of the Ante-Bellum Southwestern Frontier," *Louisiana Historical Quarterly,* 39 (1956), 199-222.
Lemay, J. A. Leo. "The Text, Tradition, and Themes of 'The Big Bear of Arkansas,'" *American Literature,* 47 (1975), 321-42.
Rickels, Milton. *Thomas Bangs Thorpe: Humorist of the Old Southwest* (Baton Rouge, Louisiana, 1962).
Utley, Francis Lee, and Others, eds., *Bear, Man, and God* (New York, 1971).

Westcott, Edward Noyes

Vance, Arthur Turner. *The Real David Harum* (New York, 1900).
Westcott, Edward Noyes. *The Teller* (New York, 1901), pp. 71-113.

Whitcher, Frances Miriam

Royot, Daniel. "Les Anti-Héroines de Frances Whitcher et la Parodie du Roman Sentimental," in *L'Humour Américain des Puritains aux Yankees* (Lyon, 1980), pp. 308-11.
Whitcher, M. L. Ward. "Memoir," in Frances Whitcher, *Widow Spriggens* (New York, 1867), pp. 11-35.

Index

Index

References to humorists are listed under given names followed by pseudonyms, if any, in parentheses. Boldface numerals cite inclusive page numbers for biographical introductions and selections by anthologized authors. Casual allusions have not been indexed. American humorous categories, schools, and traits are listed under Humor, American.

Walter Blair, professor of English, emeritus, at the University of Chicago, edited the standard anthology *Native American Humor*. He has written, among other books, *Tall Tale America, Horse Sense in American Humor, Mark Twain and "Huck Finn"* and—most recently—(with Hamlin Hill) *America's Humor: From Poor Richard to Doonesbury*. **Raven I. McDavid, Jr.,** professor of English and linguistics, emeritus, at Chicago and a scholar of American dialects, edited the abridged edition of H. L. Mencken's *The American Language* and wrote *Dialects in Culture* and *Varieties of American English*. He is editor-in-chief of *The Linguistic Atlas of the Middle and South Atlantic States* and *The Linguistic Atlas of the North-Central States*.